the
**Public
Agenda**

the
Public
Agenda
ISSUES IN AMERICAN POLITICS

LAWRENCE G. BREWSTER

San Jose State University

ST. MARTIN'S PRESS

New York

To my parents, my wife, and Mike,
for each has contributed to my growth and stability.

ACKNOWLEDGMENTS

Box 1-1, "The 'Fed' Structure and Process," © 1981 by The New York Times Company. Reprinted by permission.

Figure 1-1, "State of the U.S. Economy Since Reagan Became President," by Warren Hinckle; © San Francisco Chronicle, 1982. Reprinted by permission.

Figure 1-2, "The Great Tax Shift," reprinted from *The Los Angeles Times*.

Table 2-1, "The Structure of Energy Consumption in the Industrial World," reprinted from World Energy Information Services.

Table 2-2, "U.S. Passenger Car Efficiency, 1969–1980," from *The World Almanac & Book of Facts*, 1983 edition, copyright © Newspaper Enterprise Association, Inc., 1982, New York, NY 10166.

Table 2-3, "Average Fuel Costs to Consumers, 1975–1983," from *The World Almanac & Book of Facts*, 1983 edition, copyright © Newspaper Enterprise Association, Inc., 1982, New York, NY 10166.

Table 2-6, "Changing Attitudes Toward Conservation," © 1979 Alliance to Save Energy.

Acknowledgments and copyrights continue at the back of the book on page 300, which constitutes an extension of the copyright page.

A Note to the Instructor

I have been teaching the introductory American government course for more than ten years. To my surprise—and dismay—I have found few short, readable, and integrally written books that adequately cover the pressing issues of the day. The many collections of readings that are available have never seemed satisfactory to me. Their selections invariably differ widely in sophistication and readability as well as focus. And the books are usually too long. This volume, then, is an attempt to fill a need.

The Public Agenda is organized into eight chapters, each covering one issue, plus a general introduction that provides a framework for understanding how our democratic society deals with problems that defy easy solution. I believe the issues chosen—the economy, energy, health care, toxic wastes, the urban crisis, crime, the New Right (including the "social issues"), and the arms race—constitute most of the major public issues on the minds of many students and other Americans. Of course, there are other issues that could have been chosen. But in my own teaching I have found enthusiastic support for the discussion of these particular ones.

Early in the writing of this book I made the important decision to keep the chapters as short as possible while doing justice to the subject matter. One complaint of my students, heard loud and clear, is that American government texts are too long. Students are overwhelmed, and frequently turned off, by their texts' length even before they attempt to tackle the content. The chapters in this book, by contrast, are short. My hope is that they are also well-balanced and comprehensive.

I have put into the book a number of features that I hope will aid students in their reading and understanding of the material. Each issue chapter begins with a series of guidance questions and concludes with a selected bibliography and a glossary of key terms. Furthermore, each chapter contains several aids—boxed material, tables, charts, and/or cartoons—that should make the concepts discussed more vivid. The book is the result of a happy association with extremely creative and valued colleagues and students in the Department of Political Science at San Jose State University and Michael Weber at St. Martin's Press. The manuscript benefited from excellent reviews by Kevin Bailey, North Harris County College, Texas; Larry Elowitz, Georgia College; Lawrence J. R. Herson, Ohio State University; and Jerry Waltman, University of Southern Mississippi. Both Emily Berleth and Patricia Mansfield of St. Martin's Press were a tremendous help in making the text more readable. I also wish to thank my close friends John and Ann Marie, Kathy and Karen, Rennie, Bill, and Larry for helping me through what would otherwise have been a lonely process. And thanks must go to Adele for providing a lovely setting in which to write. None of this would have been possible without the support of my wife, Eileen—to her a special thanks.

Lawrence G. Brewster

Contents

8 THE ARMS RACE: SALVATION OR RUIN? 257

the
Public
Agenda

Introduction

Our republic is beset by problems to which no one knows the answers. We face, all at once, chronic inflation, declining productivity, high interest rates, a dangerous burden of private and public debt, diminishing ability to compete in world markets, the passing of the age of cheap energy, frightening long-term decay in the cities of the industrial Northeast, a rising crime rate, skyrocketing health costs, and damage to the ecological system. And beneath these specific problems there is a haunting fear that civilization as we know it may not survive, for the arms race continues unabated, nuclear technology and materials spread, and international tensions approach the breaking point.

These problems are particularly difficult for politicians because they get so little help from the rest of us. Political leaders rarely originate ideas—their talent lies in selection and application from the community's stock of remedies. But the private sector offers them little help these days. Our business, educational, and religious leaders are baffled and uncertain. Our economists sound a little more sure of themselves but in fact are no less baffled. We face an evident crisis in analysis. While we have some ideas why we are in poor economic shape, no one really knows, for example, the cause of chronic inflation or its cure. Even if we knew the best solution to inflation or any of the other problems facing us, there would still be the difficulty of getting people to accept the costs—*the trade-offs*—that are attached to every cure of every illness.

POLITICAL AND ECONOMIC TRADE-OFFS

We do not live in the Garden of Eden. Every decision to commit resources (including time, money, materials, and energy) to one project means that there will be fewer resources for another project. Therefore, the political and economic systems in any country are primarily means by which a decision is made as to who gets what goods and services, and to what extent. Goods and services must be *rationed* through political and economic decisions because people want more than is available. This is true of any economic system, whether it is capitalism, socialism, or feudalism. And it is true for any political system, whether democratic, autocratic, or totalitarian.

In other words, economics exists because goods and services *are* scarce. Likewise, governments exist in order to help decide (authoritatively) *how* these scarce resources will be allocated. No matter how complex economic and political systems may become, the situation or predicament is quite simple: *there just is not enough to go around.* Like so many simple and important realities, this truth is often lost sight of in the midst of complicated reasoning or emotionally powerful language. For example, people point to the existence of "unmet needs" in society as evidence of the "failure" of the economic and political systems. In fact, because economic systems are essentially systems of rationing, and governments are one means of deciding who gets what among the rationed goods and services, any successfully functioning economic and political system would have "unmet needs" *everywhere.* The alternative would be to satisfy completely all of some category of needs, but this still would leave unsatisfied needs elsewhere in the society.

For example, we could completely solve the downtown parking problem in every city in the country so that anyone could easily find a convenient parking space at any hour of the day or night—but the money to achieve this goal might be taken from municipal hospitals, schools, or the water-supply system. The mundane fact of *insufficiency* must be insisted upon and restated because so many discussions of "unmet needs" proceed as if "better" policies, practices, or attitudes would solve the problem at hand without creating deficiencies elsewhere. Typical of this attitude is the comment, "If we can send a man to the moon, why can't we . . . ," followed by whatever project the speaker favors. The fact that we sent a man to the moon is part of the reason why many other things could not be done.

Let us examine another example. Since World War II, the military supremacy of the United States has disappeared, and what has been called the "nuclear stalemate" has emerged. Both the United States and the Soviet Union have enough nuclear weapons to annihilate the major population centers of the other nations several times over—"overkill," as it is called.

We will learn in chapter 8 that the history of the Soviet-American military balance has been essentially a history of the relative decline of the American position. In 1965, the United States had several hundred more nuclear missiles than the USSR , but by 1975, the Soviets had over a thousand more nuclear missiles than the United States.[1] In 1965, the United States had more military personnel in both conventional and nuclear attack forces than the USSR, but by 1975, that ratio too had been reversed.[2] Quite simply, the relative strength of American military power declined because of political decisions during those years to *trade off* defense spending for domestic welfare programs. In 1952, military spending was 66 percent of the federal budget, but this figure decreased to 24 percent by 1977. Social welfare spending rose from 17 percent to 50 percent over the same span.[3] The Soviet government has maintained and increased its military expenditures as the United States has reduced its spending. In short, the relative decline of American military power has been largely self-imposed—we chose, for political reasons, to divert many of our limited resources to social programs.

THE NEED FOR COMPROMISE

We have stated the obvious but ignored the reality that there is not enough of everything for everyone. Consequently, political and economic decisions require trade-offs. It is this need to compromise one goal (or some part of it) for another that can cause political conflict. At times the conflict can be settled to almost everyone's satisfaction; at other times, the conflict is not so satisfactorily resolved. Still other times, the conflict results in paralysis: no decision can be reached.

For most of the significant issues facing America today, including the ones discussed in this book, *meaningful compromise* cannot be made. Therefore, the politics of confrontation are upon us like the plague. No one has the ability to impose solutions, and no solutions command universal agreement.

It is important to keep in mind that there is general agreement about the goals worth pursuing for most of the issues facing us: energy independence, revitalization of our cities, reduction, if not elimination, of crime, and so forth. *What we cannot agree upon is the best method for reaching these goals.* The reason is simple: each solution requires that someone or something be sacrificed. And not only are the people concerned unwilling to give up something, but they understand the political system enough to fight successfully against any proposed sacrifices.[4]

Most Americans accepted the moon-landing project because the sacrifice was less obvious than, say, giving up land for a transportation system, or driving the car less in order to achieve energy independence. We did not stop to think that the resources spent on the moon project could have been spent on more earthly needs. The goal was appealing while at the same time the technology for getting to the moon seemed remote and unrelated to our lives. It was, after all, the technicians' job to get us there.

DEMOCRATIC CHOICES

Looked at another way, the wide spectrum of personal values ensures that no given policy or decision will become *the* answer to a human problem. The need for health care, housing, or energy can be met in a sweeping range of ways. The methods most preferred by some will be least preferred by others. Even though no political or economic system can provide for all goals simultaneously, we nevertheless hope for or expect everything promised us when voting for a set of politicians. Whatever the merits of democracy, it has its institutional limitations, like all other systems, and operates within a set of economic constraints. The open-endedness of hopes has sometimes led to the view that a majority can or should have whatever it wants—a view defined as "the democratic fallacy."

The democratic fallacy implies unlimited possibilities. Thus, if a majority does not get what it wants, it perceives some denial of its democratic rights. Choice through the ballot box has often been equated with a market system. But one crucial difference between ballots and prices is that prices convey effective knowledge of basic limitations, while ballots do not. If I desire a Rolls-Royce and simultaneously a normal standard of living, the price tag on the automobile immediately informs me that these two things are inconsistent. But if I believe simultaneously in a large military arsenal, low taxes, a balanced budget, and massive social programs, there are no constraints on my voting for all four. Some time after a voting decision, it may become apparent that what was asked for or promised did not in fact materialize, but this disappointment can easily be blamed on the dishonesty of political candidates, with no greater public awareness that the set of options simultaneously desired was inherently unrealizable from the outset. Voters rarely perceive this message as feedback instructing them to reduce their desired options to ones that are simultaneously attainable. Instead, they interpret it to mean they should choose different leaders or different ideologies in order to continue pursuing their original set of options. Indeed, when we look back on the social progress made over the years, the temptation is to see it as the result of our having fought for the better life through the political process rather than as a result of technological and organizational changes that created a wider range of options from which to choose.

The question here is not whether voters have a right to choose whatever they want. Voters can only *choose* the process by which decisions are made and *hope* for results. Consumers, on the other hand, buy results and leave the process to those with specialized knowledge of such things. There is no argument here for denying voters their democratic choices. The point is that the terms of the choice are readily misstated politically. A good part of the art of politics is learning to misstate the options and to give the appearance of simultaneously satisfying competing claims when they cannot be satisfied in reality. We must remember this fact when thinking about the issues in this book.

POLITICAL LABELS

To help ourselves act with more confidence and intelligence (at least in terms of our perceived interests), we often try to put ourselves and others into neat political categories. The most common of these categories are labeled *liberalism* and *conservatism*. Although these labels have been recently used with so many different, and often conflicting, meanings that they have been robbed of much of their clarity and usefulness, we shall attempt to define them here.

Whenever issues are discussed, a common question is: Are U.S.

citizens basically liberal or conservative in their political opinions? The answer we get depends on how we define "liberal" and "conservative," the issues we ask people about, and when the research is conducted. Naturally, because of the many different approaches to this question, analysts offer many different answers.

A Useful Distinction

When asking whether the majority of Americans are liberal or conservative, it is useful to make the distinction between economic and noneconomic liberalism-conservatism.[5] The *economic* dimension basically refers to attitudes toward issues associated with the FDR New Deal reforms. *Economic liberals* have generally endorsed the extension of the welfare-planning state and have backed government policies and expenditures to improve the lot of the less privileged, the poor, the unemployed, the elderly, and the sick. They have favored a progressive income tax hitting hard at the wealthy and at corporations. They have supported trade unions and the regulation of business. *Economic conservatives* have generally opposed such policies.

The *noneconomic* or social dimension, as it has come to be called in recent years, supports civil liberties (protection from arbitrary government interference) for unpopular groups, the rights of criminals, the claims of minority groups and women, new social and cultural values, and most recently, environmental issues. On this dimension, those called conservatives, though not overt opponents of the rights of political and social minorities, or of efforts to improve the environment, have tended to be less enthusiastic about involving the government actively. They have been more hard line on issues of law and order and have been unhappy about changes in conventional morality.

Are Most Americans Liberal or Conservative?

Over the years, polls have consistently shown that most people (about 75 percent) can apply "liberal" or "conservative" to some of their political positions, but that people generally place themselves near the "middle-of-the-road" position.[6] Though year-to-year variations occur, the middle position is always the most popular. Measured this way, then, we can say that most people are moderates, not extremists, on the liberal-conservative scale.

Does poll information of this type provide a conclusive answer to our question? Some analysts claim that many people who use terms like *liberal* or *conservative* have little understanding of what these labels mean in either the economic or noneconomic dimensions. Therefore, when people label themselves liberal or conservative, this says little about the actual policies they favor. For example, a 1970 Gallup Poll asked, "What is the first thing that comes to your mind when you think of someone who is a liberal (conservative)?"[7] Many responses were vague and had little to do with government action. Common answers were "open-minded, fair," "gives things away, spends too freely," or "cautious." About a third of the respondents could offer no definition of the terms. Such answers suggest that we must be cautious when interpreting what people mean when they describe their political orientations.[8]

Inconsistency in Opinion

The matter is made more difficult when we acknowledge that opinions are often personal and emotional. This dimension, combined with a low level of understanding of many issues, can lead to unstable and inconsistent public opinion. So it is also true that a person holding the liberal position on one issue may hold the middle-of-the-road or conservative position on others. For example, a person may favor equal rights for women (a liberal position) yet also oppose the legalization of marijuana (a conservative position).[9]

It All Depends

To return to our original question of whether citizens are liberal or conservative, the answer is—it depends. If we simply ask people to describe themselves as liberal or conservative, we find that most consider themselves moderate. If we claim that liberal or conservative labels mean little to most people, and instead examine opinions on an issue-by-issue basis, no simple pattern emerges. Depending on the issue, people tend to be liberal, conservative, or middle-of-the-road. The problem is even further complicated because many people who use terms like *liberal* or *conservative* disagree on what they mean.

TIME

When thinking about the democratic process and the hoped-for results from that process, it is important to consider *time*. Issues like the ones included in this book require both short- and long-term plans and have both short- and long-term consequences—both intended and unintended.

Unfortuantely, most politicians have relatively short time horizons. Cynics, in fact, say that they think no further ahead than to the next election. Although voters may have a longer time horizon than politicians, we do not anticipate the long-term consequences of most issues at the time we are asked to vote. Furthermore, the connection between a decision on an issue and our self-interest is not always clear. It is sometimes difficult to know what a particular decision made in Washington, or our state capital, or even by our city officials, means for us. Finally, most of us are not programmed to plan very far into the future. While we may think further ahead than the two or four years until the next election, we are not likely to think ten, fifteen, or twenty years down the road. Yet many of the issues facing us require that kind of long-term planning.

When planners decided in the 1950s to build an interstate high-way system, most voters, if they were aware of the decision, thought only about the immediate benefits of faster and easier travel. Neither the voters nor the planners thought about the probable increase in highway deaths, loss of land, division of neighborhoods and cities, traffic jams, or an energy shortage. In other words, consequences that take time to become visible are less likely to be understood by the average voter. And given the turnover of elected and appointed officials, the prospect of long-run negative consequences may be of little concern to them at the time they make the decision.

The Value of Political Parties

When there is a strong political party system or a powerful political machine concerned with its long-run officeholding prospects, decisions that favor sacrificing the future for the present are discouraged. The costs to society of decisions that primarily favor individual politicians are internalized to some extent, and a somewhat longer time horizon is enforced. However, with the growth of "independent" (or perhaps "charismatic") politicians, the political time horizon tends to shrink back to the individual's own office-holding years. It may be significant, for example, that New York City's financial crisis of the 1970s grew out of policies and practices adopted during the administration of one of its most charismatic and independent mayors during the 1960s, and that the contrasting financial solvency of Chicago at the same time was maintained in one of the last bastions of municipal machine politics.

Members of a political machine have a large investment in its future election prospects, which relate to their own prospects of advancement to higher office. The more independent individual politicians are, the less their fates are tied to the long-run consequences of their decisions in a particular unit of government. Negative consequences after they have departed from office can even be used as evidence of their superiority to those who follow. What matters to independent politicians is how their *current* decisions in their *current* position promote their *immediate* prospects for higher positions elsewhere. If a given set of policies enhances Mayor Smith's presidential prospects, he is not concerned with the possible damage of those policies to the city after he is in the White House.

Time and Fixed Costs

The reader must also consider the relationship of time to economic decisions involving "fixed costs"—costs that do not vary in the short run. Bridges and bus, sewer, and water lines, for example, have large fixed costs for their basic structure and equipment relative to the other kinds of costs—such as labor costs—which vary with the use of the facility or service. Municipal bus lines can continue to operate without adding to taxpayers' burdens as long as the fares cover the short-run costs, such as the purchase of gasoline and the drivers' pay. For the longer run, however, the fares must also cover the fixed costs of replacing the buses as they wear out. At any one point, the need to raise bus fares to cover both kinds of costs can be politically denied without fear of feedback within a politician's time horizon. As long as the existing fares continue to cover the cost of gasoline, drivers' salaries, and similar short-run costs, fare increases can be postponed without any immediate reduction in the quantity or quality of bus service or any increase in taxes—regardless of how inadequate the fares may be in long-run terms. That is a problem for future riders, taxpayers, and administrations. At the moment of decision there are obvious political gains to be made by protecting the public (or the poor) from higher fares. However, when the buses age and begin breaking down, leading to more overcrowding in those remaining, longer waits between buses, and less comfortable rides, this affects not only the transportation system but also the social ecology of the city. Those who find the municipal transit system intolerable have incentives to use their own automobiles or stay at home. Both traffic congestion and a loss of business for shopowners in the city will result. We will learn in chapter 5, for example, that today's taxpayers will be forced to pay the high cost of replacing the vital parts of aging cities because politicians and planners have for too long ignored repairs of roads, water and sewer pipes, and other elements of the infrastructure.

THE DESIRE FOR A RISK-FREE SOCIETY

One last point should be made. Most people in developed nations, including Americans, seek to make *their* world *risk-free*, or nearly so. The instrument for doing this is government.[10] Whenever possible, we ask government to reduce or shift the risk carried by individuals.

A new form of society has evolved. It started with a reliance by citizens on government for the solution to certain economic, social, and cultural problems and grew to include pressures on government to minimize almost every risk any individual might be asked to bear. The costs of many of the new government protection programs, as well as some of the old ones, are not covered by taxation, nor are they shown in a government budget or even in any official report or document. Rather, the government achieves its objectives through laws, regulations, and licenses. As a result, government is much bigger than most people realize. Its ability to disguise its vast size is partly what makes the new society work.

At first, government's role grew because certain people were concerned about questions of morality and equality. They recognized that an uncontrolled free market economy might lead to what they considered socially unacceptable income and wealth distribution. These considerations, as we have already learned, were reinforced by a gradual shift in the distribution of political power. The combination of moral considerations and the increasing political power of the poor and minorities has led to more and more government programs and protections. The richer the country became, however, the louder were the demands for an expanded role of government.

In his *No-Risk Society,* Yair Aharoni claims that we have moved beyond the welfare state to an insurance state.

> The welfare state has turned into an insurance state, as all individuals are protected against a whole array of risks by shifting the burden of their consequences to a larger group or the whole community or simply by eliminating them.[11]

He goes on to say,

> We are insured against a variety of mishaps that range from earthquakes and other natural disasters to poor health, unemployment, and the infirmities of old age. Safety in terms of workplace and working

hours is regulated; ailing firms are supported; research and development is subsidized by guarantees and grants; quality is controlled, information and social insurance supplied, foreign competition checked, extreme weather conditions and technological changes insured against, and even social status protected.[12]

We will learn in chapter 1 that some, like Aharoni, argue that the role and size of the federal government should be limited. They blame inflation and stagnant economic growth in Western nations on government policies directed toward protecting citizens from a great number of risks. However, others, while decrying extensive government taxation, spending, and regulation, warn against the opposite extreme, complete laissez-faire. They advocate a balance between big government and laissez-faire. The composition of this balance, if it ever can be achieved, will affect most political and economic issues in this country.

Have We Gone Too Far?

In short, a growing number of people are asking if we have gone too far. In the new society, some feel they have lost rights as others have gained them. Management is less free to hire and fire workers or make decisions that have an ecological impact. Workers who tend to be risk takers have found that their rights to take risks for extra compensation have been reduced through social and regulatory legislation. Young people who would rather spend today than save for tomorrow are constrained from doing so by, among other things, Social Security taxes. On the other hand, equal opportunity for women and minority groups and access to health care for the poor are increasing, though many argue that the present degree of equality of opportunity is not enough. Big government, mounting regulations, and ever higher taxes lead some to complain that governments "route too much of income away from productive private uses, . . . high tax rates destroy the rewards of production, and capricious economic policies and tenacious inflation destroy the climate for investment to produce jobs and income."[13]

As with everything else, there is a *need for balance* in discussions of the role of government in solving today's problems. Perhaps we are beginning to accept the idea that government is not the all-knowing, all-seeing savior of the human race. Some problems, after all, are insoluble, and a no-risk society *is* impossible. Perhaps there will be a more realistic appraisal of what is possible, and an understanding that neither competitive individualism nor benevolent management by government can deliver the necessary goods and services that will solve all problems. If so, then we will also learn to live with unsolved problems and unsatisfied human desires, while never losing hope that a solution may ultimately be found.

NOTES

1. The Library of Congress, Congressional Research Service, *United States/Soviet Military Balance* (Washington, D.C.: Government Printing Office, 1978), p. 43.
2. Ibid., pp. 43, 45.
3. Roger Freeman, *The Growth of American Government* (Stanford, Calif.: Hoover Institution, 1977), pp. 6–7.
4. For an excellent discussion of this change in American society, see Lester C. Thurow, *The Zero-Sum Society* (New York: Basic Books, 1980).
5. The most common definition of liberalism-conservatism stresses the role of government in economic matters. For example, someone favoring more government financial assistance to poor people is a liberal. However, on noneconomic issues, this more-government versus less-government distinction becomes less clear. On the abortion controversy, for instance, the liberal position is usually associated with no government intervention while conservatives endorse government regulation.
6. See, for example, poll data for the years 1972, 1974, 1976, and 1980 on the position of Americans on liberal-conservative scales conducted by the Center for Political Studies, University of Michigan, Ann Arbor.
7. On the public's understanding of the government's role in society vis-à-vis the terms *liberal* and *conservative*, see Philip E. Converse, "The Nature of Belief Systems in Mass Publics," in *Ideology and Discontent*, ed. David E. Apter (New York: Free Press, 1964), pp. 219–27.
8. Gallup Poll, *Public Opinion 1935–1971*, III (New York: Random House, 1971), pp. 244–45.
9. See Lloyd Free and Hadley Cantril, *Political Beliefs of Americans* (New York: Simon and Schuster, 1968).
10. See Yair Aharoni, *The No-Risk Society* (Chatham, N.J.: Chatham House, 1981).
11. Ibid., p. 1.
12. Ibid., pp. 1–2.
13. Editorial in *Wall Street Journal*, September 7, 1977.

SUGGESTED READINGS

Beard, Charles A. *An Economic Interpretation of the Constitution of the United States.* New York: Free Press, 1965.

Dolbeare, Kenneth M., ed. *American Political Thought.* Monterey, Calif.: Duxbury, 1981.

Edelman, Murray. *The Symbolic Uses of Politics.* Urbana, Ill.: University of Illinois Press, 1964.

Harris, Louis. *The Anguish of Change.* New York: Norton, 1973.

Hartz, Louis. *The Liberal Tradition in America.* New York: Harcourt Brace Jovanovich, 1955.

Hofstadter, Richard. *The American Political Tradition and the Men Who Made It.* New York: Knopf, 1948.

Kristol, Irving. *On the Democratic Idea in America.* New York: Harper & Row, 1972.

Roelofs, H. Mark. *Ideology and Myth in American Politics: A Critique of a National Political Mind.* Boston: Little, Brown, 1976.

1
The Political Economy

How does the government affect the economy?

What are the economic goals of government?

How have presidents, beginning with John F. Kennedy, attempted to manage the economy?

How do President Reagan's economic policies differ from those of his recent predecessors?

Has the government become too involved in the economy?

Americans have not been a nation united by common ancestry or religious beliefs. Instead, we have been united by economic and political factors. Yet most of us know very little about the economic system or its relationship to the political system. Traditionally, Americans have thought of economics and politics as separate activities. Even today many of us do not see the connection between our jobs, the overall economy, and government policies. Or, more likely, we do not realize that the costs of such things as a steak dinner are determined in part by government action.

The truth is that no economic decision is completely divorced from politics. Political decisions are made about every aspect of the economy, including the value of the dollar, interest rates, tax rates, the uses of private property, business regulations, and so forth. There is good reason, however, why we don't understand the economic system, let alone its relationship to politics: it is incredibly complex. Almost everything is somehow related to everything else—even an event in another country can be as important to you as something that happens in your neighborhood or city.

Because the economic system *is* so complex, it is tempting to leave the economic decision-making to experts. After all, with their fancy computer models and statistics, most economists give the impression they know how to fix what is wrong. But even when they are able to offer solutions to economic problems, political decisions take precedence over purely technical decisions. The U.S. economy is *not* like an engine that has to be correctly tuned up by master technicians following a service manual. There are many different ways, but no single "correct" way, of solving economic problems. Through the political process, we establish our priorities and the particular solutions we shall use. A professional economist could show us that production is exceeding demand and suggest a tax cut as a solution. However, the seriousness of this problem and the question of *who* will get the benefit of a tax reduction are *political,* not technical, matters. We saw in the introduction that all economic decisions have costs. A tolerable cost for one person may be a disaster for another. Such a dilemma poses a political question, not an economic one.

This chapter examines important questions dealing with the relationship between politics and economics. We will examine what causes a nation's economy to expand or contract—what causes inflation and unemployment, and more recently, stagflation (high inflation and unemployment at the same time). We also want to know how a nation's economic health and performance can be improved. Our investigation of these questions must include definitions and explanations of some basic concepts and tools of macroeconomics—the branch of economics that studies the national economy as a whole.

THE LANGUAGE OF MACROECONOMICS

Aggregate Supply and Demand

When talking about macroeconomics, it is important to think in terms of aggregate supply and aggregate demand rather than the supply and demand of microeconomic theory. *Aggregate supply* is the capacity of a nation's total resources, at full employment, to produce goods and services. It is more or less fixed at any given moment, but it can grow over time—as the labor force grows, as industry invests in new plants and equipment, as the government builds more schools, highways, airports, and other capital improvements, and as science, technology, and human knowledge advance. In the short run, however, aggregate supply sets a limit on what the economy can produce, a limit that may or may not be exceeded by aggregate demand. *Aggregate demand* is all the money that people, businesses, and governments spend on goods and services. Problems arise in a national economy when aggregate demand and aggregate supply are not balanced.

Inflation

No subject is as much discussed and as little understood as inflation. What we call inflation is, always and everywhere, primarily caused by an increase in the supply of money and credit. In fact, inflation *is* the increase in the supply of money and credit. It is sometimes defined as the "undue *expansion* or increase of the *currency* of a country, especially by the issuing of paper money not redeemable in specie" (emphasis added).

In recent years, however, the term has come to be used in a radically different sense. This is recognized by a second definition usually given: "A substantial *rise of prices* caused by an undue expansion in paper money or bank credit" (emphasis added).[1] Obviously, a rise of prices *caused* by an expansion of the money supply is not the same thing as the expansion of the money supply itself. The use of the word *inflation* with these two quite different meanings leads to endless confusion.

The word *inflation* originally applied solely to the quantity of money. It meant that the volume of money was inflated, blown up, overextended. However, because the word *inflation* is now so commonly used to mean "a rise in prices," it would be difficult and time-consuming here to keep avoiding or refuting it on every occasion. The word has almost universally been used ambiguously. Sometimes it is used in the first sense—to mean an increase in money stock—but much more often it is used in the second sense—to mean a rise in prices.

Let us see what happens under inflation, and why it happens. When the supply of money is increased, people have more money to offer for goods. If the supply of goods does not increase—or does not increase as much as the supply of money—then the price of goods will go up. Each individual dollar becomes less valuable because there are more dollars. Therefore more of them will be offered against, say, a pair of shoes or a hundred bushels of wheat than before. A "price" is an exchange ratio between a dollar and a unit of goods. When people have more dollars, they value each dollar less. Goods then rise in price, not because they are scarcer than before, but because dollars are more abundant and thus less valued.

In other words, an excessive increase in the supply of money allows total demand to increase fast and hence cause inflation. This is known as *demand-pull inflation.*

Inflation may also result from the pressure of labor, industrial monopolies, or international cartels driving up costs faster than productivity; this is *cost-push inflation.*

It is often argued that to attribute inflation solely to an increase in the volume of money is oversimplification. This is true. Many qualifications have to be kept in mind. For example, the "money supply" must be thought of as including not only the supply of hand-to-hand currency, but the supply of bank credit—especially in the United States, where most payments are made by check.

It is also an oversimplification to say that the value of an individual dollar depends simply on the *present* supply of dollars outstanding. It depends also on the *expected future* supply of dollars. If most people fear, for example, that the supply is going to be even greater a year from now than at present, then the present value of the dollar (as measured by its purchasing power) will be lower than the present quantity of dollars would otherwise warrant. Thus the expectation of inflation may be a self-fulfilling prophecy as every seller of goods and services raises prices and wages in an effort to keep ahead of expectations of increased costs. The wheel spins on and on in a process known as *momentum inflation.*

Again, the value of any monetary unit, such as the dollar, depends not merely on the *quantity* of dollars but on their *quality.* When a country goes off the gold standard (as did the United States), it means in effect that gold, or the right to get gold, has suddenly turned into mere paper. The value of the monetary unit therefore usually falls immediately, even if there has not yet been any increase in the quantity of money. This is because the people have more faith in gold than they have in the promise or judgment of the government's monetary managers. There is hardly a case on record in which departure from the gold standard has not soon been followed by a further increase in bank credit and in printing press money.

In short, the value of money varies for basically the same reasons as the value of any commodity. Just as the value of a bushel of wheat depends not only on the total present supply of wheat but on the expected future supply and on the quality of the wheat, so the value of a dollar depends on a similar variety of considerations. The value of money, like the value of goods, is not determined merely by mechanical or physical relationships, but primarily by psychological factors which may often be complicated.

Unemployment

Instability also occurs when aggregate demand falls below aggregate supply in the form of unemployment. This creates a "capacity gap," with part of the nation's labor force and some of its industrial plants standing idle.

The demand for labor is a "derived demand"—derived from the demand for goods and services. The way to cure unemployment generally is to expand the total demand for the goods and services that the economy is capable of producing.

Unemployment also results, in the case of particular workers, from other factors such as a lack of education or skills that employers can use. Job discrimination against ethnic minorities, older people, or women, and minimum wage laws that set wages above the productive value of some workers, such as inexperienced teenagers, can also be specific causes of unemployment.

Urban decay, social unrest, and crime doubtless contribute to unemployment. Employers may move their plants or offices away from troubled city centers to the suburbs or other states (see chapter 5), and workers may be unable to follow because of family circumstances, inadequate transportation, or lack of housing in the new area.

Regions of chronic underemployment, such as Appalachia or parts of the industrial Northeast, may suffer high unemployment due to industrial stagnation and the immobility of labor. Unemployment resulting from social, locational, technological, and specific market factors unrelated to overall weakness in the economy is called *structural unemployment.*

But when unemployment increases by the hundreds of thousands or millions over the course of a single year, you can be sure the change is due not to structural factors but to a business slump—and insufficient aggregate demand. This condition existed in 1983, for example, with unemployment greater than 10 percent.

Stagflation

Stagflation is economic stagnation combined with inflation. What should fiscal policy be when the economy is suffering from the economic disease of simultaneous inflation and unemployment? No one knows for certain. The treatment requires some combination of economic balance, juggling, guessing, luck, improvisation, and specific measures aimed at specific aspects of inflation and unemployment.

In dealing with stagflation, planners must first decide whether inflation or unemployment is the more serious problem and whether the economy is moving toward worse inflation or worse unemployment. If inflation is seen as the greater menace, national fiscal and monetary policy should be aimed at restraint. But if unemployment is held to be the greater danger, a fiscal and monetary stimulus should be applied. Republicans traditionally favor restraint, and Democrats prefer stimulus.

Setting aggregate demand so that it is neither too strong nor too weak—a fine line that may be impossible to locate—does not in itself give the whole answer to how to deal with stagflation. If inflation persists, even without excess aggregate demand, specific attacks should be launched on the forces pushing up wages and prices faster than productivity. Efforts could be made to increase productivity as a means of curbing inflation; for instance, one might call for an investment tax credit or more liberal depreciation allowances to induce industry to invest more in productive equipment. But it is extremely difficult to raise national productivity, especially in the short run.

We do not know how to stop an ongoing inflationary spiral without throwing the economy into recession. Direct wage and price controls may have some shock value, but they are likely to become less effective and more disturbing to the economy as time goes by. Direct controls go against the free enterprise philosophy of the Republicans and against some of the political interests of the Democrats. Labor, strong in the Democratic camp (although labor shifted some support to President Reagan in the 1980 elections), opposes wage controls, fearing that it will lose ground because wages are easier to control than prices. And business interests, as well as the Republican party, are usually against price controls because they see them as a blow to profits, a source of inefficiency, and a curb to their own autonomy.

Stagflation has also called forth a host of other proposals for reducing unemployment without a more rapid increase in aggregate demand (which, it is feared, would worsen inflation). The proposed means of attacking structural unemployment include public service job programs; youth-employment programs; attacks on racial discrimination and other restrictive practices, such as archaic building codes and apprenticeship rules; federal subsidies to cities without the financial means of maintaining adequate police, fire, educational, and other services; reform to encourage those on welfare to seek employment without a dollar-for-dollar loss of benefits; and community services, such as day care for young children, that would enable more parents on welfare to work.

The economists advising President Reagan are skeptical about the ability of such programs to solve structural unemployment problems, and they believe that more emphasis should be put on eliminating the minimum wage, which keeps young and low-productivity workers out of jobs. In a moment we will examine other proposals for solving stagflation advocated by President Reagan and his economic advisers. In fact, in part because of Reagan's policies, it appears that stagflation has been defeated—for the moment anyway. That is, the recession beginning in 1981 has brought down inflation, although at tremendous cost in unemployment (see Figure 1-1). We will have more to say about Reagan's programs later in this chapter.

Now that we have a better understanding of some basic concepts of macroeconomics, let us look at four changes since the Great Depression of the 1930s that have helped to stabilize the economy in this country. The changes are of course interrelated. In different ways, all mark a tremendous increase in the importance of what happens in Washington.

STABILIZING THE ECONOMY

Government Employment

In 1929, the federal government employed 579,559 civilians. Just over half worked for the Post Office. Not quite 20 percent were attached to the War and Navy departments. Only about 30 percent of the total—180,000 people—worked for the other branches of the federal government. Counting both these civilian employees and the military (roughly 255,000 soldiers, sailors, and marines), the federal government in 1929 employed slightly less than 2 percent of the labor force. State and local governments employed another 2.5 million, or about 5 percent of the labor force. All told, one American worker in fifteen worked for government at some level.

Today the Defense Department alone employs more civilians (just over a million) than the whole federal government did back in 1929. The federal government as a whole employs approximately three million civilians and more than two million military personnel

Figure 1-1 STATE OF THE U.S. ECONOMY SINCE RONALD REAGAN BECAME PRESIDENT

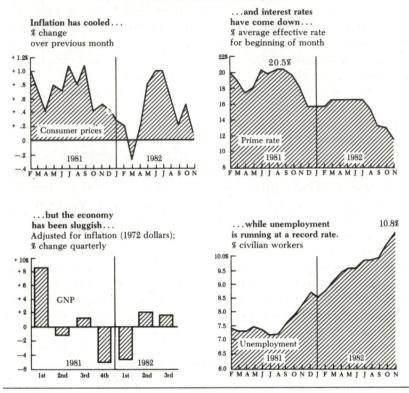

Source: *San Francisco Chronicle,* December 26, 1982, sect. D, pp. 1–2.

on active duty. State and local government employment has bur-
geoned to almost thirteen million. Counting the armed forces, government at some level now employs about 17 percent of the labor
force. Indirect government employment—people working for
firms with government contracts, for example—has been estimated
to include another 11 percent of the labor force. More than a quarter of U.S. workers now depend directly or indirectly on government expenditures.[2]

From the employee's point of view, working for the government is pleasant because one seldom gets laid off. The
well-publicized cutbacks of city workers during the past few years
don't contradict this statement; they're just the exception that
proves the rule. When twenty police officers lose their jobs, it's a
scandal; when two thousand rubber workers lose theirs, it's a fact
of life. Unemployment rates for people who have worked in govern-

ment are lower than for any other major occupational group: these rates are usually less than half the national average. The reason, of course, is that businesses lay off workers any time sales drop, or whenever the future looks bleak. Governments don't face the same constraints. Only when a particular jurisdiction finds it hard to raise taxes—New York City, for instance, or Cleveland—will it even begin to think about layoffs. And even then the federal government (which always has plenty of money, for reasons we'll get to shortly) can often be called in to help.

From the economist's point of view, all these government workers are an immense stabilizing force on the economy. When business is slow, industries begin laying off workers. Production falls; so does purchasing power. Things immediately look worse than they did before. More businesses then lay off workers, and the downturn becomes more severe. Not so with the government. Business may be bad, but children still have to be taught, roads maintained and criminals put in jail. Moreover, Congress may decide to fund a new missile system or build a new dam—thereby increasing government employment—precisely because business looks bad. Thus the business cycle is stabilized or even counteracted by a large government sector.

Transfer Payments

State and local government employment has grown considerably in recent years. It more than doubled, for example, between 1960 and 1982. Civilian and military federal employment, however, has increased only a little since the late forties and has actually fallen off in the last ten years. What has accounted for the recent growth in federal spending is transfer payments.

Transfer payments are essentially an invention of the last fifty years. In 1929, the only money the federal government paid out to individuals other than its employees went to veterans and bondholders. In 1981, transfer payments (*excluding* interest on bonds) were well over $200 billion, or roughly 40 percent of total federal outlays. In the 1970s alone, transfer payments increased 76 percent in real terms.

The increase of federal spending in this area relative to state and local government spending continues despite President Reagan's efforts to return authority to the states. The relative growth in federal spending was not what Reagan had in mind when he took office in 1981. Except for military spending, he advocated reducing outlays and letting states pick up affected programs. The Advisory

Commission on Intergovernmental Relations, a nonpartisan research group established by Congress in 1982, attributed the federal increase in transfer payments to an aging population that has
put more demands on Social Security and Medicare.

Although citizens frequently conclude that welfare recipients
are gobbling up more and more of their tax dollars, the fact is most
of the transfer payments represent programs that we don't usually
think of as "welfare." Let us divide a hypothetical 1981 tax dollar
going to transfer payments—hypothetical only because the taxes
that actually pay for these programs come from many different
sources. About 78¢ will go to cash benefits—47¢ to social security,
11¢ to retired federal employees, and 5¢ each to veterans, welfare
recipients, the unemployed, and miscellaneous other beneficiaries.
The other 22¢ goes to in-kind benefits: food stamps, public housing,
and (the largest) Medicare.

From the recipients' point of view, these transfers make retirement or lack of work a lot more tolerable than they otherwise might
be. They also provide something of an alternative to jobs that pay
too little, or jobs where the employer tries to cut wages. From the
point of view of the whole economy, transfers are a tremendously
important way of stabilizing purchasing power. The poor and the
elderly have considerably more income to spend than they otherwise might. Workers who lose their jobs get unemployment benefits, giving them some money to spend. In the past, even the threat
of a slump led people to cut their spending; the slump itself might
reduce their incomes to zero. Today recessions can be painful (as
we learned in 1982–1983), but our incomes fall nowhere near as far
or as fast as they once did. The downturn is apt to be less severe,
and recovery is that much quicker.

Fiscal Policy

Government spending of all kinds adds up to about a third of the
Gross National Product (the total dollar value of all goods that have
been bought for final use and services during a year). More precisely, in 1982, combined federal, state, and local outlays exceeded the
$1 trillion mark or about 35 percent of the GNP. Washington's dis-
bursements alone account for more than a fifth of the GNP. All this
spending helps anchor the economy through the business cycle,
maintaining people's purchasing power during bad times and good.
The federal budget also plays another role: it can counteract the
business cycle by running in deficit when the economy is slow and

running in surplus when the economy is booming. This "countercy-clical" effect, as economists term it, reflects the government's fiscal or tax-and-spending policies.[3]

A budget surplus is simple enough to understand. Washington, in effect, is taking more money out of the economy than it is putting back in. Purchasing power is thus less than it otherwise would be. People buy less, workers produce less, and the economy slows down. Insofar as that eases pressure on prices and wages, inflation should slow down too.

Deficits are a little harder to comprehend. The government is simply borrowing the extra money that it is spending. The factory worker who is busy saving bonds on a payroll-deduction plan and the New York bank that buys a million dollars' worth of Treasury bills are both lending the government money to cover its deficit. As the government borrows, the national debt increases. But this is not, in most cases, a cause for alarm. Just as a company can borrow more and more every year as long as business is good and the firm is growing, the government can borrow more and more as long as the economy is growing. The national debt has increased in dollar terms every year since 1950. But debt as a proportion of GNP has grown smaller almost every year. The debt "burden" on the taxpayers is thus decreasing although government deficits in the 1970s hit record levels.[4]

More worrisome than the national debt is what might happen if the government does not run a deficit. Without a deficit there's a good chance that purchasing power (recall that economists call it aggregate demand) won't be sufficient to keep the economy going at full speed. Why this should be so is no mystery. Suppose, for example, that you make $20,000 a year. According to the way these things are figured, you have produced $20,000 worth of goods or services that somebody now has to buy. But you may not want to spend your whole $20,000. You may want to put a little in the bank, or maybe buy some stocks or bonds. In good times, businesses are looking for ways to expand: building a new plant, say, or replacing old machinery with the latest model. To do so they need to borrow money. So they sell you a bond, or they go to the same bank you put your savings in, borrow your savings, and spend them. In that case every dollar that has been earned gets spent, and the economy keeps humming.

But suppose business looks bad, and companies aren't doing much investing. Your savings and everybody else's start to pile up in the banks. Now you have "produced" more dollars than you're spending. Everybody else who's doing any saving has done the same thing. Unsold goods begin to pile up on the shelves. Companies notice this and begin to cut back production. A recession threatens.

Here's where the government steps in. If it borrows your money (either directly or from the bank) and spends it, the money you saved will stay in circulation. Everything that is produced will be bought. There will be no unsold goods on the shelves, and no cutbacks. In fact, business will look good: companies too will want to borrow so they can expand, and the economy will grow. But note that the government must run a deficit in order to assure this happy result. It must spend all it takes in in taxes, borrow some more, and spend that too. It has to spend your savings as well as its "own" money. It can run a surplus only when it's willing to risk recession (to fight inflation, say), or when it believes that business will invest enough on its own to keep the economy moving (Reagan's hope).

The government budget's countercyclical effect varies automatically with what the rest of the economy is doing. When unemployment rises, spending for jobless benefits and other relief programs goes up too. Yet tax revenues fall, since people who aren't working don't pay taxes. So the federal balance sheet tilts toward a deficit. When the economy is booming, on the other hand, tax revenues rise and spending falls, thereby tending to create a surplus.

In principle, whatever administration is in power sets its fiscal policy by adjusting tax and spending levels to achieve the desired effect. If recession threatens, the government should cut taxes or increase spending, thereby boosting purchasing power. If inflation is thought to be the greater danger, the supposed cure is to increase taxes or reduce spending. In real life, of course, the choice is seldom so simple. The trade-off between inflation and recession (as we shall see in a moment) is not always clear. And political considerations always impart a certain asymmetry to fiscal policy changes. Any politician will find it easier to increase spending, thereby keeping various interest groups and federal agencies happy, than to cut it—even in good times.

Fiscal policy therefore more often focuses on stimulating the economy than on slowing it down. In the past twenty years, the budget has been in significant surplus exactly twice. The result is higher levels of employment and fewer (or milder) recessions than we otherwise might have had. Another result, however, is more inflation.

Monetary Policy

Like an engine that runs on gasoline, the economy runs on money. If there isn't enough, the economy won't run very fast and will be prone to fits and starts. By itself, plenty of money will not ensure a fast-growing, smoothly working economy; we need people, businesses, and governments willing and able to spend that money. But if we don't have the money, we can't have the spending.

The word *money* in ordinary terms usually refers to currency: bills and coins. Those who accuse the government of cheapening the dollar frequently accuse it of "printing too much money," as if the presses that turn out $5 bills were working overtime. In reality, of course, most of what we use as money isn't currency at all; it's the "money" that is in our checking accounts.

This money is neither more nor less than a bookkeeping account on the bank's ledgers. It is created, in part, by the banking system itself.

Suppose you take $1,000 in cash to a bank and open an account. You now have a brand-new checkbook, and you know you can write checks up to a total of $1,000. Suppose at the same time your neighbor applies to the same bank for a loan of $1,000. When she gets the loan, the bank doesn't necessarily give her your $1,000 in cash; more likely it also gives her a checkbook and credits her account with $1,000. Now you and she have a total of $2,000 to draw on, but the bank, let us assume, only has your original $1,000 in currency. As long as neither of you wants $1,000 in cash at the same time, the bank is sitting pretty. By this process the supply of money—that is, the total deposits the banking system carries on its books plus currency in circulation—grows well beyond the volume of cash that is in circulation at any given time.

Obviously, there has to be some limit on the amount of money so created. If banks lend money to all comers, they'll soon find themselves in trouble (which in fact happens from time to time). And if the banking system creates too much money in relation to what there is to buy, the excess purchasing power will drive prices up. The dollar will be worth less simply because there are too many dollars in circulation.

The growth of the money supply can be limited in two ways. One is the way of "hard" money, fiscal responsibility, reliance on the market. The other is the way of "soft" money and political interference with the market. By all the standards of good conservatism, the first sounds preferable. When it was tried, however, it had two rather severe drawbacks. Coping with these drawbacks led to the inflationary monetary system we have today.

Under the traditional system of managing the money supply (in effect in this country throughout much of the nineteenth century and changed only gradually in the twentieth), every paper dollar is theoretically redeemable in gold. The government can issue only as much currency as it can safely cover with the gold in its vaults. Banks have to have access to enough currency or gold to satisfy any of their depositors who want it. The gold standard thus imposes rather severe limits on how fast the money supply can grow.

A country's gold supply depends on how much of the metal is being mined, and on how much is coming in from abroad to purchase goods and services. Its need for money, however, depends on how much real economic activity there is—how much people want to borrow and spend. If people want to borrow and spend more money than is easily available with the existing gold supply, interest rates shoot up. Banks make fewer loans, and businesses don't invest. The supply of money can thus limit economic growth. It may even provoke a recession. That's why the Populists of the late nineteenth century—William Jennings Bryan and his followers, for instance—fought so hard against the gold standard. If more money were available (if, for example, all the currency could be backed by silver as well as gold), then booms would be longer, panics fewer. The price of this—inflation—was one the Populists were willing to pay.

In a series of steps beginning with Roosevelt's 1933 ban on gold transactions and ending with Nixon's renunciation of the international gold standard in 1971, the United States went "off gold." The particular reasons for each step were different. Ultimately, however, gold is too inflexible a standard for a rapidly growing economy. If we were still on the gold standard, we would either be limiting ourselves to a very slow rate of growth (essentially the rate at which gold could be obtained) or else we would constantly be making the dollar worth less in terms of the amount of gold it would buy. The former choice would be disastrous for the economy. The latter, though theoretically possible, would appear to undermine ("devalue") the currency repeatedly by deliberate government action. A rapidly expanding economy can't work with a money supply that is fixed either by fiat or by custom, any more than a growing number of automobiles can easily run on the oil produced by a fixed number of wells.

So the dollar today has no "gold backing" at all. If you take a

$1 bill to the Treasury and ask for metal, you will probably be given a Susan B. Anthony copper-and-nickel coin, worth less than 3¢ melted down. Instead, limits on the money supply are set, through a variety of devices, by the Federal Reserve System (see Box 1-1). The Fed tells banks how much money they can lend in proportion to their "reserves" (currency and money the banks keep on deposit at the Fed). It sets the discount rate at which it will loan money to banks, thus influencing other interest rates. And it buys and sells government securities on the open market, thus pumping money into the system (when it buys) or taking money out of the system (when it sells).

The details of these procedures are intricate. The only people

Box 1-1

THE "FED" STRUCTURE AND PROCESS

**Board of Governors—seven members, fourteen-year terms
twelve regional Federal Reserve banks
5,426 member banks (as of August 1980)**

1. *The Federal Open Market Committee decides monetary policy.*
   Voting members are the seven governors, the president of the New York Fed, and the presidents of four other regional banks, who serve rotating one-year terms. The seven other presidents attend but do not vote.

2. *The "morning call."*
   A daily conference call links staff specialists in Washington with their counterparts at the New York Fed, which handles trading for all the regional banks and the system itself. The Federal Reserve chairman and the New York Fed president often take part. The daily instructions to the Fed's trading desk come out of this meeting.

3. *The Federal Reserve Bank of New York.*
   Its System Account, or trading desk, handles day-to-day buying and selling of securities. The department also prepares frequent estimates of commercial banks' reserves, a key indicator in carrying out monetary policy.

The Federal Reserve affects the supply of money by buying and selling government securities. It trades with about three dozen "primary" dealers. When the Fed buys securities, it pays the seller by adding to the seller's checking account at a commercial bank, thus increasing demand deposits (checking accounts), the largest component of the money supply. When the Fed sells, the buyer's payment comes from its bank account, thus reducing this component of the money supply.

Source: New York Times, May 3, 1981.

who really care about them are those who get paid to do so. For the rest of us, the important point is simple enough. The rate at which the money supply is allowed to grow is now determined not by gold or any other impersonal force, but by the Federal Reserve. The Fed officials who determine how fast the money supply will grow are not elected; they are appointed by the president and are not wholly insensitive either to his wishes or those of Congress. If they keep too tight a lid on the money supply, recession is likely to threaten. Recessions are not popular with elected officials, particularly with presidents seeking second terms. (We will have much more to say about President Reagan's willingness to put the country into a major recession in order to curb inflation.) In ordinary times, therefore, the Fed has a strong incentive to let the money supply grow. As it does, prices tend to rise.

Fiscal and monetary policy—tax-and-spending policies on the one hand, regulation of the money supply on the other—fit together in an important way. In real life, there is no such thing as running a deficit exactly big enough to make sure that "everything that is produced will be bought," as in the simplified explanation above. Instead the government tries to run whatever deficit it thinks is necessary to stimulate the economy. An expanding economy, however, typically requires *new* money, which is exactly what the Fed provides when it buys a bond from the Treasury. (The Fed typically pays for its bonds by crediting the Treasury's account on its books. The effect is the same as if it paid for the bonds with newly printed Federal Reserve Notes—currency.) The deficit is thus "monetized," in the language of economics, and both total ·spending and the money supply expand.

On the other side of the ledger, an expansionary fiscal policy ensures that expansionary monetary policy will work. In the 1930s, remember, the money supply failed to grow despite the rock-bottom interest rates: nobody was doing any borrowing. A big government deficit, though, means that new money will automatically be spent. Again, total spending and the money supply increase together.

The federal fiscal and monetary policies that we have been describing are based in part on the economic theories of John Maynard Keynes. Keynes (1883–1946) was a brilliant British economist and lecturer at Cambridge University.[5] Although many of Keynes's ideas were represented in President Roosevelt's New Deal, it was the Kennedy administration that made Keynesian economics accepted doctrine. And every president since Kennedy, except Reagan, has used Keynesian principles to guide his economic policies. Before we discuss why and how President Reagan's policies differ from those of his predecessors, let us review the history of economic management beginning with Kennedy's administration.

THE KENNEDY-JOHNSON YEARS: THE CLASH OF POLITICS AND ECONOMICS

We have noted that the economists that John Kennedy brought to Washington in 1961 were all disciples of Keynes who believed in the power of aggregate demand. There were, however, differences within the Kennedy administration on how to strengthen demand. John Kenneth Galbraith, for example, kept urging greater emphasis on social spending programs, which he saw as a means of using one stone to kill two birds, unemployment and poverty. But the President's Council of Economic Advisers put greater emphasis on the practical and political benefits of tax cuts to boost aggregate demand. They were perfectly willing to support enlarged public spending but thought that the amounts the president could extract from a reluctant Congress would be too small to cure unemployment and get the economy moving fast enough.

President Kennedy himself was reluctant to call for major tax reduction at first; a major theme in his election campaign had been a call for national sacrifice—"Ask not what your country can do for you, but what you can do for your country." Asking people to accept a tax cut did not fit this theme. However, with Chairman Walter Heller of the Council of Economic Advisers waging an effective educational campaign for tax reduction both inside and outside the administration, the president gradually came around. He accepted a tax cut in business investment in 1962 and started to campaign for massive tax cuts in individual and corporate taxes.

President Kennedy was assassinated before he could get Congress to enact the latter tax cuts, and it was President Johnson who swiftly pushed the tax cut through Congress in early 1964. Although it is certainly easier to get a tax cut than a tax increase through the legislature, Congress was reluctant to approve a tax cut of over $10 billion at a time when the federal budget was already running $10 billion in the red. As Walter Heller remarked, the nation was still dominated by the "Puritan ethic," which in fiscal matters meant "balance the budget, stay out of debt, live within your means." The tax cut, said Mr. Heller, would help *close* the budget gap, not widen it, because it would raise national output, national income, and therefore the tax yield to the federal government. Under pressure from LBJ, Congress bought the concept and voted for a big tax reduction while the budget was still deep in deficit. This was a victory for the ideas represented in Keynesian economics.

The economy responded vigorously to the big tax cut—it was worth $14 billion to taxpayers—just as the Keynesians, now called the "New Economists," said it would: national economic output surged forward, unemployment declined, and the gap in the federal budget narrowed as rising national income resulted in higher tax payments. The miracle had worked, and the prestige of Keynesian doctrine and of the New Economists soared to a historic high.

By the end of 1965, unemployment had fallen to 4 percent of the labor force, the level that Walter Heller had at first called the "full-employment" target and later, under political criticism, had relabeled an "interim target." But with unemployment down to 4 percent and still declining, prices began to rise. Johnson's economic advisers (by then Gardner Ackley had succeeded Walter Heller as chairman of the Council of Economic Advisers, and the council's other two members were Otto Eckstein and Arthur Okun) now wanted economic policy gradually switched from stimulus to restraint. In accordance with the New Economics, which they saw as symmetrical, they began to urge an *increase* in taxes rather than a tax cut. They feared that the president's decision to escalate the war in Vietnam might rapidly raise defense expenditures, thus overburdening an economy already experiencing full employment. LBJ would not allow his economists to "go public" with their campaign for a tax increase; they carried it on cautiously, nervously, within the administration.

But the president was unwilling to accept his economists' advice; instead, he decided to go for a "guns-*and*-butter" economic policy, hoping to pay for what still seemed like a relatively small war in Vietnam with the extra resources flowing from an expanding economy. LBJ apparently chose this course for two major reasons: to avoid a raucous debate in Congress over Vietnam, and to avoid having a Congress that did not want to raise taxes deny him the Great Society antipoverty funds and other social programs he sought. He wanted these as the contribution that would give him his place in history beside Franklin D. Roosevelt as a friend of the "forgotten man."[6]

President Johnson's hope that he could find the extra resources to deal with the nation's military and social needs without a tax increase, and without inflation, failed. By the middle of the summer of 1966, the administration was battling to prevent the complete collapse of its economic policy.

Successive blows, first by labor, then by industry, left the administration's wage-price guidelines for containing inflation so battered that they could not be salvaged. The airline machinists overwhelmingly rejected the settlement their leaders had worked out in the White House with Johnson himself. And Inland Steel Corporation—which once had helped beat down a steel industry price increase during the Kennedy administration—announced a price increase that the rest of the industry quickly followed. Johnson's unwillingness to use fiscal policy in the form of a tax increase had put unbearable pressure on the wage-price guidelines.

When inflation began to speed up in 1966 and 1967, it proved harder than LBJ or his economists had expected to turn policy toward restraint. Congress and the nation resisted a tax increase, and the president did not want a public defeat. In August 1967, Johnson asked Congress for the tax increase his economists had long counseled. He did not get it, however, until the summer of 1968. By then inflationary expectations were so strong that the 10-percent surtax on personal and corporate income had less effect than anticipated.

Thus, war, inflation, and the long-delayed tax hike sealed the doom of LBJ and the Democrats. These factors also badly hurt the reputation of the New Economists. In 1968 and 1969, their stock fell far below the peak it had reached in 1964 with the highly effective $14-billion tax cut. Politics had triumphed over economics—and the economists.

NIXONOMICS: AGAIN POLITICS WINS THE DAY

As unemployment was the main problem faced by John F. Kennedy when he reached the White House in 1961, so inflation was the nation's primary problem for President Richard Nixon in 1969.

Nixon had been counseled on economic policy during his campaign by Professor Milton Friedman of the University of Chicago and several of his monetarist disciples. Professor Friedman had been trying for years to stage a counterrevolution against the Keynesian revolution, which he criticized for its relative neglect and downgrading of monetary policy, for its overemphasis on fiscal policy, and for its endorsement of so much government interference in the private economy.

The economists that Nixon named to his Council of Economic Advisers had been much influenced by Friedman's theory that gradual growth in the money supply would check inflation without causing a recession or much rise in unemployment. Friedman himself preferred to stay outside Washington and at his academic post, though he remained influential.

A test of Friedman's "new, new economics" was now to be made, to stop inflation. In his book *Capitalism and Freedom,* Friedman had put the formula very succinctly: "I would specify that the reserve system shall see to it that the total stock of money . . . rises month by month, and indeed, so far as possible, day by day, at an annual rate of X percent, where X is some number between 3 and 5." He chose a money-supply growth rate between those two numbers because the U.S. economy's long-term growth rate lies between 3 and 5 percent annually. Friedman dismissed the complications regarding which definition of the money supply to use—there are at least ten according to the calculation of Henry C. Wallich, a member of the Federal Reserve Board—or precisely what numerical growth rate to follow, saying that these make "far less difference than the definite choice of a particular definition and a particular rate of growth."[7]

Friedman's theory obviously had strong appeal to an administration that did not want to increase taxes as a means of stopping inflation, and that in any case regarded Johnson's tax increase as a failure. Friedman's theory was also attractive to Nixon in that it did not require the administration to intervene in the wage and price decisions of labor and business. Nixon was particularly anxious not to offend business the way the Kennedy and Johnson administrations had done. The Friedman theory asserted that such government intervention would only distort the use of resources and be unfair to particular companies, industries, or workers. It would in any case have no effect whatsoever on inflation, as inflation is a result of too rapid an increase in the money supply.

During President Nixon's first years in office, the money supply was held down to a rate of growth of only 2.5 percent. But consumer prices climbed at an annual rate of about 6 percent until the second half of 1970, when the inflation rate slowed to about 4.5 percent. But in the first half of 1971, inflation appeared to be picking up again.

On the other side, with the slowdown in the money supply, the economy had gone into recession and unemployment had risen from 3.5 percent to over 6 percent. President Nixon and his economic advisers said that they would use the concept of a "full-employment budget," in which revenues would equal expenditures only if the economy were at full employment, while accepting sizable deficits if the economy were well below full-capacity use. Nixon's economists clearly did not like having their fiscal policy branded "liberal." Herbert Stein, who had provided an early post–World War II formulation of the full-employment budget, insisted that the doctrine had a good, conservative, Republican lineage.

At the same time, Nixon's economists now sought to persuade the Federal Reserve Board, under the chairmanship of Arthur F. Burns, Nixon's appointee, to increase the rate of growth of the money supply faster than the Friedman formula of 3 to 5 percent, and faster than Burns himself thought prudent. The President's Council of Economic Advisers maintained that monetary growth at a rate of more than 6 percent—perhaps as much as 9 percent—was essential to restore full employment by the end of 1972. And the council felt that as long as it were not continued too long, so rapid a rate of monetary growth would not reactivate inflation.

To buy a little extra anti-inflationary insurance, the Nixon administration began to shift away from its strong opposition to wage and price restraints and to adopt, though somewhat reluctantly, an "incomes policy." As an administration spokesman explained, "In order to help assure that the inflation rate moves down as the real economy moves up, the administration has become increasingly active in using its influence to restrain directly price and wage increases in particular industries."

The cautious steps taken, however, were not enough to satisfy Chairman Burns of the Federal Reserve Board, the administration's most important critic in view of his control of the money supply. In March 1971, Burns told the Senate Banking and Currency Committee: "I don't think our fiscal and monetary policies are sufficient to control inflation." He again urged the Nixon administration to establish the type of wage and price review board that he then regarded as central to an effective incomes policy. The findings of such a board, said Burns, could be used not only to create a case-law basis for wage-price guidelines but also to support the president's efforts to deal with inflationary actions by labor or industry. Walter Heller, Gardner Ackley, Arthur Okun, and other Kennedy-Johnson economists could not have agreed more.

President Nixon was furious with Burns for hectoring and pressuring him. He unleashed Charles Colson to launch a flank attack on Burns via the press. But the banking and business reaction in support of Burns caused Nixon to back off quickly.

On August 15, 1971, Nixon suddenly froze wages and prices,

following the advice of Secretary of the Treasury John B. Connally. The adoption of controls staggered Nixon's free enterprise economists. They quickly adjusted, rationalizing the president's move as having been forced upon him by the Democrats and the Eastern Establishment press, especially the *New York Times*.

Politics had again triumphed over economics, and the economists licked their wounds and made the best of it. Only this time the wounded economists were Nixon conservatives and Friedmanians, not LBJ liberals and Keynesians.

The Ford and Carter administrations were little different in their attempts to control inflation through wage-price controls and a slowdown of the economy (thereby putting us into recessions in 1975 and 1979). It wasn't until the election of Ronald Reagan in 1980 that a new approach to solving stagflation was offered: *supply-side economics*.

REAGAN AND THE SUPPLY-SIDE THEORISTS

In an astonishingly short time, supply-side economics has captured the public imagination, eliciting nods of approval from politicians of both parties and acknowledgment from economists of almost every theoretical stripe.

But while supply-side economics has turned into a buzzword, it has come to mean different things to different people. To most economists, including the long-standing Keynesian and 1980 Nobel laureate Lawrence R. Klein as well as conservative Martin S. Feldstein of the National Bureau of Economic Research, it means shifting resources from consumption to investment. To achieve this goal, planners must tilt tax cuts away from stimulating consumption toward stimulating investment.

Supply-side economics stresses tax-rate incentives rather than use of the federal budget (which Keynesian economics encourages) to stimulate productivity and economic growth. This emphasis, rooted in the idea of Adam Smith and other classical economists, has a long history.[8] The classical economists emphasized the importance of positive incentives on saving, investment, and capital formation. In the words of Adam Smith:

> High taxes, sometimes by diminishing the consumption of taxed commodities, and sometimes by encouraging smuggling, frequently afford a smaller revenue than what may be drawn from more moderate taxes.[9]

Adam Smith's Heirs

The basic idea of supply-side economics is described by Arthur Laffer, an economist at the University of Southern California; Paul Craig Roberts; and Norman Ture, an economic consultant in Washington, D.C. (All three draw on the insights of Harvard economist Robert Mundell.) According to these men, increased tax rates deter economic activity, drive it underground, or cause it to switch into legal but untaxable outlets.

Awareness of the importance of increased tax rates on economic behavior increased during the 1970s as inflation and a progressive income tax intensified the effects of "bracket creep." Whereas only 2.9 percent of taxable returns faced a 25-percent or higher marginal tax rate in 1960, this figure had increased to 38.2 percent by 1976.[10] There is a growing recognition that increasing tax rates affect incentives and responses of taxpayers generally, not just those of people in higher tax brackets.

Specific prescriptions of supply-side economics are:

- Large and sustained cuts in personal tax rates and business taxes to induce increased work effort and capital investment. (See Figure 1-2 for changes in the tax structure since Reagan took office.)
- Relatively restrained monetary management, with the aim of bringing monetary growth in line with the long-run growth potential of the economy. This may require moving to some form of a gold standard.
- An end to fiscal and monetary fine-tuning and greater reliance on the internal dynamics of a free market economy.
- A slowing of the growth of government spending to halt the continuing rise in the nation's tax burden relative to GNP and also to free financial resources for private investment.

The basis of the pure supply-side approach is a rejection of Keynesian demand management and a resurrection of Say's Law of Markets that says "supply creates its own demand."

The Government's Failure

The supply-siders are convinced that Keynes's belief that "demand creates its own supply" was wrong. They claim that Keynesian policies have failed to boost aggregate real output (although Mundell

Figure 1-2 THE GREAT TAX SHIFT, 1981–1988 (FEDERAL REVENUE AS A SHARE OF GNP)

Before Reagan

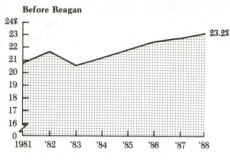

Tax law when Reagan took office in 1981 called for federal revenues to take a steadily growing share of the nation's output of goods and services.

Reagan's 1981 proposal

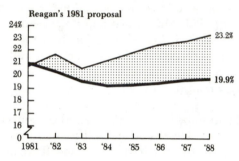

Reagan asked Congress for a 30% individual income tax cut that would have trimmed Washington's share of GNP to about 20%.

The actual 1981 tax cut

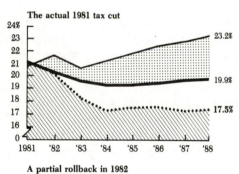

The bill that Congress passed and Reagan signed cut taxes far more than he had proposed — by liberalizing corporate credits and deductions, easing the marriage penalty, etc.

A partial rollback in 1982 but a gap remains

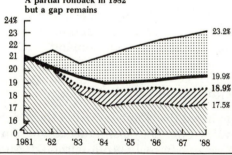

Panic over huge deficits and backlash against corporate tax benefits led Reagan and Congress to agree on two tax-increase measures, one to close alleged loopholes, the other to raise gasoline taxes. But even after the 1982 increases, Washington is claiming less in revenue than it would have received under Reagan's original proposal.

Source: Los Angeles Times, January 31, 1982, pt. IV, pp. 1–3.

disagrees with his colleagues on this point) and that the policies have laid the groundwork for the nation's twin problems of high inflation and slow growth—in other words, stagflation.

Remember that ideally, Keynesian economics calls for symmetrical offsetting policies at different stages of the business cycle: monetary ease, higher spending, and tax cuts during a recession, and tight money, spending cuts, and tax increases during a boom. In practice, however, the government, while quickly increasing spending, cutting taxes, and easing money in a downturn, has failed to reverse course sufficiently or soon enough on the upside.

Most economists—from liberal-leaning Nobel laureate Paul Samuelson to archconservative Nobelist Friedrich von Hayek —remain highly skeptical of supply-side economics. While acknowledging that the incentive effects of tax policy have received too little attention in the past, they believe that the impact of such policies is being grossly exaggerated by the supply-siders. More important, they see little evidence that large tax cuts combined with monetary restraint can produce a rapid increase in real output and productivity. Rather, they see big tax cuts as a risky program that could lead to still higher interest rates, cause greater inflation, and shrink capital spending.

Still, it does appear that the Keynesian prescriptions of the past are inapplicable to the present. And the idea of virtually painless therapy that would simultaneously put more money in everyone's pockets, vanquish inflation, and accelerate real growth—all of which has been promised by President Reagan—is a compelling political vision. Not everyone is satisfied, however, that Reagan's economic programs will be painless for all groups of people. Furthermore, many think important environmental and health costs will be associated with his policies. Certainly, in the short run at least, it appears these concerns are justified for the following reasons.

UNEMPLOYMENT: A "NEW" OLD PROBLEM?

Just as President Reagan's policies have eased the burden of inflation, mounting unemployment once again is posing a threat to the security of many Americans. (Unemployment in 1982–1983 was at its highest since the Great Depression.)

The rising unemployment represents not only the declining situation of those who have long been out of the economic mainstream but also the shrinking opportunities for workers in such basic American industries as automobiles and steel. More important, even if the economy improves and unemployment declines again, as most economists expect, they are concerned that joblessness will remain higher than it was before the 1981–1982 recession, continuing a decade of upward creep.

Already the specter of joblessness felt in the slums of the South Bronx has spread through the idled industrial plants of Pittsburgh and Detroit and is reaching into the white-collar jobs of the middle class. The Reagan administration concedes it miscalculated the depth of the problem, and most economists agree that things will become worse.

Indeed, the figures have soared. Unemployment, which was at 7 percent in July 1981, reached 8.9 percent in December and in February broke through the 9-percent postwar record set in May 1975. Although the first official unemployment figures were not issued until 1940, some experts have estimated that unemployment hovered around 18 percent throughout much of the 1930s and reached a high of 25 percent in 1933.

A total of 11.4 million people were counted as unemployed in March 1983, meaning they held jobs and were laid off, or they wanted to work but could not find a position. This number is not expected to decline significantly until 1984. According to figures released by the Bureau of Labor Statistics, unemployment rose from July 1981 to July 1982 in forty-eight states and the District of Columbia, with only North and South Dakota showing shrinking unemployment lines. The seasonally adjusted unemployment rate for March 1983 was 10.1 percent—the highest since an annualized 9.9-percent rate in 1941, before monthly figures were compiled. (Reagan was correct when he said it was not fair to compare today's unemployment figures with those of 1941. Today many more women are working than in 1941, thus accounting for some of the increased percentage of unemployment figures.) For some segments of the population, such as adult males and blacks, unemployment is already at its highest levels since World War II. Blacks, for example, show a 17.4 percent unemployment rate, while all adult males are at 8.8 percent. As already noted, many economists predict that these rates will rise further.

What troubles economists most, however, is not so much the present bulge in unemployment as the longer-term upward creep in the figures. While unemployment above 3 or 4 percent was considered unacceptable in the early 1960s, now 6 or 7 percent appears to be taken as "normal." Economists are puzzled by what has happened recently: after each recession ends, unemployment falls but does not drop to its previous low. Labor experts are beginning to conclude that the causes of unemployment are more complex than they were thought to be a decade or two ago, and that reducing unemployment is more difficult as well.

Of course, even with unemployment creeping upward, the economy has proved remarkably fruitful in creating jobs. There are now nearly 111 million people in the civilian labor force. Nearly two out of every three people are seeking jobs, but more people are also finding them. Roughly 100 million people are now employed, as against 57 million in 1947.

An additional problem today is the shrinking of the system of "cushions" that was created to ease the pain of unemployment. In large part, this shrinkage results from the budget cuts pushed through Congress by President Reagan. After the Great Depression, Congress enacted unemployment insurance and social welfare provisions to tide over those who were out of work. New programs with more generous benefits were adopted in the 1960s and 1970s. In the view of many labor experts, those cushions made unemployment a less serious national problem than before and made relatively high levels of unemployment less of a political liability to presidents and members of Congress. Now the steady upward trend of fifty years is being reversed.

Reagan's underlying premise is that in the long run, unlimited economic growth is still possible and that everyone will gain from this growth. In other words, the old game of political compromise will continue with an expanding economic pie. Reagan's critics say his policies may result in growth, but at the expense of the poor and to the benefit of the wealthy. The one thing most agree upon is that the material deficit is growing and shows no signs of decreasing under Reagan's programs.

A HOPELESS DEFICIT?

Unemployment is not the only major problem facing Reagan and his supply-side economists. The United States government is falling into a financial hole that may have no exit. Year after year, it is spending far more than it is collecting in taxes, and piling up debt faster than ever before in peacetime. The Treasury Department reported, for example, that the government finished fiscal 1982 with a record deficit of $110.7 billion.

For the first time, it is not certain that federal revenues will catch up with outlays again, even when the economy recovers. So

far, the government has managed to pay its bills by massive borrowing—an estimated $145 billion in 1982 and $170 billion in 1983. But
if the deficits continue, the Treasury will absorb a majority of the
available credit, squeezing out private individuals and business bor-
rowers. Interest rates could be pushed back up, choking off car and
home sales and blocking job-creating investments. Inflation could
be renewed and an economic recovery strangled in its cradle.

Deficits, of course, are nothing new. In 89 of the 194 years since
its founding, the government failed to raise as much as it spent. In
the last fifty years, it has operated in the black only eight times, and
in the past twenty years only once. But the present situation is
alarmingly different. Past deficits were a by-product of war or depression. After the immediate cause was over, the budget soon
swung back into balance. This time no surplus is visible. The
self-correcting mechanism has been damaged, and even when the
recession ends, enormous deficits that threaten economic recovery
lie ahead. Although Congress passed a $99-billion tax increase in
the summer of 1982, the government's income for fiscal 1982 fell
$110.7 billion short of its expenses. As Figure 1-3 shows, govern-
ment spending—driven by defense and social security—is rising

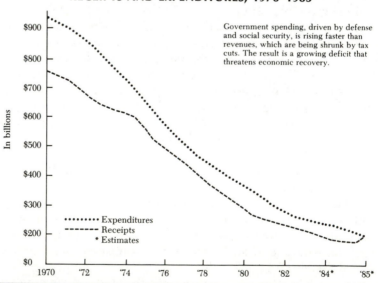

**Figure 1-3 THE WIDENING GAP BETWEEN GOVERNMENT
RECEIPTS AND EXPENDITURES, 1970–1985**

Government spending, driven by defense
and social security, is rising faster than
revenues, which are being shrunk by tax
cuts. The result is a growing deficit that
threatens economic recovery.

In billions

········· Expenditures
------- Receipts
* Estimates

Source: Office of Management and Budget, Congressional Budget Office.

faster than revenues, which are being shrunk by tax cuts. The 1982 shortfall was the thirteenth straight deficit and nearly double the previous record.

Deficits have grown not only in dollars but also, more ominously, as a share of the country's total wealth. They averaged less than 1 percent of the GNP from World War II until 1970. In the last eleven years, however, the average was 2.4 percent. Now the Congressional Budget Office (CBO) predicts they will average 4.1 percent from 1982 to 1985, with a peak of 4.7 percent in 1983. Some experts fear deficits in the 5-percent range for years to come.

I noted in the introduction that politicians and citizens share responsibility for the problem. Pollsters have consistently found that Americans want a strong defense, security in old age, pure food and water, good highways and parks, and protection against floods, crop failure, and plane crashes. They also dislike high taxes to pay for these services. But the three main culprits in the deficit crisis are tax cuts, military spending, and social security.

THE THREE WORST PROBLEMS

Tax Cuts

As we have learned, President Reagan insists the best way to control the government's spending is to reduce its income, but this approach is making it almost impossible to balance the budget. The president's massive tax cuts are depriving the Treasury of so much revenue that the government can't pay its bills without going deeper into debt.

As a result, the president has been forced to put off indefinitely his dream of a balanced budget. Although Congress made him accept a $99-billion, three-year tax increase in the summer of 1982, the 1981 tax reduction act will mean a cumulative total of $879 billion in lost revenues from 1982 to 1987 (see Figure 1-4) compared with what would have been collected under the old law. Even with the tax cuts, the government's income continues to rise, from $517 billion in 1980 to a projected $757 billion in 1985. But spending is mounting even more rapidly, from $577 billion in 1980 to an estimated $910 billion in 1985, leaving huge deficits each year.

Furthermore, the president and Congress agreed to index tax rates to the cost of living, starting in 1985. That means taxpayers will no longer be pushed into higher tax brackets as their incomes go up. The Treasury will lose $12 billion in 1985, $51 billion in 1987,

Figure 1-4 REVENUES LOST THROUGH NEW TAX LAWS, 1982–1987

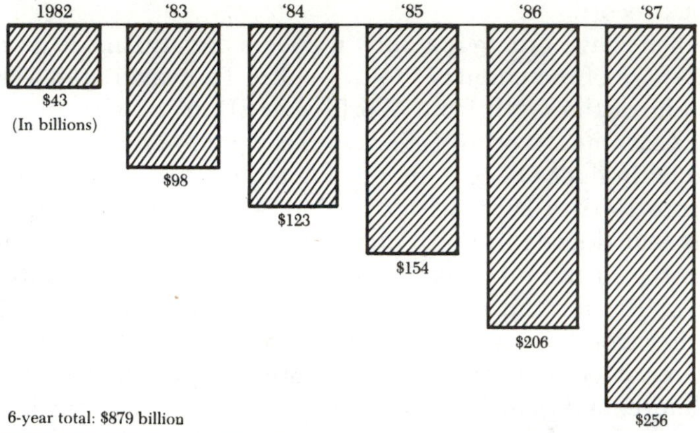

1982	'83	'84	'85	'86	'87

$43
(In billions)

$98

$123

$154

$206

6-year total: $879 billion

$256

Source: Office of Management and Budget, Congressional Budget Office.

and more every year afterward. Indexing means future deficits won't automatically be eliminated as they were in the past.

Military Spending

For reasons discussed in chapter 8, President Reagan is pushing for massive increases in the military budget for the next five years. Consequently, national defense is the most powerful force driving up federal spending. After years of decline, the military budget is expanding rapidly, both in dollars and as a share of the total budget.

Between 1982 and 1987, defense outlays are scheduled to double, from $188 billion to $365 billion. In 1983, defense will cost $222 billion—$50 billion more than Social Security, the next-biggest government program. By 1987, the Pentagon will take 37 percent of the budget, up from 24 percent when Reagan took office and its largest share since 1970. In the six years before Reagan, military expenditures, after adjusting for inflation, grew by only 1.8 percent a year. From 1982 to 1987, however, annual real growth will be 8.1 percent, more than four times as fast, unless Congress forces a slowdown.

Social Security

As America's population grows older, Social Security costs grow heavier. By 1987, nearly twenty-five cents out of every dollar the government spends will go for Social Security, up from twenty

cents in 1980. Over the last twenty years, payments to retired workers and their dependents have risen from $14 billion to $155 billion.
They are expected to hit $242 billion five years from now.

This rapid growth is partly due to an increase in the elderly population and partly due to higher benefits. For the past thirty years
of the program, Congress has voted every few years to raise benefits. In 1969, President Nixon proposed that future increases be
made automatic and tied to the cost of living. Congress approved
this proposal in 1972, and indexing began in 1975. In fact, Social
Security payments have risen faster than average wages and faster
than inflation (see Figure 1-5). From 1960 to 1980, the real value
of the average monthly benefit nearly doubled, from $183 to $341,
in 1980 dollars. Over the last eight years, wages rose 71 percent
while Social Security benefits went up 80 percent.

The problem is that all three of these culprits have been politically untouchable. A consensus is building, however, that these sa-
cred cows must be confronted. A growing number of prominent
Republicans and Democrats, if not the president, recognize that
new sources of revenue must be found, the explosive growth in
military outlays slowed, and future increases in Social Security
benefits trimmed. Leaders in both parties argue that there simply
is not enough money in other government accounts to eliminate
the deficit without sacrifice by taxpayers, the military, and future
retirees.

Figure 1-5 INCREASES IN WAGES AND SOCIAL SECURITY BENEFITS, 1960–1982

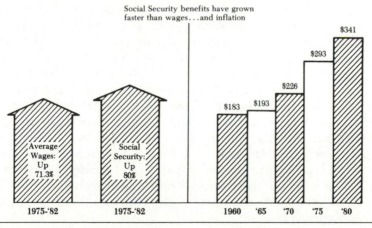

Social Security benefits have grown
faster than wages...and inflation

$341
$293
$226
$183 $193

Average Wages: Up 71.3%

Social Security: Up 80%

1975-'82   1975-'82   1960   '65   '70   '75   '80

Source: Office of Management and Budget, Congressional Budget Office.

SUMMING UP

The Industrial Age has held disappointments for us before, but perhaps none so great as the growing belief that our civilization is out of control. By every conventional measure, the postwar world born in 1945 was a huge success. More goods were produced and sold than ever before. More people were working; the standard of living had never been higher. But the suspicion grows that this era is ending, and there is a pervasive sense that something is deeply wrong. We are used to rapid change, but we have a new and uncomfortable feeling that we are in a racing car without a driver. A Gallup Poll published in July 1981, for example, showed a majority of Americans no longer believe that the president is able to control inflation. If Americans no longer believe the president is able to control inflation, then who do they believe can do it?

The new mood is no conventional pessimism but rather a loss of faith rooted in a sense of betrayal. We worked hard, we educated our children, we believed in the future, we followed all the rules of success. And yet, somehow, it has turned out wrong. As the postwar era began, economists promised a managed prosperity through "fine tuning" of the economy, and as it ended, they threw up their hands. The remedy for galloping inflation and nagging unemployment had yet to be discovered. As the *Wall Street Journal* summed it up, "The economic ideas and policies employed during the Great Depression and through a long era of Post World War II prosperity seem to have worn out."

We learned that in order to stop inflation, recent administrations chose to tighten monetary and fiscal policies to produce idle capacity. Whatever the merits of idle capacity in the fight against inflation, it exacts a stiff price in slower growth of productivity. With idle capital, incentives to invest diminish. There is little need for new, more productive facilities. Knowing that they do not need to expand, firms often cut back on research and development for new production processes. With high unemployment, workers fear that technical progress will cost them their jobs and that alternative work will be hard to find. Consequently, they push for more restrictive work rules to stop technical progress. The result is a stagnant economy with a productivity slowdown on top of a basic productivity growth rate that already puts us at the bottom of the industrial league—with about one third the productivity growth of Japan.

Unless this decline can be reversed, and unless productivity can be accelerated to the levels being achieved by West Germany and Japan, it is only a question of time until we slip into relative backwardness. Few major countries have been brought down by foreign enemies; many have disappeared because of their internal failures. How are we to eliminate our failures and make our economy more dynamic than it ever has been? President Reagan's answer is supply-side economics. We must wait to see if he is correct.

The future success or failure of President Reagan's economics depends a great deal on the answers to two questions. These questions, however, cannot be answered here. First, is the world really running out of everything, as some claim? On the answer to that question hangs the whole future of politics. A world of scarcity, after all, is a world of inevitable conflict.

The other question has to do with the *control* of resources. Who decides which resources are developed, what they cost, and where they go? Clearly the two questions are related. Whether there is scarcity or abundance of particular materials at particular times and places depends on human decisions. We do know that the power to make those decisions is, in many cases, shifting.

NOTES

1. The most common measure of inflation in the United States is the Consumer Price Index (CPI), a number published each month by the government's Bureau of Labor Statistics. If the CPI in January is 1 percent higher than the CPI for December, inflation (which is usually reported on a yearly basis) is said to have hit 12 or 13 percent.
2. Three reference books are indispensable to anyone interested in economic statistics: *The Economic Report of the President,* issued annually; the *Statistics of the United States, Colonial Times to 1970;* and the *Statistical Abstract of the United States.* Figures in this section are derived from these books.
3. For an interesting discussion of the tough decisions involved in the budget-making process, see William Greider, "The Education of David Stockman," *The Atlantic,* 6 (December 1981), 27–54.
4. *Burden* is the wrong word in any case. To understand why, imagine what would happen if the debt were suddenly paid off. A company that is in debt owes money to "outsiders"—banks, bondholders, and so forth. A government that is in debt owes money for the most part to its own taxpaying citizens. Suppose Congress votes tomorrow to pay off the national debt this year. The move requires a stiff new tax—nearly $800 billion—but Congress passes it, the taxpayers pay it, and everyone holding a U.S. government security is paid off.

    The immediately effect in cash terms is an enormous redistribution of income. Those who own no government bonds are a lot poorer, and those who own many are a lot richer. But the bondholders no longer have the assets they once had: no savings bonds for their old age, no Treasury bonds to pass on to their grandchildren. Doubtless, they will be looking for something to do with all their new-found cash. Doubtless too, the federal government will want to borrow some money to finance all the food stamps, unemployment benefits, and the like made necessary by the tax-induced impoverishment of everybody else. Maybe the people who have just been paid off would like to lend their money again—U.S. government bonds, after all, are probably the safest investment in the world. So the debt, in a short time, is recreated.

5. For an excellent discussion of Keynesian economics, see Robert H. Heilbroner, *The Worldly Philosophers: The Lives, Times, and Ideas of Great Economic Thinkers* (New York: Simon & Schuster, 1961), and *The Making of Economic Society* (Englewood Cliffs, N.J.: Prentice-Hall, 1962). For an opposing view of his economic theories, see Allan H. Meltzer, "Keynes' General Theory: A Different Perspective," *Journal of Economic Literature,* 49 (March 1981), 34–64.
6. For a fascinating study of Lyndon Johnson and, in particular, his desire to become the second Franklin Roosevelt, see Robert A. Caro, *The Path to Power,* vol. 1 of *The Years of Lyndon Johnson* (New York: Random House, 1982).
7. Leonard Silk, *Nixonomics* (New York: Praeger, 1972), p. 184.
8. Robert E. Keleher and W. P. Orzechowski, *Supply-Side Effects of Fiscal Policy: Some Historical Perspectives,* Working Paper Series (Atlanta: Federal Reserve Bank of Atlanta, 1980), p. 57.
9. Adam Smith, *An Inquiry into the Nature and Causes of the Wealth of Nations* (New York: Random House, 1937), p. 835.
10. James D. Gwartney and Richard Stroup, *Economics: Private and Public Choice,* 2nd ed. (New York: Academic Press, 1980), p. 280.

GLOSSARY

Cost of living: The cost of maintaining a particular standard of living measured in terms of purchased goods and services. The rise in the cost of living is the same as the rate of inflation.

Credit crunch (liquidity crisis): The period when cash for lending to business and consumers is in short supply.

Deficit spending: The practice whereby a government goes into debt to finance some of its expenditures.

Depression: A long period of little business activity when prices are low, unemployment is high, and purchasing power decreases sharply.

Devaluation: The official lowering of a nation's currency, decreasing its value in relation to foreign currencies.

Disposable income: Income after taxes which is available to persons for spending and saving.

Federal Reserve System: The entire banking system of the United States, incorporating twelve Federal Reserve branch banks and all national banks and state-chartered commercial banks and trust companies that have been admitted to system membership. The system wields a great deal of influence on the nation's monetary and credit policies.

Gross National Product (GNP): The total dollar value of all goods that have been bought for final use and services during a year. The GNP is generally considered to be the most comprehensive measure of a nation's economic activity. The *real GNP* is the GNP adjusted for inflation.

Inflation: An increase in the average level of prices; double-digit inflation occurs when the percentage of increase rises above ten.

Money supply: The currency held by the public, plus checking accounts in commercial banks and savings institutions.

National debt: The debt of the central government as distinguished from the debts of the political subdivisions of the nation and private business and individuals.

National debt ceiling: Limit set by Congress beyond which the national debt cannot rise. This limit is periodically raised by congressional vote.

Per capita income: The nation's total income divided by the number of people in the nation.

Prime interest rate: The rate banks charge on short-term loans to their large commercial customers with the highest credit rating.

Public debt: The total of the nation's debts owed by state, local, and national government. This is considered a good measure of how much of the nation's spending is financed by borrowing rather than taxation.

Recession: A mild decrease in economic activity marked by a decline in real GNP, employment, and trade. It usually lasts six months to a year and is characterized by widespread decline in many sectors of the economy. Not as severe as a depression.

Seasonal adjustment: Statistical changes made to compensate for regular fluctuations in data that are so great they tend to distort the statistics and make comparisons meaningless. For instance, seasonal adjustments are made in mid-winter for a slowdown in housing construction and for the rise in farm income in the fall after the summer crops are harvested.

Stagflation (slumpflation): The coincidence of a high rate of inflation and a high rate of unemployment.

Supply-side economics: The school of economic thinking which stresses the importance of the costs of production as a means of revitalizing the economy. It advocates policies that raise capital and labor output by increasing the incentives to produce.

Wage-price controls: A policy under which the level of wages, salaries, and prices is set by law or the administration.

Wage-price spiral: The phenomenon that takes place when workers obtain pay raises greater than their increase in productivity. Since the higher wages mean increased cost to the employers, prices tend to increase; the resulting higher prices give workers an incentive to bargain for even higher wages.

SUGGESTED READINGS

Boulding, Kenneth E. *Economics as a Science.* New York: McGraw-Hill, 1970.

Bunke, Harvey C. *A Primer on American Economic History.* New York: Random House, 1969.

Friedman, Milton. *Capitalism and Freedom.* Chicago: University of Chicago Press, 1972.

Galbraith, John Kenneth. *Economics and the Public Purpose.* Boston: Houghton Mifflin, 1973.

Grossman, Gregory. *Economic Systems.* Englewood Cliffs, N.J.: Prentice-Hall, 1973.

Harrington, Michael. *Socialism.* New York: Saturday Review Press, 1972.

Heilbroner, Robert L. *Understanding Macroeconomics.* Englewood Cliffs, N.J.: Prentice-Hall, 1972.

Owen, Henry, and Schultze, Charles L. *Setting National Priorities: The Next Ten Years.* Washington, D.C.: The Brookings Institution, 1976.

Schultze, Charles L. *National Income Analysis.* Englewood Cliffs, N.J.: Prentice-Hall, 1972.

Schumpeter, Joseph A. *History of Economic Analysis.* New York: Oxford University Press, 1954.

———. *Capitalism, Socialism, and Democracy.* New York: Harper & Row, 1962.

Terkel, Studs. *Hard Times: An Oral History of the Great Depression.* New York: Avon Books, 1971.

2

Energy, Vulnerability, and Crisis: Alternatives for America

How have energy problems affected the political, economic, and social systems of the United States?

How did the American political system respond to the energy crisis?

How have the costs and benefits of the oil crisis been distributed in this country?

How are these problems interacting with such basic trends as the evolution of technology, shifts in the balance of power, and other changes such as shifts in values between generations?

What are the dangers and risks both to national stability and to the international order?

When World War II ended in 1945, Americans feared that the United States would plunge back into a depression. But this did not happen. Certainly we had our disappointments, but for the most part Americans were living more comfortably and securely than they had imagined possible.

America was not alone in reaching high levels of economic growth and stability. Japan and Western Europe also can look back on a very impressive—some might even say stunning—achievement. Between 1950 and 1973, Japan's Gross National Product increased tenfold; Western Europe's increased almost three and a half times; and that of the United States was multiplied by almost two and a half.

Many factors caused this sustained surge of growth: the momentum of postwar reconstruction and recovery, successive waves of trade liberalization, the stability provided by an international economic regime based on the dollar, European integration, technological innovation and higher productivity, managerial dynamism, various government policies—and energy, in particular, oil.

In fact, most people equated economic growth with energy; the first could not happen without the other.[1] High and growing levels of energy use were a sign of the advance of civilization. They were something to be looked upon with pride. But the energy crisis has helped to change our thinking. Today energy is a source of worry and insecurity. Because energy is central to modern life, the insecurity extends beyond concerns about the price and availability of energy to fundamental questions about the possibilities for sustained economic growth and the stability of society, and about war and peace.

Economic growth means much more than an increase in the production and distribution of goods and services. It also provides a way to resolve social and political conflicts and tensions within society and between nations. It becomes in itself a "social good . . . the source of individual motivation, the basis of political solidarity, the ground for the mobilization of society for a common purpose."[2]

A seemingly endless supply of cheap energy played an important role in economic growth. First in the United States and then in other industrial economies, energy came to mean cheap oil. Between 1950 and 1973, petroleum reserves in the free world increased eightfold. Almost 90 percent of that growth was in the Middle East and Africa, where the costs of extraction were very low. This increasing abundance was reflected in the price of oil, which in real terms declined by 50 percent during those years. Industrial and individual consumers responded, and some governments encouraged switching to oil as a way to modernize their industries and to escape the social problems of coal-mining. The growth was awesome; oil consumption in the free world increased fivefold between 1950 and 1973, and oil came to play a larger and larger role in the total energy mix (see Table 2-1). To give one example, between 1950 and 1973, the share of coal—the traditional fuel of industrial society—in Western Europe's total energy mix declined from 86 to 25 percent, while oil's share rose from 12 to 59 percent.[3] Oil truly was the fuel of economic growth during this period.

The dependence on oil was most clear in transportation and living patterns, but it was also evident in the commercial and industrial sectors. Moreover, it was generally taken for granted (although the assumption was rarely closely examined) that the growth of energy consumption at a vigorous rate was necessary to maintain satisfactory rates of economic growth.

To repeat, the energy crisis of the last decade has severely shaken previous assumptions. Low-cost reliable supplies of energy, especially oil, do not appear available. Consequently, assumptions

Table 2-1
**THE STRUCTURE OF ENERGY CONSUMPTION IN THE
INDUSTRIAL WORLD**

	1950	1973	1980
Oil	29%	52%	47%
Natural Gas	12%	23%	24%
Coal	57%	22%	25%
Primary Electricity*	2%	3%	4%

Source: World Energy Industry Information Services.
*Hydropower, nuclear, geothermal.

about the inevitable correlation of energy consumption with economic growth now require close examination. Perhaps growing energy consumption can no longer be considered a necessary concomitant of economic growth. It is possible, in fact, that an actual reversal has happened: the growing demand for energy under the present circumstances may pose a threat to sustained economic growth.

Our purpose here is to look at the economic, social, and political consequences of the energy problem that were manifested in the 1973 Arab oil embargo. We begin with questions: What kind of system developed in the era of cheap and easy oil? How has the system responded to stringency so far, and what has shaped those responses? How have costs and benefits been distributed? We will end the chapter with some alternative paths that can be taken toward a solution of the energy crisis.

THE AUTOMOTIVE-PETROLEUM COMPLEX

George W. Pierson of Yale has identified the decisive element in American history as the "M-Factor." What made Americans different was their mobility. With the end of the frontier, the whole country became a place to wander in. Once the oil began to flow and the internal combustion engine was invented to burn it up, the restlessness of the American spirit was packaged for sale. If Pierson's theory is true, then oil has made it possible for our society to be in perpetual motion.[4]

In fact, the energy industry in this country is built on the ability to sell trips. It was not so long ago that oil companies sponsored "take to the road for fun" campaigns and invited every American to join the "getaway people." About 53 percent of America's oil goes for motion of one sort or another, compared with 28 percent among Europeans. Motion is a basic American need growing out of the national character. We are a nation of go-getters, comers, movers, shakers, ever contemptuous of the "stick-in-the-mud" and always ready to respond to political slogans like John F. Kennedy's promise to "get the country moving again."

It was inevitable that the American love affair with the car would lead to a variety of offspring. The Interstate Highway and Defense System, a $27-billion program to transform the face of the country, was as much an expression of manifest destiny as the push to the frontier. This essential playground for the nation's cars was originally sold as a civil defense measure. Of course the idea that high-speed highways would save lives rather than take them now looks a little foolish. But highways and cars, as the president of the American Association of State Highway Officials put it, had become "the keystone of the American way of life."

But if you build highways, then you must also build motels, fast-food restaurants, extra hospitals to service the victims of highway mayhem, an outdoor-life and sporting industry, and the culture of suburbia. The roads cut up cities, divided farmlands, and connected markets. The highway system was the nation's only physical plan, and more than anything else it determined the appearance of cities and the stretches in between.

In choosing the car as the engine of growth, the highway and automotive planners scrapped mass transit. General Motors, Exxon (then Esso), and the Goodyear Tire Company bought up the San Francisco trolley system, tore up the track, and replaced it with Esso-drinking buses rolling on Goodyears. In the name of progress, GM, Firestone, and Standard Oil of California ripped up the Los Angeles interurban train system. In all, one hundred electric railway systems in forty-five cities were destroyed as a result of similar conspiracies. (General Motors's treasurer, H. C. Grossman, was fined one dollar for sacrificing the antitrust laws to the automobile.)

AN ENERGY CRISIS IN AMERICA—NEVER!

It is not in the American experience to think about limits on energy. We have already noted that American patterns of social and industrial development have us consuming the lion's share of the world's oil supply (approximately one third in 1981–1982). Yet by the late

1960s and early 1970s, limits on the energy base in this country began to surface.

One cause was a process of social change that rearranged national priorities. A new political force, *environmentalism,* became evident. Although its roots went back at least to the publication of Rachel Carson's *Silent Spring* in 1962,[5] it became more visible after the blowout of an oil well in the Santa Barbara Channel of California in 1969, which paved scenic beaches with tar. In 1970, one hundred thousand people paraded down Fifth Avenue in New York City to mark Earth Day. The nation, people argued, was now rich enough to correct for the negative externalities of industrial society. Environmentalism made its influence felt in a large number of ways: in such legislation as the National Environmental Policy Act, the Clean Air Act, the Clean Water Act, and the Endangered Species Act; in the establishment of environmental impact statements; in the creation of the federal Environmental Protection Agency; and in the development of the significant new industry of pollution control.

As far as energy was concerned, environmentalism had its major impact on the burning of coal. Concern about air pollution led to fuel-switching, especially by electric utilities, away from domestically produced coal to low-sulfur oil, which had to be imported. Although not particularly noticeable at the time, this change led to a significant increase in the demand for oil. Between 1968 and 1973, oil consumption by electric utilities more than tripled. Much of this was low-sulfur imported oil.

Another limitation on our energy base was fundamental. The United States was an aging producer. It was outrunning its geological base. But this highly relevant fact was not represented in either the consumption pattern or in prices. Indeed, controls in the early 1970s resulted in prices that increasingly gave the "wrong" information to consumers. The United States was continuing to consume as though it were essentially self-sufficient, but additions to the oil and gas reserves were not congruent with this trend (see Figures 2-1, 2-2). The reserve base for oil and gas could not sustain the kind of growth that it had supported in the past. The marginal source of energy was one that had previously been very small, oil imports. The turning point came in 1970, when U.S. oil production reached its peak and then began to decline. Self-sufficiency had, at least in terms of energy, come to an end. The differences in foreign and domestic oil were more than just a matter of sulfur content and specific gravity. Imported oil could not be regarded in the same light as domestically produced oil. It was a separate fuel source, and it became the one that balanced supply and demand.

But so deeply ingrained was the assumption of abundance that many people could not accept the notion of limits. At the end of the 1960s, the headquarters staff in Michigan for Dow Chemical, one of the nation's largest industrial energy users, became convinced that pressure would mount on natural gas prices. But the company's managers in the Texas division, home of the great postwar petrochemicals development, were reluctant to accept such projections. "People had gone down there when gas was cheap," recalled a senior corporate official. "The people in Texas said, 'It can't happen here.' " It could, and it did.

Yet the assumption of unlimited abundance is so deep-seated that even a decade later, in 1980, the Republican presidential candidate was predicting that "with decontrol, we could be producing enough oil to be self-sufficient in five years."[6]

It would be a mistake, however, to think that the United States entered an era of scarcity. While oil was more difficult and more expensive to find, and was more likely to be found in smaller fields, the United States was still a significant oil producer in the early 1980s. It then produced a sixth of all the oil used in the world. Unfortunately, there was a catch. America, with only one-sixth of the world's population, was also accounting for one third of total consumption.

The United States was also becoming more and more integrated into the world market just as the market was undergoing a number of significant changes—including the rapidly growing demand for oil throughout the industrial world, the growing nationalistic assertion of oil-producing nations, the rise of the independent oil companies, the erosion of the position of the major oil companies, the running down of coal, and the growing environmental consciousness, which tended to favor oil consumption. All of these factors combined to put pressure on the world market.[7]

In this changed picture, a political-military crisis erupted, leading to the embargo and the first "oil shock" in 1973–1974. A second oil crisis hit the American people in 1979 with the collapse of the shah's regime in Iran. The interruption of oil supplies, the ensuing panic, the new prices, and international crises all delivered some very important messages to American society. The assumption of abundance was no longer plausible; oil and energy in general could no longer be considered a free good; imported oil was not a neutral energy source; and its role should be reduced. If this were not done,

Figure 2-1 U.S. OIL: THE PASSING OF SELF-SUFFICIENCY, 1960–1980

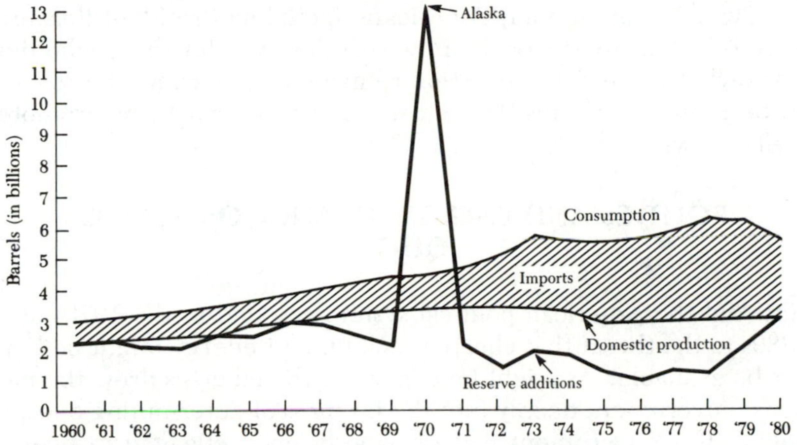

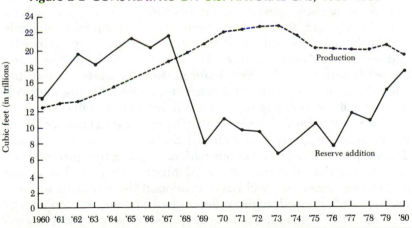

*Natural gas liquid not included in production and consumption.

Source: Energy Information Agency, *Report to Congress,* 1981, pp. 58, 59.

Figure 2-2 CONSTRAINTS ON U.S. NATURAL GAS, 1960–1980

*This figure does not include 26 trillion cubic feet at Prudhoe Bay that cannot be marketed because of lack of transportation facilities.

Source: Energy Information Agency, 1981, U.S. Energy Department.

there would be a continuing series of crises and perhaps a catastrophe.

Even so, a great many Americans, including President Reagan, were reluctant to accept the new realities. And for those who did acknowledge them, the question remained: How could the role of oil be reduced in ways that did not decrease growth or promote inefficiency?

POLITICS AND ENERGY: CHANGE OR STATUS QUO?

How did the American political system respond in the 1970s and 1980s to the threat that cheap and abundant energy might no longer be available? As might be expected, the oil crisis drew the national government deeply into the business of determining energy policy. The government had previously been engaged in everything from building dams to developing nuclear power to regulating natural gas to setting oil import quotas. Nevertheless, all this was done in a highly fragmentary way, with policies for specific fuels and with little effort at coherence.[8]

The Nixon Years

During the first Nixon administration, 1969–1973, the warning signs about possible pressures in energy supplies first appeared both domestically and abroad. The result was a considerable struggle within the administration to establish some coherence, authority, and urgency in energy matters. The effort was bedeviled by many obstacles—inflation, ideological and personality clashes within the administration, environmental concerns, and conflicting demands by politically powerful groups such as independent refiners. Coherence was not achieved before the 1973 embargo. However, three weeks afterward, Nixon announced the goal of energy independence by 1980: "Let us set as our national goal, in the spirit of Apollo, with the determination of the Manhattan Project, that by the end of this decade we will have developed the potential to meet our own energy needs without dependence on any foreign energy sources."[9] But Watergate, not energy, was on the mind of the president and his crumbling administration, so the desire and ability to do much about energy were sharply limited. Ironically, an administration strongly committed to the free market ended up regulating and rigidifying the petroleum market with price controls, an allocation system that froze buyer-seller relations, and entitlements that encouraged oil imports and inefficient refiners.

This was a heavy legacy for the Ford administration, which devoted much effort to an attempt to unravel the controls and regulations. But in response to Watergate, voters had sent a heavily Democratic Congress back to Washington in the 1974 elections. Some of the new members, highly critical of "big oil," wanted to roll back oil prices through further controls. With inflation still a primary concern, price decontrol was not exactly a popular issue.

Yet there were two highly significant achievements during the Nixon-Ford years. One involved a major environmental compromise. In the immediate aftermath of the embargo, Congress gave a green light to the Alaskan pipeline, ending three years of debate. This made possible the single most important contribution to the American energy supply in the 1970s, the buildup of Alaskan oil production to 1.5 million barrels a day. Without it, the second oil shock, in 1979–1980, could have been a great deal worse. Second, in 1975, Congress set fuel efficiency standards for the automobile industry. By 1985, fleet averages would have to double to 27.5 mpg. Since one out of every nine barrels of oil used in the world every day was burned as gasoline on American highways, such a change would have a major impact not only on America's oil balance but also on that of the world (see Table 2-2).

The Ford Years

Ford maintained the Project Independence theme with what might be called a "high-production" strategy. In January 1975, he called for a ten-year program to build 200 nuclear power plants, 250 major coal mines, 150 major coal-fired power plants, 30 major oil refineries, and 20 major synthetic fuel plants.[10]

This strategy proved unrealistic for a variety of reasons. First, the environmental movement had been gaining momentum since the late 1960s. The strongest impact had initially been on the strip-mining and burning of coal, but in the mid-1970s it was felt on nuclear power. By 1974, a national movement opposing atomic energy had taken clear shape. Environmentalism was not solely responsible for the opposition to nuclear power; rather, it interacted with economics—continually rising costs, inflation, and, later, high interest rates—to place major roadblocks in the way of nuclear power's further development.[11] Some of the increasing costs could be assigned to delays that resulted from the activities of the en-

Table 2-2
U.S. PASSENGER CAR EFFICIENCY, 1969–1980

Average Fuel Consumed Per Car		Average Miles Traveled Per Car	Average Miles Per Gallon
Year	Gal.		
1969	718	9,782	13.63
1970	735	9,978	13.57
1971	746	10,121	13.57
1973	763	9,992	13.10
1974	704	9,448	13.43
1975	712	9,634	13.53
1977	706	9,839	13.94
1978	715	10,046	14.06
1979	664	9,485	14.29
1980	603	9,135	15.15

Source: *The World Almanac and Book of Facts,* 1983 edition (New York: Newspaper Enterprise Association, 1982), p. 144. Data for 1972 and 1976 not available.

vironmentalists, but some could also be attributed to poor management, to the government's changing specifications in midstream, and to a rapid scaling-up of plant size in the industry without sufficient operating experience. A renewal of concern about nuclear proliferation also slowed the development of nuclear power. By the end of the Ford administration, the ordering of new plants had just about come to a halt in a de facto moratorium.[12]

There was another reason why Project Independence plans would prove unrealistic. The plans were based on the notion that energy demand would continue to grow at a relatively high rate. Expectations were basically determined from the recent past with some lowering of demand curves due to higher prices. These expectations were embodied in a number of forecasts in the early 1970s that estimated U.S. energy consumption would double by the year 2000.[13] The forecasts were based on what seemed the altogether reasonable premise that continued high rates of energy growth were necessary to assure economic growth. As we have seen, this assumption was the commanding idea well into the middle 1970s.

A change was at hand, however, and it was being expressed in a naive question—"Why?" Why did energy consumption have to grow so substantially? This question had been asked by a few dissenters years earlier; it had been posed by S. David Freeman within the administration at the very beginning of the 1970s and in a controversial Ford Foundation study in 1974.[14] But by the middle 1970s, the debate was in full swing.

The Carter Years

This basic shift in ideas, gathering momentum in the mid-1970s, explains the considerable difference in emphasis between the Nixon-Ford and Carter administration positions. In April 1977, less than a hundred days into his term, Carter came forward with a National Energy Plan which put much greater emphasis on conventional coal use (to be doubled in 1985) and conservation, gave greater attention to renewable sources, and sought to break out of the pricing impasse through a crude-oil equalization tax. In what was clearly a shift of attitude, the new president declared that a major transition was at hand, no less significant than that from wood to coal at the beginning of the Industrial Revolution or that from coal to oil and gas in the twentieth century. Moreover, reflecting the change in the commanding ideas on energy, Carter raised conservation to a first priority—"the cornerstone of our policy . . . our first goal . . . the cheapest, most practical way to meet our energy needs and to reduce our growing dependence on foreign supplies of oil."[15]

The first Carter program was thoroughly worked over by a Congress whose members reflected the many contradictory values and interests of a diverse nation. The most significant achievement was the complex compromise on natural gas which ended an exhausting eighteen-month battle on Capitol Hill. In the autumn of 1978, legislators reached a compromise providing for a merger of the interstate and intrastate markets on natural gas and its quasi-decontrol by the mid-1980s. There were also additional incentives for conservation, solar energy, and utility pricing reform. Because of a growing concern about nuclear weapons proliferation, brakes were applied to both the breeder-reactor and nuclear fuel–reprocessing programs.

The Carter administration had sufficiently experienced the skepticism and contradictory pressures engendered by the energy problem when the second oil shock occurred in 1979. The president took a bold step in April when he finally broke the logjam on oil prices and announced that domestic oil price control would end by September 1981. He also called for a windfall tax on the additional revenues that would flow to oil producers.

Gas lines in the next two months, however, created national hysteria. Thrown on the defensive by public and congressional clamor, the administration fell back on a technological fix. In July 1979, the president offered a second energy program, built around an $88-billion synthetic-fuels effort—primarily liquids from shale, and liquids and gas from coal. The scale was reminiscent of the Nixon-Ford proposals. Essentially, it was a strategy to mobilize investment and reduce risk by channeling revenues from a windfall profits tax.

The development of a synthetic fuels know-how and capacity was, at the very least, a reasonable insurance policy. But this program was very large. There were important questions about how rapidly such technologies could be perfected and scaled up, about costs, about environmental consequences. When would those technologies be available? Would the simple fact of the existence of such a program help to prevent further price eruptions or severe cuts in supply? Many concluded that even if the program were very successful, only a modest effect could be felt even by the early 1990s; and Congress proceeded to scale back the program to more manageable dimensions.

The Reagan Years

The election of Ronald Reagan clearly indicated that there was not yet a consensus on the energy problem in the United States. Indeed, the Reagan administration set its agenda in conscious opposition to that of the Carter administration. Three strands formed its outlook. First, the government was seen as the real source of the energy problem. In 1978, at the time of congressional action on Carter's National Energy Plan, Michael Halbouty, who in 1980 became head of the Reagan administration's energy task force, declared:

> There is no question that the public is confused about the energy situation. I would like to clarify a flagrant misconception by making it perfectly clear that there is no energy crisis in the United States. This country has a tremendous amount of energy potential. But there is a very serious energy problem—in fact, the problem is a crisis—namely, Washington has politically manipulated, interfered, and imposed dictatorial controls and regulations which severely stymied discretionary productive efforts by the energy industries.[16]

Second, energy efficiency was seen not only as a sure recipe for a nongrowth economy but also as a rejection of the American experience. The "policy theme" of the Reagan transition team report was that "much has been done. But what has been done is to impede production and curtail consumption. The government has acted on the principle that the way to deal with energy is to do away with it. . . . The price of energy failure is not just economic stagnation, but social upheaval."[17] This view was pungently summed up by Reagan himself a month after his election. Conservation, he said, means "we'll be too hot in the summer and too cold in the winter."[18]

These two strands both amounted to an assertion that the United States had not outrun its geological base and that it was possible to return to the energy economy of the 1950s and 1960s. Here was an explicit reassertion of the belief in essentially unlimited abundance. Obviously, such views emphasized the positive role of energy producers—quite a change from the dominant view of the preceding years.

The third strand of the Reagan administration's energy policy was shaped by a broader shift in national attitudes concerning the role of government in American society. Through the late 1960s and the 1970s, government, especially the federal government, had become more and more active in almost every realm of American life. The 1980 election was seen as a mandate to roll back government influence, intervention, and regulation. This certainly applied both to direct government intervention in the energy area and to government's much expanded role in the related area of environmental pollution. Those holding this view in the Reagan administration were not inherently hostile to energy efficiency; indeed, they favored "economy" and regarded conservation as a relatively cheap and attractive option. They emphasized the need to "free" the market to make whatever adjustments made the most sense on a decentralized basis.[19] Market prices would, they believed, lead to the optimal adjustment.

These three views led to a rejection of much of what had happened in the preceding ten years. The Reagan administration virtually eliminated conservation and solar budgets, greatly reduced support for synthetic fuels development, and eschewed planning for emergencies and disruptions. It speeded up the leasing of public lands and offshore areas for energy development and sought to roll back a decade of environmental protection programs. In the one major exception to its oft-repeated commitment to the market system, it actually increased government support for nuclear power. Symbolizing its drive to downgrade the importance of the energy question, the administration sought to eliminate the Department of Energy (as Reagan said in his presidential campaign, "The Department of Energy has not produced one barrel of oil") and disperse its functions among other agencies, though there was no evidence that this would save money or improve efficiency.

Although much good can be said about Reagan's concern over excessive government regulation of energy and the importance of infusing "market principles" into the energy arena, one can't help but be alarmed at his apparent attitude that there is no geological clock ticking. The bulk of evidence in the early 1980s suggests that it is risky to assume we can return to the energy economy of the 1950s and 1960s and restore the era of energy abundance.

Perhaps of even greater danger is the Reagan administration's desire to divorce U.S. energy issues from their global context. Other industrial nations remain acutely aware that the United States, as the world's largest importer of oil, has a major impact on the world market, and they are alarmed by what they see as a new American "energy nationalism," indeed, "energy isolationism."

Finally, the approach of the Reagan administration contrasts with those of the Nixon-Ford administrations as well as that of the Carter presidency. After all, it was those earlier Republican administrations that saw a "crisis," controlled prices, and promoted large government subsidies to capital-intensive projects. Although the Ford administration had certainly sought to do so, it was the Carter administration that had actually initiated decontrol.

American Energy Policy—A Mixed Bag

These lurches in policy demonstrate certain key themes that characterize America's response to the energy problem:
1. sharp shifts from sense of crisis to complacency
2. a strong desire to return to "business as usual"
3. a drive to find a technological fix, a miracle solution
4. considerable difficulty in balancing energy concerns with equity and environmental considerations
5. a basic debate over what the sources of the "energy problem" are and over the role of various actors
6. a denial of the significance of America's integration into the world market

7. an inability to weld domestic energy issues to fundamental foreign policy and security considerations

In consequence, no firm consensus has yet emerged. Perhaps the problem has not been severe enough. According to one analyst, "The embargo of 1973–74 caused temporary inconvenience to many, but it fell short of being a disaster. That is to say, it was just irritating enough to give rise to a search for scapegoats without being so painful as to create a nationwide front in the face of adversity."[20]

Consensus is made more difficult by fragmentation, for it is inescapably true that the energy problem is really many different problems that have converged in a short period and that are experienced and viewed differently by different groups. No matter what the specific issue, many competing interests are affected. Thomas (Tip) O'Neill, speaker of the U.S. House of Representatives, aptly described the energy issue as "perhaps the most parochial issue to hit the floor of the House."[21] In other words, representatives in Congress vote on energy questions based on the interests of their hometown folk rather than in the interest of the nation.

THE DISTRIBUTION OF COSTS AND BENEFITS

We turn now to the third question asked at the beginning of this chapter: How have the costs and benefits of the oil crisis been distributed in this country? This question takes us to the related question of price controls. What is the appropriate, sensible, and fair way for energy prices to be determined? No other energy question in the 1970s generated as much political controversy as did this one.

The question of whether to insulate domestic consumers against higher world oil prices has bedeviled all industrial nations.[22] But the issue has taken on a special importance and intensity in the United States. The persistence of controls is based in America's situation as a significant oil producer as well as the world's major consumer. Out of this "split personality" arises a series of endemic tensions, expectations, and suspicions. As Thomas Schelling has observed, these conflicts led to a bitter debate as to whether price is part of the problem or part of the solution.[23] Some have argued that free pricing alone can solve the problem. Others warn about the dangerous economic impact of higher oil prices; many OPEC meetings have been preceded by the pleas of leaders of the industrial nations against price increases. When Americans rate inflation as one of the most important problems facing both the nation and themselves personally, it is difficult to see high prices as a "good." And when faced with the possibility of a surge in inflation, even strong free market advocates in various administrations have wavered in their commitment to remove controls.[24]

As paradoxical as it has sounded to many on both sides of the debate, the truth is that price is both a significant part of the problem and a significant part of the solution. When the price of domestic oil is increased fourteen times over—as occurred between 1965 and 1981—and six times over in constant dollars, economic pain is inflicted on segments of the public (see Table 2-3).[25] Insofar as those higher prices are paid to foreign producers in the context of large price shocks, they inflict considerable damage on the national economy. Yet those upward movements in price also reshape consumption patterns and encourage additional domestic production of oil and other energy sources. In summary, higher prices "today" reduce American oil imports, thus increasing the slack in the world petroleum market and so helping to prevent much higher and more damaging price increases at some unspecified "tomorrow."

Why did this argument prove so difficult for so many to accept? To begin with, major questions of income distribution are involved. Wealth is transferred from the United States to foreign oil producers. That is a national loss. But the United States is also a significant producer as well. It is the third largest producer of oil and the largest producer of natural gas. Thus, considerable transfers of income also take place within the United States—from sector to sector, from region to region, from social group to social group. This shift of wealth means that there are winners and losers. The stakes are very large. The value of U.S. oil and gas reserves was about $200 billion in early 1973 at world oil market prices. Those same reserves today, even allowing for depletion, are worth $2 trillion at world oil prices.[26] So the battle over pricing has been a struggle over how to distribute the income generated by the production of these hydrocarbons.

The sectoral transfer—from such energy-consuming industries as chemicals to energy producers—can have a significant and negative impact on the ability of the former to mobilize investment, including investment in more energy-efficient capital stock. Obviously, higher energy prices mean higher costs for firms. Nevertheless, the business community has generally favored decontrol, for the commitment to market pricing and reduced government regulation is deep-seated and decontrol seems more likely to assure reliable supplies over the longer term.[27]

Table 2-3
AVERAGE FUEL COSTS TO CONSUMERS, 1975–1983

Fuel	1975	1976	1977	1978	1979	1980	1981	1982	1983
Leaded Regular Gasoline (cent/gal)*	43.7	43.1	43.2	41.0	49.8	119.1	131.1	121.	116.1
Residential Heating Oil (cent/gal)	29.3	30.2	31.2	31.7	40.8	97.8	120.5	119.	115.5
Residential Natural Gas (cent/Mcf)†	132.8	145.4	162.2	163.5	185.3	391.5	455.7		
Residential Electricity (cent/Kwh)†	2.73	2.77	2.81	2.76	2.66	5.36	6.20		

Source: The World Almanac and Book of Facts, 1983 edition (New York: Newspaper Enterprise Association, 1982), p. 143.

*1972 constant dollars.

†Mcf = million cubic feet; Kwh = kilowatt hours.

Table 2-4
ESTIMATED AVERAGE ANNUAL EXPENDITURES BY INCOME
CLASS, 1981

Estimated Household Income	Estimated Average Home Energy and Gasoline Expenditures	% of Income	% of All Households
Less than $7,400	$1,140	23	15
$ 7,400–$14,799	$1,550	14	21
$14,800–$22,099	$2,010	11	19
$22,100–$36,899	$2,580	9	28
$36,900+	$3,230	6	18

Source: Congressional Budget Office, *Low Income Assistance,* June 1981, p. 7.

Tension over energy prices reflects a regional-class split. Lower-income people expend proportionally more of their income on direct energy expenditures. In 1980, low-income households spent more than a quarter of their income directly on energy. This was two and a half times as much as middle-income households spent (Table 2-4). Low-income families have the least capacity to adapt, the least discretion in what they buy. They are locked into a way of life without access to the capital or means to change. Moreover, many see energy as a basic necessity, like food. In a modern industrial welfare state, an attempt is made to assist those so seriously affected. Price controls came to be the chosen instrument, although there were also programs of direct assistance. But two further points need to be made. If one includes indirect consumption of energy, embodied in goods and services, then the distribution is less regressive.[28] Second, even when the benefits of price controls are measured only in direct expenditures, the groups that in absolute terms receive by far the largest benefits are the middle classes. One might well suspect that it is in the response to their needs that controls were maintained.

Moreover, there is a very substantial redistribution of income among regions as a result of changes in oil and gas prices, taxation, and investment flows. Ten states produce over 90 percent of the nation's domestic oil. According to an estimate made during the windfall tax debate, these states will collect in excess of $128 billion in increased revenues as a result of decontrol, through tax receipts and royalty income.[29] At the same time, those living in energy-deficient regions will pay more for energy. For instance, it was estimated that in 1980–1981, it cost residents of the Northeast about 30 percent more than the national average to supply adequate energy to their homes.[29]

Thus, energy has greatly aggravated tensions between the Sunbelt, the South, and the West, on the one side, and on the other, the Frostbelt, the established industrial states of New England, and the Great Lakes region. Legislators from the latter group of states tended to exert the main pressures for continued price controls, while those from the Southwest were most vigorously opposed. But the geographical distinctions are not absolute; there are discrepancies within regions as well. Officials in Iowa who had to cut the state budget three times in one year can be just as angry at Montana's severance tax on coal as at Texas's tax on oil.

Yet by the end of the decade, the debate on price control had pretty much moved toward resolution. We have already learned that this occurred first in 1978 in the case of natural gas, when President Carter managed to get Congress to agree to a merger of the interstate and intrastate markets and quasi-decontrol by the mid-1980s. Although slower in coming, decontrol of oil prices was to happen by September 1981. This date was moved up by the newly elected Reagan to February 1, 1981.

ALTERNATIVE PATHS

We end this chapter by looking at the two energy paths most often described as reasonable approaches to solving the energy problem. But first a word should be said about the efforts already made by Americans to adjust and adapt to the changed energy world. Important changes have been made on both the supply side and the demand side of the energy curve; these changes will contribute to a solution regardless of the path or paths selected. For instance, in the search for new sources of oil and gas, the number of crews engaged in seismic exploration and the total footage of wells completed both increased more than two and a half times between 1973 and 1981. Coal production increased 34 percent in that period, while coal consumption increased 21 percent.[30] Moreover, for the first time in years, the amount of oil reserves added in 1980 almost equaled the amount produced.

But the most dramatic impact has been on the demand side, where a considerable process of adjustment has taken place. This process began in the early 1970s when industrial consumers first noted a tightening in natural gas prices, and it took on real momentum in the aftermath of the 1973 embargo. Growth in demand for energy slowed, and in recent years it has actually flattened.

The change becomes quite apparent when we compare energy use per unit of GNP in 1973 with that in 1981 (see Table 2-5). In 1981, the United States consumed 35.1 million barrels a day of oil equivalent—the same level as in 1973. In the meantime, the U.S. economy had grown. If every unit of GNP generated in the United States had required the same amount of energy in 1981 as in 1973, then the country would have consumed 7.3 million barrels a day of oil equivalent more than it actually did in 1981. Thus, the United States was about 17 percent more energy-efficient in 1981 than in 1973.

To many, this kind of adaptation comes as a surprise. "Conservation of energy was never regarded all that seriously as a primary method for cutting the nation's appetite for imported fuel," *Busi-*

Table 2-5
U.S. ENERGY CONSUMPTION, 1960–1981

	Energy Consumption (Mbdoe)*	Energy/GNP†	Petroleum as % of Total Energy Consumption
1960	20.8	59.8	45.2
1965	25.0	57.0	43.9
1970	31.5	61.6	44.2
1971	32.2	60.9	44.7
1972	33.8	60.4	46.0
1973	35.1	59.5	46.7
1974	34.3	58.3	46.0
1975	33.3	57.3	46.3
1976	35.1	57.3	47.2
1977	36.0	55.6	48.6
1978	36.9	54.4	48.6
1979	37.2	53.3	47.0
1980	36.5	51.5	44.9
1981	35.1	51.5	43.2

Source: U.S. Department of Energy, Energy Information Administration, *Annual Report* to Congress, 1980, II: *Monthly Energy Review,* February 1982; and U.S. Council of Economic Advisers, *Economic Report of the President,* 1982.

*Millions of barrels daily of oil equivalent.
†1,000 BTUs per 1972 $ of GNP.

ness Week noted in 1981. The magazine quoted one analyst as saying, "Conservation has taken hold much faster and produced larger savings than anyone could anticipate."[31]

Certainly the dominant view after the 1973 embargo focused on increasing conventional supply and downplayed efficiency. This accorded with the fact that most prominent figures in the energy field, naturally enough, came from the energy *supply* industries. But it was also in line with the powerful traditions of the American experience. Frederick Turner's frontier thesis stated in 1893: "Not the Constitution, but free land and an abundance of natural resources open to a fit people, made the democratic type of society in America for three centuries."[32]

In 1979 and 1980, the attitudes, perceptions, expectations, and values of the American consumer underwent a profound change. Even if they continued to be suspicious of oil companies, consumers concluded that there was a real energy problem. Moreover, there was a movement away from regarding conservation in negative terms—as deprivation—to regarding it in a positive light—as efficiency, as a way to adjust to a changed situation in order to preserve certain goals (distribution of expenditures, comfort, mobility). Thus, in 1979, one poll found that for the first time, a majority of people (65 percent) regarded conservation as a way to avoid "severe cutbacks" in life-style (Table 2-6). Recent polls have confirmed this positive shift and support of conservation.

These shifts in attitude facilitated another key change, an ero-

Table 2-6
CHANGING ATTITUDES TOWARD CONSERVATION

If the United States continues to use energy as we do now, ten years from now we will be very low in energy resources and will face severe cutbacks in our life-styles.

Response	Percent
Strongly Agree	30
Agree	35
Disagree	17
Strongly Disagree	7
Don't Know	11

Source: Alliance to Save Energy, *American Attitudes toward Energy Conservation* (July —August, 1979), p. 38.

sion of the "first-cost mentality" that has traditionally underlain in-vestment decisions in the United States. What has mattered has been the initial cost, not the life-cycle costs, not the operating costs—including those for energy—over the years. This perspective was reasonable as long as these costs were relatively insignificant. The attitude certainly prevailed in the residential and commercial sectors, where structures were built with the goal of minimizing construction costs and therefore selling prices. Little attention was given to the goal of minimizing long-term energy consumption and costs. Much the same was true in the purchase of automobiles, where selling price, performance, size, and design all mattered much more than operating costs.

The need for higher energy efficiency has stimulated a vigorous effort to use existing technology better and to develop new technol-ogies and improved materials. But the availability of *capital* consti-tutes one of the greatest questions hanging over the adjustment process of American industry. Much higher rates of investment are required—General Motors estimates that its rate of investment in the first half of the 1980s will be twice that of the 1970s for exam-ple—but it is difficult for industry to mobilize such capital when the overall health of the economy is poor. Moreover, the *external envi-ronment* also has its impact, for capital investment is highly sensi-tive to interest rate fluctuations, which in turn means that the na-tional effort to control inflation can severely retard industry's ability to mobilize the capital for adaptation.

The Two Energy Paths

In terms of solving the supply side of the energy equation, the choices most talked about can be classified into two categories: hard versus soft energy paths. *Hard* technologies are centralized, capi-tal-intensive, and for the most part dependent upon depletable re-sources. The usual proposed hard path solution is the rapid expan-sion of three sectors: coal (mainly strip-mined, then made into electricity and synthetic fluid fuels); oil and gas (increasingly from Arctic and offshore wells); and nuclear fission (eventually in fast-breeder reactors).

Soft technologies, on the other hand, use to the greatest possi-ble extent nondepletable resources like sun, wind, and vegetation. They emphasize diversification and dispersal of energy sources so as to avoid in the future the sort of dependence we now have upon fossil fuels. They are flexible, which means that recovery from the

effects of wrong decisions is possible. (A wrong decision about nuclear wastes, in contrast, is irrevocable. Once they have been produced and it turns out that there is no safe way to get rid of them,
the damage has been done.) Soft technologies employ easy-
to-understand, adaptable processes that encourage the wide dispersion of skills, not the creation of a small energy priesthood. They
are designed to flow with nature to the greatest possible extent, to
emphasize decentralized delivery to the people who need energy,
and to avoid creating huge centralized banks of energy which are
inefficient and vulnerable. (A blackout of a generator serving a city
is a different order of disaster from a power failure in a generator
that serves a neighborhood.)[33]

The Debate Goes On

In the debate over hard versus soft technologies, the issue of jobs
is central. The soft-technology advocates agree that the too much
emphasis has been given to replacing human labor with capital, energy, and materials and that job creation in developed societies
through aggregate growth is not happening and will not happen.
The argument that energy-guzzling is necessary for creating jobs
is disputed by scholars like Bruce Hannon of the University of Illinois's Center for Advanced Computation, who calculates that each
large power station destroys about four thousand more jobs than
it creates.

Similarly, according to a study quoted by Senator Edward Kennedy at a Joint Economic Committee hearing, the Fortune 500 used
80 percent of the total tax credit and 50 percent of all industrially
consumed energy and created seventy-five thousand jobs over
seven years.[34] Six million small businesses, using far less energy, created nine million new jobs in the same period.

No government agency has yet analyzed the impact of alternative energy policy on employment, but individual case studies lend
strong support to the soft-technology faction. A 1978 survey by the
California Public Policy Center estimates that if space and water
heating needs in the 1980s were met by small-scale solar energy,
the classic symbol of soft technology, some 376,000 jobs would be
created.[35] This is far more than the jobs that would be lost in fossil
fuels. A better comparison is provided by a comparative study of
the employment impact of a nuclear power plant and the introduction of certain conservation measures and solar energy technologies
on Nassau and Suffolk counties in New York. The study, prepared

by the Council on Economic Priorities, concluded that conservation and solar energy would provide about four times more employment in the regional economy than would the proposed nuclear power plant.[36]

Centralized Versus Decentralized Control

There is passion on both sides of the debate because different technologies lead to very different configurations of power. Specifically, the more centralized the control of energy resources, the more concentrated the power is in a few hands. And although some resources lend themselves better than others to decentralized control, it is possible to pursue soft or hard systems with respect to virtually any energy source. Consider solar energy. In 1952, the Paley Commission report on the future of natural resources in the United States estimated that by 1975 technology for trapping the sun's rays could be supplying 10 percent of our total energy needs. Thirteen million solar-heated homes, the report concluded, was a reasonable goal. Yet in 1978, only thirty thousand homes had solar heating, and the secretary of energy, James Schlesinger, predicted that the 10-percent figure would not arrive until the year 2000.

There is nothing new about using the sun for power. A solar still for producing fresh water from salt water was built in Chile in 1872, and a solar irrigation pump for the Nile was installed in 1913. A range of solar technologies is being developed. One of the most significant is the redesign of buildings to enable them to take better advantage of the sun—in the jargon of the trade, "passive solar technology." In 1974, a study by the American Institute of Architects calculated that efficient design alone could save 12.5 million barrels of oil a day.[37]

Nearly three hundred patents for solar heating have been issued since the 1850s. Before 1940, none went to the large companies. Since the mid-sixties, thirty of forty-seven patents have gone to Mobil, GE, GM, Du Pont, Boeing, United Aircraft, and other giant corporations. Diversification into solar energy is a primary reason for the dramatic acquisition of copper mines by oil companies. Each solar collector for heating and cooling systems requires about a pound of copper, and oil companies now control almost 60 percent of domestic copper production in the United States.

The ultimate in "hard" solar technology is the solar-power satellite, which is being developed by Grumman, Raytheon, and other aerospace companies. According to a study by Peter Glaser of Arthur D. Little, photovoltaic cells in space would generate ten times the electricity such cells could produce if located on earth.[38] All that is needed is a fifty-eight-thousand-acre ground station, about $36.5 billion for each satellite and launch vehicle, and some way to keep the deadly microwaves produced in space away from the customers in their kitchens.

Thus, solar energy lends itself to extremely simple technology. In India, a simple solar cooker sells for $6.70. A space heating system that can be built in Oregon for $650 saves as much as $250 a year in electric bills. But solar energy can also be used in the most expensive and complex systems. Despite the unique advantages of decentralization, flexibility, and competition inherent in power through sunlight, government research favors big centralized technology. Ninety-five percent of all federal solar funds, according to a Citizens Energy Project report, go to large companies and universities for developing centralized delivery systems.[39] Solar satellites are a way for energy and aerospace companies to meter the sun. Among the leading vendors of sunlight power are Alcoa, GE, GM, Grumman, Honeywell, and Reynolds Metal.

Until recently, energy and high technology companies disparaged solar energy, stressing its high cost and uncertain operation. Worried that every rooftop could become its own power plant and sensing that the cry for solar energy was a revolt against huge companies, utilities, and staggering electric bills, large corporations spent a share of their public relations budget playing down the solar "messiahs." At the same time, they began buying up solar technology companies. President Carter's interest in solar energy, the tax incentives to encourage solar installation passed in 1978, and the growing public fascination with this most obvious and available renewable energy source have caused the companies to change their tack. An emphasis on solar energy would be a "real mistake," says Roland W. Schmitt, vice-president for corporate research and development at General Electric, but "if the nation decides it wants to go solar, we'll be ready to respond."[40] The role of the big corporations is a bit less passive than that. GE, along with Boeing, Lockheed, RCA, Martin Marietta, McDonnell-Douglas, and others, formed Sunsat to lobby for solar satellites. They want sixty of them by the year 2025 at a cost of $1 trillion.

The physical characteristics of the sun make decentralized small-scale technology efficient and cost-competitive. This is also true for wind, which is another free resource that has been used for years by individuals on a small scale. In the nineteenth century, six million windmills were built in the United States; about 150,000 are still functioning. But research efforts are biased toward the development of big centralized turbines rather than small decentralized units.

SUMMING UP

What the American people believe about the nature of the energy problem, its impact on their lives, and their ability to cope with it will determine to a great extent how the nation ultimately responds. And we know from the introduction to this book that *time* is critical. We cannot predict with any confidence which technologies will be the chosen ones in two or three decades. But we do know that the innovation and deployment of new technologies on a scale large enough to be meaningful in American society cannot happen overnight. Such change takes not only money, organization, and consistency in policy, but also time. And the time is provided by greater energy efficiency. For this reason more than any other, American attitudes, perceptions, expectations, and values about energy are critical.

Unfortunately, for several years there was what proved to be a misguided effort to control prices and so deny reality. This view has been succeeded in some circles by a passionate belief that prices will do everything. The second approach also denies reality—the considerable market imperfections, the gap between short-term private interests and long-term national interests, time pressures, geological and technical limits, and the possibility for disruptions similar to the 1973–1974 and 1979 catastrophes. Moreover, blind insistence on price as the be-all and end-all can result in a breakdown in the balance between energy and equity concerns, setting the stage for renewed clashes between social classes and different regions in this country. The effort to deny reality takes another form as well: the passionate desire to believe that temporary calms in the oil market—a momentary leveling of prices—mean long-term economic and political security.

We can hope that Americans are moving toward a deeper appreciation of how much and how rapidly the energy supply system has changed. Yet whatever the level of acceptance, there is still a great deal of skepticism, confusion, anger, and uncertainty—which reflect the uncertainty that hangs over the entire energy picture. Moreover, it is still possible that tensions will develop between the acceptance of the need for adjustment to a new energy environ-

ment and the character of the American culture. It has been observed that this culture

> has long been dominated by a growing psychology of entitlement and
> a greater emphasis on the freedom of the individual. One result of the
> new psychology of entitlement has been to catch Americans in a
> strange cross current of pressures between cultural trends that tell the
> individual "you have a right to a greater freedom of choice, even in
> material well-being," and economic trends that signal the individual
> American that "the good times may be coming to an end."[41]

The inflation and unemployment that owe so much to the energy problem accentuate this clash, and in the clash rests the potential for even greater political and social upheaval. Speeding up the
move toward energy efficiency and adaptation to a changed energy
picture offers a reasonable way to mediate between these two
trends.

Yet the lifeboat ethic is undermining the legitimacy of the federal government and its ability to insist upon a consistent energy
policy for the nation. Before the age of scarcity, the federal government could be an arbiter of competing interests and a mollifier of
class and regional conflict. But today these functions are more difficult. The Southwest resists "subsidizing" the Northeast with controlled natural gas prices. South Carolina resists being the reposi-
tory of nuclear wastes from generators that light up the cities of the
East and Middle West. California talks about "self-sufficiency." Because the federal government has failed to develop a plan for the
economic integration of the nation that appears equitable to the
various regions, the nation faces internal strain that can only cause
harm. Regional and local loyalties are becoming more intense, and
antipathy to central authority is rising everywhere. The current bad
repute of "big government" is due to its distance from and insensi-
tivity to local concerns.

The rebellion against federal regulation, represented by the
election of Reagan, has obscured the important nonregulatory functions that government can perform—in stimulating research and
development, spreading information, assisting capital investment
flows, and helping strengthen market signals. Canada and the
United States are two countries facing similar energy issues. Yet the
federal government of Canada, a nation with one tenth the population of the United States, is spending twenty times more for energy
conservation than is the American federal government. In fact,
under the Reagan administration, one would have to say that government policies have become a drag on the process of energy effi-

ciency. For instance, in 1981, the administration sought to suppress the Solar Energy Research Institute report that sketched efficiency possibilities for the United States.[42]

But perhaps the real problem is that the federal government is caught in the middle. It is neither large enough to plan on a global scale, as in environmental controls and resource allocation, nor small enough to be accountable to people where they live. As a consequence, much of what we call "national" is a facade. Neither political party has a national program. Each is a loose coalition of local duchies which rises like a phantom every four years to elect candidates for high office. Allegiance to these "national" parties has declined sharply. The national purpose that once united class and region—Manifest Destiny, Cold War, the American Dream—has become elusive.

The conservative columnist Kevin Phillips attributes the prolonged paralysis of leadership to the resurgence of "tribalism and balkanization" in America.[42] The last three elected presidents have found the country ungovernable. None succeeded in carrying through a major domestic program. Each spent time making and unmaking foreign commitments, ordering weapons, and performing other tasks more amenable to presidential initiative than solving the energy crisis.

The job of our national leaders to develop a coherent and consistent energy policy would be made easier if energy choices were merely technical ones. But they are not. They directly determine who will feel the effect of inflation and who will pass those costs to others. (A 1978 survey showed that one out of every five older Americans had to choose between buying groceries and paying the utility bill.)[44] Energy choices involve the most basic decisions about values: What is efficiency and what do we sacrifice for it? Is interdependence good or bad? Is it avoidable? Is simplicity better than complexity? In asking these questions, we must remember that when a society buys an energy system, it is also buying a particular path of development. By choosing to burn up imported fossil fuels, to develop new coal technologies, to take the nuclear option, or to develop new alternatives—solar energy, fusion, harnessing of the ocean winds—leaders are also making decisions about how dependent society will be on scarce minerals, how much water it will use, how many jobs will be created, which cities and regions will rise and which will fall, and who will hold political power. Some energy systems lend themselves to decentralization and others to centralization. In a decentralized system, local communities can determine energy prices for their citizens rather than letting the oil companies, the sheiks of Arabia, or the U.S. government decide how much of each dollar earned will go to drive the car or heat the home.

Unfortunately, such questions do not determine energy policy. Instead, energy choices are made explicitly on other grounds. Comparative cost projections are prepared on the basis of incomplete information, energy company plans, corporate influence, bureaucratic inertia, and the like—and the value questions are decided implicitly without public discussion or even public notice.

However energy decisions are made, the fundamental issue for the 1980s is not whether energy costs can be avoided—because they cannot. It is rather how they are to be distributed, internationally and within our national economy. The pattern of distribution, rather than the aggregate cost, will determine the impact of energy on the relative power of nations, social classes, and regions. But it is the total cost that will ultimately measure the impact of energy on the overall prosperity of the world economy, from which no nation can entirely divorce itself.

From that flows the basic dilemma for everyone concerned with energy policy: whether to maximize national advantage (or minimize national loss) by exploiting particular energy assets separately and to the utmost, without regard to regional or global repercussions, or to assume some larger share of an irreducible total cost in the interest of wider security and stability.

At the moment, the Reagan administration is clearly favoring the maximization of our national advantage at the possible expense of less advantaged countries. While this approach may help to preserve the American way of life a little longer, it may well have serious and irreversible economic and military consequences in the longer run.

NOTES

1. Economic growth is usually defined to mean the expansion over a period of years of an economy's capacity to produce real goods and services. The concept of economic growth is based on an analogy with growth in biological organisms. But what is an economic organism? It is not the flow of goods and services that issues forth every year (or every day or hour), but the complex of people, factories, stores, farms, rivers, dams, banks, and information that produces the stream of goods and services. In the industrial-postindustrial age, oil must be included.
2. Daniel Bell, "The Public Household," *The Public Interest*, 10 (Fall 1974), 42–43.
3. Information on reserves is from the American Petroleum Institute, *Basic Petroleum Databook*, II-1, IV-3, I-6; information on price is from Hollis Chenery, "Re-

structuring the World Economy: Round Two," *Foreign Affairs*, 59 (Summer 1981), 1105; data on consumption and shares are from United Nations, *World Energy Supplies, 1950–1974*, ser. 5, no. 19 (New York, 1976).

4. George W. Pierson, *The Moving American* (New York: Random House, 1973).
5. Rachel Carson wrote *The Silent Spring* (Boston: Houghton Mifflin, 1962) to warn the public of possible ecological disaster. She said: "The earth's vegetation is part of a web of life in which there are intimate and essential relations between plants and animals. Sometimes we have no choice but to disturb these relationships, but we should do so thoughtfully, with full awareness that what we do may have consequences remote in time and place" (p. 278).
6. *Wall Street Journal*, September 5, 1980.
7. For constraints on U.S. oil production, see Richard Nehring with E. Reginald Van Driest II, *The Discovery of Significant Oil and Gas Fields in the United States* (Santa Monica, Calif.: Rand Corporation, 1981), R-2654/1, USGS/DOE.
8. A remark by a Johnson staff member exemplifies this approach of the federal government. See Crawford Goodwin, ed., *Energy Policy in Perspective: Today's Problems, Yesterday's Solutions* (Washington, D.C.: Brookings Institution, 1981), p. 399. The discussion that follows on the internal administration struggles in the Nixon and Ford years draws on this book.
9. U.S. Congress, Senate Committee on Energy and Natural Resources, *Executive Energy Documents*, 95th Congress, 2nd sess., July 1978, no. 95-114.
10. Ibid. However, following the accident at Three Mile Island in 1979, no new reactors have been ordered and thirty-four orders have been canceled. See Michael Gold, "To Breed or Not to Breed," *Science*, 212 (May 1982), 82.
11. Questions and doubts about the use of nuclear power continue to grow. This has been especially true since the accident at the Three Mile Island nuclear power plant in Pennsylvania in March 1979. During this accident, the plant spewed radioactive poisons into the air, dumped hundreds of thousands of gallons of radioactive water into a river, generated widespread anxiety and fear, and brought us to the very brink of a nuclear catastrophe. The worst did not happen, but the near-miss alerted people to the possible dangers of nuclear power.

   There has been a steady stream of reports about radioactive leaks and discharges from nuclear plants. Storage facilities for nuclear wastes have also leaked, and uranium-mining operations in the West have spread radioactive poisons. A federal study in 1980 concluded that an acceptable solution to the problem of containing and disposing of radioactive wastes remains as remote as ever. Some of these wastes will remain deadly for thousands and even hundreds of thousands of years.

   Protests and bans have lately greeted the transportaion of nuclear materials. Uranium that could be used to build atom bombs disappeared from a plant in Pennsylvania, and there is good reason to believe that it was diverted to Israel. Plans to evacuate people in the event of a nuclear accident have been found to be nonexistent or woefully inadequate. Finally, directions for construction of homemade nuclear weapons continue to appear in publications accessible to all citizens.
12. I. C. Bupp and J. C. Derian, *The Failed Promise of Nuclear Power: The Story of Light Water* (New York: Harper & Row, 1981), pp. 132–35, 153–69; Daniel Yergin, "The Terrifying Prospect: Atomic Bombs Everywhere," *Atlantic Monthly*, 239 (April 1977), 46–75.
13. John H. Gibbons and William U. Chandler, *Energy: The Conservation Revolution* (New York: Plenum Press, 1981), p. 28. Also see Marc Ross and Robert Williams, *Our Energy: Regaining Control* (New York: McGraw-Hill, 1981).
14. Goodwin, *Energy Policy*; Ford Foundation, Energy Policy Project, *A Time to Choose: America's Energy Future* (Cambridge, Mass.: Ballinger, 1974).

15. U.S. Congress, Senate Energy Commitee, *The President's Energy Program: A Compilation of Documents,* 95th Cong., 1st sess., 1977 (Washington, D.C.: Government Printing Office, 1977), pp. 2–10.
16. *Wall Street Journal,* October 1, 1978, p. 2.
17. *Report of the Energy Policy Task Force,* November 5, 1980, p. 3.
18. *National Journal,* 12 (December 6, 1980), 2075.
19. *Report of the Energy Policy Task Force,* November 5, 1980; Ronald Reagan, *National Journal,* 12 (December 6, 1980), 2075.
20. Daniel Boggs, session of the Harvard Energy and Security Seminar, November 2, 1981.
21. Neil diMarchi, "Temporary Inconvenience," in Goodwin, *Energy Policy,* p. 513.
22. On energy prices and consumers in the Organization for Economic Cooperation and Development, see International Energy Agency, *Energy Conservation: The Role of Demand Management in the 1980s* (Paris: OECD, 1981).
23. Thomas Schelling, *Thinking Through the Energy Problem* (Washington, D.C.: Committee for Economic Development, 1979), p. 112.
24. For public opinion, see Barbara C. Farhar, Charles T. Unseld, Rebecca Varies, and Robin Crews, "Public Opinion About Energy," *Annual Review of Energy,* 5 (1980), 143, 149, 155–56. For worries in the Ford administration, see Goodwin, *Energy Policy,* p. 507.
25. Although by January 1983 gasoline and fuel oil prices had plunged sharply in relation to prices for 1981. The government's consumer price index for January 1983 showed gasoline prices fell 3.3 percent in January, which meant that gas costs were 10.6 percent below their peak level of March 1981. Home heating oil prices plunged 4.1 percent, the biggest fall since records were first kept in 1952. The declines were attributed to a variety of factors, including the oil surplus, the recession, and the mild winter weather. However, natural gas prices rose 1.7 percent. Gas prices rose a record 25.4 percent for all of 1982. Analysts generally attribute the surge to the 1978 legislation decontrolling new gas costs.
26. Robert Stobaugh and Daniel Yergin, eds., *Energy Future: Report of the Energy Project at the Harvard Business School* (New York: Ballantine, 1980), pp. 273–74.
27. For concern about the possible "crowding out" of energy-efficiency investment, see remarks by William Sneath, the chairman of Union Carbide, in *Energy User News,* October 8, 1979, and Bankers Trust Company, *U.S. Energy and Capital: A Forecast, 1980–1990,* November 1, 1979, pp. 23–34.
28. The issue is analyzed in Harold Beebout, Gerald Peabody, and Pat Doyle, "The Distribution of Household Energy Expenditures and the Impact of Higher Prices," in *High Energy Costs: Assessing the Burden,* ed. Hans Lansburg (Baltimore: Johns Hopkins University Press, 1981).
29. For state tax revenues, see *National Journal* (March 27, 1980), 47–71. For New England, see Congressional Budget Office, *Low Income Energy Income Assistance* (Washington, D.C.: General Printing Office, 1981), p. 9.
30. Energy Information Administration, U.S. Dept. Energy, *Monthly Energy Review.*
31. *Business Week,* April 6, 1981, p. 58.
32. Frederick Jackson Turner, *The Frontier in American History* (New York: Holt, 1920), p. 293.
33. See, for example, Amory B. Lovins, *Soft Energy Paths: Toward a Durable Peace* (New York: Harper & Row, 1979).
34. "Energy and Labor in the Consumer Society," in *Environmentalists for Full Employment,* Washington, D.C., July 1976.
35. *Creating Solar Jobs: Options for Military Workers and Communities,* a report

of the Mid-Peninsula Conversion Project, Mountain View, Calif., November 1978.
36. Council on Economic Priorities, *Jobs and Energy: The Employment and Economic Impact of Nuclear Power, Conservation, and Other Energy Options* (New York, 1979).
37. American Institute of Architects, *Energy Conservation in Buildings: Some United States Examples* (Washington, D.C., 1974), p. 8.
38. Peter E. Glaser and Raymond F. Walker, eds., *Thermal Imaging Techniques* (New York: Plenum Press, 1964).
39. Scott Denman, *Solar and Big Business,* Citizens Energy Project, March 1979.
40. *Business Week,* October 9, 1978, p. 88.
41. Daniel Yankelovich and Bernard Lefkowitz, "National Growth: The Question of the Eighties," *Public Opinion,* 3 (December–January 1980), 48–49.
42. *A New Prosperity: Building a Sustainable Energy Future* (Hanover, Mass.: Brick House, 1981).
43. Kevin Phillips, "The Balkanization of America," *Harper's,* May 1978, p. 37.
44. Gallup Poll, *San Francisco Chronicle,* April 10, 1978, p. 2.

GLOSSARY

Active solar energy systems: These use outside energy to operate the system and to transfer the collected solar energy from the collector to storage and distribute it throughout the living unit. Active systems can provide space heating and cooling and domestic hot water.

Environmental impact: The effect on an environment of entering a new substance or activity into it. For example, milling uranium leaves large amounts of radioactive tailings that give off radon gas. The gas results in a statistically expected number of lung cancers and other health effects.

Fossil fuels: Fuels such as coal, crude oil, and natural gas, formed from fossil remains of organic materials.

Fuel cycle: The sequence of steps needed for the production and combustion of fuel to produce nuclear energy. Included are mining, milling, conversion, enrichment, transportation, and waste storage.

Half-life: The number of years required for the decay of half the radioactivity in a radioactive substance.

Irradiation: Exposure to radiation. People are irradiated when they absorb a dose of radiation.

Manhattan Project: A code name for the project, begun in 1942, that developed the first atomic bomb.

Meltdown: A serious nuclear accident in which the cooling system in a nuclear reactor does not prevent the nuclear fuel core from melting. A potential release of large amounts of radiation is associated with meltdown.

Nonpotable: Water that is not suitable for drinking or cooking purposes.

Nonrenewable energy source: A mineral energy source which is in limited supply, such as fossil (gas, oil, and coal) and nuclear fuels.

Payback: The time needed to recover the investment in an energy system.

Peak load: The maximum instantaneous demand for electrical power. It determines the generating capacity required by a public utility.

Renewable energy source: Solar energy and certain forms derived from it, such as wind, biomass and hydro.

Retrofit: To modify an existing building by adding a solar heating system or insulation.

Shutdown: The halting of the nuclear fuel cycle as a means of generating electrical power. After shutdown, further activity of the nuclear industry would consist of waste handling and containment, decontamination, and possible conversion of existing nuclear facilities to other methods of power generation.

Solar collector: A device which collects solar radiation and converts it to heat.

SUGGESTED READINGS

Blair, John. *The Control of Oil.* New York: Random House, 1976.

Commoner, Barry. *The Politics of Energy.* New York: Knopf, 1979.

Engler, Robert. *The Politics of Oil.* New York: Macmillan, 1961.

———. *Brotherhood of Oil: Energy Policy and the Public Interest.* Chicago: University of Chicago Press, 1977.

Mosley, Leonard. *Power Play.* New York: Random House, 1973.

Simpson, Anthony. *The Seven Sisters.* London: Hodder & Stoughton, 1975.

Solbert, Carl. *Oil Power.* New York: Mason Charter, 1976.

Stobaugh, Robert, and Yergin, Daniel, eds. *Energy Future: Report of the Energy Project at the Harvard Business School.* New York: Ballantine, 1980.

3
The Cost of Health

Where does the money come from for health care, and who gets it?

Why are we spending so much for health care in the United States?

Are we getting our money's worth?

How much longer can we pay for high-priced health care?

What can be done to cut health care costs?

The average American does not think about health care or its cost until he or she is ill enough to seek it. Yet in 1981, health care expenditures amounted to $1,225 per person.[1] It is important to remember that each of us paid for the expense of health care in some form, whether it was by direct payment for services, insurance premiums, increased taxes, or increased prices for goods and services resulting from employee health expenses facing employers. Clearly, this means that decisions about the quantity and quality of health care are public ones. Gone are the days when the treatment of disease was a matter for the patient and doctor alone.

If the actual cost of health care is not cause enough for concern, its rapidly increasing burden upon total resources is a source of anxiety. Health care consumed nearly 10 percent of the Gross National Product in 1981 compared to only 6 percent in 1965. It is estimated that it will constitute 12 percent of GNP by 1990. In light of this type of increase, we must question to what extent needs other than health care are not being met. At what point does health care take priority in maintaining society's welfare?

*This chapter was written by Eileen Cunningham (RN, MBA), Quality Assurance Coordinator, Mount Zion Hospital and Medical Center, San Francisco, CA.

It is important to keep in mind that consumers, providers of health care, and public policymakers do not always agree about the causes of skyrocketing health-care costs nor the ways to remedy the situation. For this reason, the problem of rising costs in the health care system promises to be a volatile issue in the 1980s.

In this chapter, we will examine some of the issues surrounding today's crisis. We will begin with an overview of the different components of the health care delivery system and how they interrelate.

THE HEALTH CARE DELIVERY SYSTEM

Third Party Payers

The modern American health system had its beginning in the 1940s when private insurance was developed. Health insurers act as financial agents for the consumer of health care as they assume the risk of medical or hospital expenses. They can be either privately or publicly financed and are known as *third party payers.* Since third party payers take care of 94 percent of hospital bills and 66 percent of physicians' bills, it is essential that we understand their role.[2]

The third party reimbursement system works like this: A patient (first party) who is "covered" by insurance obtains a health service, for instance from a physician or hospital (second party). The insurer (third party) pays for the service, in full or in part, *after the service is provided.* This is known as *fee-for-service* and is the traditional way in which health care has been financed in the United States. (Alternatives to this system will be discussed later in the chapter.)

Government entered the health care field as an insurer in 1965, when the first health insurance provisions were added to the Social Security Act. With the implementation of Medicare (care for the aged) and Medicaid (care for the poor) in 1966, the federal government made a major commitment to help pay for those least able to afford private health insurance.

Physicians

It is not patients who determine when their appendixes should be removed, when they need a prescription drug for high blood pressure, or when a test should be performed to diagnose anemia—it is physicians. The physician is the gatekeeper of health care. There are more than four hundred thousand "gatekeepers" who distribute care to the sick and "worried well." It is estimated that 70 percent of all health-care spending is a result of the "doctor's order." Each American visits the doctor an average of 4.7 times a year.[3] At these visits, the doctor prescribes the course of treatment for the particular complaint or illness, whether it be aspirin, a trip to a specialist, or admission to the hospital.

What is not well known is that most physicians are not employed by hospitals, but rather serve as voluntary staff. This arrangement gives them access to the hospital for treatment of their patients. One consequence is that doctors have considerable flexibility in selecting hospitals for their patients. Hospitals therefore are eager to provide the latest in technology, the best support services (nurses, technicians, dietary personnel), and the cleanest and most attractive facilities in order to attract physicians *and* their patients.

The role of physicians in shaping this country's system of health care delivery cannot be overstated. The American Medical Association (AMA) spends more money on lobbying activities than any other private organization. The likelihood of whether a piece of health-related legislation becomes law largely depends on the support of the AMA.

Hospitals

Most health-care dollars are spent in the hospital. There are approximately seven thousand hospitals in the United States, of which more than six thousand are referred to as general, acute, short-term facilities—or in other words, the "community" hospital. Hospitals can be run for profit or can be nonprofit. They can also be run and financed by the government. At present, the majority of hospitals are not-for-profit, but the number of for-profit hospitals is steadily increasing.

Hospitals are complex organizations. They offer a multitude of services ranging from an ordinary ward where a patient recovers from a gallbladder operation to an intensive care nursery where babies of one and one-half to two pounds fight for life. The size of hospitals varies considerably as well. A hospital may have as few as twenty-five beds or as many as fifteen hundred.

The already high cost of medical care in the United States is increased by an overabundance of hospital beds—approximately one hundred thousand too many. The average hospital-occupancy rate in 1979 was 73.9 percent.[4] Empty beds raise costs and encourage overutilization of services.

HOW MUCH IS TOO MUCH?

In 1981, health costs in the United States reached $287 billion. Of this, $255 billion, or $1,090 per capita, was spent for personal health care.[5] While this figure alone is impressive, it is the rate at which health care costs are rising which is most alarming.

Rising Costs

Figure 3-1 illustrates the dramatic increase of national health expenditures by type during the sixteen years between 1965 and 1981.

The growth of personal health expenditures has averaged 13.1 percent annually since 1965, exceeding that of other goods and services. Price inflation is the major factor influencing the rising cost of health care. Medical care goods and services worth one hundred dollars in 1965 cost $329 in 1981.

The predictions for the future are grim. It is estimated that by 1990, health care will cost more than the total 1980 budget. In fact, by the year 2000, $2.3 trillion could be spent if the present rate of increase continues.[6]

Figure 3-1 NATIONAL HEALTH EXPENDITURES BY TYPE OF EXPENDITURE FOR SELECTED CALENDAR YEARS, 1965–1981

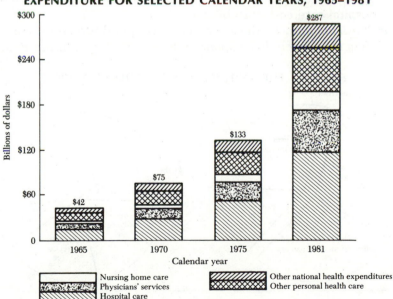

Source: Health Care Financing Review 4 (September 1982), 4.

Where Does It Come From?

The question of who pays for health care is easy to answer. It is you, the consumer. You may pay in the form of taxes, insurance premiums, higher prices for goods and services, or out-of-pocket payment for services, but health care ultimately is paid for by all Americans.

The actual sources of health financing for 1981 are shown in Figure 3-2. Public funding accounted for 42 cents of each dollar spent. Federal monies, primarily consisting of Medicare and Medicaid expenditures, totaled 29 cents, while state contributions were 13 cents. Private insurance benefits and other private funds contributed 29 cents, and consumers paid "out of pocket" the same amount for services.

Where Does It Go?

We have been speaking about a general term—health care. But what makes up the actual goods and services provided in our health care system and what does each of these goods and services cost? Figure 3-2 indicates how the health dollar was spent in 1981.

- *Hospital care* constituted the largest expenditure—41 cents of each dollar. Hospital care refers to all inpatient and outpatient care provided in both public and private hospitals, excluding the services of physicians not employed by the hospital. In 1981, hospital care cost $118 billion.
- *Physician services,* the second largest expenditure, represented 19 cents of each dollar spent on health. Included in this figure

Figure 3-2 THE NATION'S HEALTH DOLLAR IN 1981

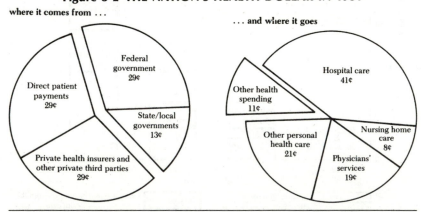

where it comes from . . .

. . . and where it goes

Federal government 29¢

Direct patient payments 29¢

State/local governments 13¢

Private health insurers and other private third parties 29¢

Other health spending 11¢

Hospital care 41¢

Other personal health care 21¢

Nursing home care 8¢

Physicians' services 19¢

Source: Health Care Financing Review 4 (September 1982), 2.

are services provided in physicians' offices, hospital care by private physicians, and tests in independent laboratories ordered by physicians. In 1981, physician services totaled $55 billion.

- *Nursing home care* cost $24 billion or 8 cents of each health care dollar.
- *Other personal health care* accounted for 21 cents. This category includes drugs and medical sundries ($21.0 billion); dental care ($17.0 billion); and other health services, such as home health agencies and industrial care, orthopedic appliances, eyeglasses, and so on ($19.6 billion).
- *Other health expenditures* represented two major categories of spending: (1) $18.5 billion for the net cost of private insurance as well as the administrative costs of government and charitable programs which advance the general health of the population and (2) $13 billion for construction of medical facilities and nonprofit research activities.

CAUSES FOR INCREASED HEALTH SPENDING

Why has the price of health care risen faster than the general inflation rate? In this section, we will look at some of the causes of the current crisis in the health care system. Most economists and policymakers agree that the following factors are important:
1. advances in technology
2. third party reimbursement
3. an excess supply of medical care
4. an aging population.

Advances in Technology

We can do more than we could fifty years ago. Technological advances in medicine have enabled physicians to diagnose and treat more diseases than ever before.

For example, coronary artery disease has been the focus of a great deal of clinical research. Coronary bypass surgery, which was developed in the late 1960s, has become almost a routine procedure. In 1980, one hundred thousand of these surgeries were performed. At approximately $15,000 each, this represents a significant expenditure of resources.

Other surgical advances have included replacement of joints such as hips, knees, and even fingers. Transplants of kidneys, corneas, hearts, and livers, unheard of twenty-five years ago, are being

**"I don't really want a diagnosis. What diseases
have you got for under $50?"**

done at many major medical centers across the country. Some say
the ultimate was accomplished in December 1982, when an artificial heart replaced a human one.[7]

Entire new modalities of care, such as the intensive care nursery, have emerged. Infants born prematurely or with life-
threatening birth defects who would have died almost immediately
after birth twenty years ago are today treated in highly sophisticated, technically intensive nurseries. Many of these babies survive
and go home. Their care can cost as much as $1,000 a day. As with
other of today's medical feats, many argue that intensive care nurseries are not cost-effective.

The computerized axial tomography (CAT) scanner, an innovation in X-ray technology introduced to hospitals in 1973, is a classic
example of how a technical advance can increase health costs. By
1979, only six years after the first CAT scanner was purchased,

1,200 of them had been installed in the United States. This rapid and widespread distribution is apparently the result of the desire of hospital administrators to attract physicians by obtaining the latest technology. Because the CAT scanner costs almost a million dollars for purchase, installation, and first-year operation, it has contributed significantly to health care spending.[8]

Third Party Reimbursement

We have already said that third parties are those who pay the bill, whether they are private insurers or the government in the form of Medicare or Medicaid. Under the provisions of insurance plans, the forces which normally control price and demand are removed. Patients do not shop around for the physician with the lowest fee for an office visit or a hospital with the lowest charge per day. At the same time, providers of care realize that for most patients with insurance coverage, cost is not an issue. They therefore do not offer lower-cost options.

Dr. Alain C. Enthoven provides a helpful analogy to illustrate this point:

> Imagine that you and nineteen friends belong to a lunch club. You agree that you will each pay 5 percent of the total lunch bill for the group. Each member is free to choose whatever he or she wants. Consider the incentives. Suppose you go to lunch one day, feeling that a $2 salad would satisfy your desires and be just fine for your health. You watch your friends order. One orders filet mignon; another, lobster. You calculate that if you order the $12 filet instead of the $2 salad, it will cost you only $.50 more. There is little economic incentive for you to choose the less costly meal. If the waiter expects a tip equal to 10 or 15 percent of the bill, imagine which dishes he will recommend. And if everybody in town is a member of this or a similar club, there is not much incentive for anybody to open an economical restaurant that specializes in healthy $2 salads.[9]

Consider an example closer to our subject. Mrs. Jones is a patient in the hospital recovering from back surgery. She has been walking in the hall for two days. The incision has healed well, and the doctor says that she may go home today. "My son is out of town and won't be able to take me home until tomorrow," says Mrs. Jones. Dr. Smith replies, "Fine, we'll discharge you in the morning." In this case, both patient and doctor ignore the fact that one day of convenience costs $300.

Insurance company policies often foster unnecessary expenditures. For instance, insurance usually pays for most if not all of the costs associated with hospitalization but provides little or no coverage for services rendered outside the hospital. Therefore, patients needing procedures that can be performed on an outpatient basis are hospitalized so that insurance will pay for the service.

There are two aspects of third party reimbursement which particularly influence the overall cost of health care: cost reimbursement for hospitals and fee-for-service for physicians. *Cost reimbursement* simply means that hospitals are paid whatever it costs them to provide the service. That may sound reasonable, but consider that the cost of a gallbladder operation includes a great deal more than the salary for the operating room nurses for an hour and supplies used. Included in each service are the costs for *all* hospital administrative functions—housekeeping, maintenance of empty beds, depreciation, bad debts, and so forth. Since Medicare, Medicaid, Blue Cross, and other insurers pay based on total cost, there are absolutely no incentives to control expenditures.

Fee-for-service, the traditional system under which physicians are reimbursed, means exactly what it says—payment based on each service provided. After the service is provided, the third party is billed. Typically, the more services provided, the more the cost to the patient or third party and the more money the physician earns. There are no agreed-upon standards establishing the minimum amount of diagnostic testing required to determine the cause of a certain symptom, how frequently a patient needs to be seen for a given diagnosis, or when elective surgery is advisable. These determinations are made by the individual physician with little or no outside input. The recent campaigns encouraging "second opinions" for elective surgery are an effort to correct this problem.

It should be noted that third parties usually do set limits on physicians' fees through the usual, customary, and reasonable (UCR) method. This method has been criticized because it is based upon existing physicians' fees, and it is generally recognized that this standard was high to begin with.

Excess Supply

Demand for health care outweighs need. *Need* is defined by medical experts as the amount of services required by individuals to maintain optimal health. Although influenced by need, *demand* quite often is excessive due to such factors as cultural heritage, level of education, and social class. Excess in the supply of health services is both the cause and result of this demand. Providers have been cited for prescribing types of treatments and services which are not needed.

First, as already noted, the United States has an overabundance of hospital beds, perhaps more than one hundred thousand more than are needed. Including personnel, equipment, and overhead, each hospital bed costs about $20,000 a year to maintain. Hospitals with empty beds encourage physicians to fill them, resulting in overutilization. The Hill-Burton Act of 1946, which subsidized the building and expansion of hospitals during the 1950s and 1960s, is partly to blame for this situation. The passage of this act was in response to a demand for easier access to health care. Unfortunately, a by-product of this effort has been to raise the cost of health care for everyone.

Likewise, beginning in the 1960s, there was a push to increase the number of physicians to fill gaps in health care. State and federal assistance to medical schools led to a rapid growth in the number of medical students. By 1975–1976, for example, 13,561 students were graduated from medical schools compared with 7,574 in 1965–1966.[10]

It is projected that by 1990, there will be 242 active physicians per 100,000 people. In 1960, there were only 140 doctors for each population of 100,000.[11] At what point do we reach a surplus of physicians? Opinions vary, but it is clear that a maldistribution of physicians exists. In metropolitan areas such as San Francisco and New York City, the number of physicians per capita far exceeds the average. Similarly, in specialty fields, general surgery for instance, there is an oversupply of practitioners. Medicine behaves contrary to normal market forces in that an increase of doctors in a given location or specialty does *not* result in lower prices. Economist Frank Sloan of Vanderbilt University conducted a survey showing that "fees for common surgical procedures were 50% higher in Manhattan than in nearby Bergen County, even though the physician/population ratio in Manhattan was double that in the suburb." Economists explain this phenomenon by means of the "target income hypothesis." They suggest that when physicians are faced with an oversupply of other physicians in their area of practice, they will still maintain their desired income level by either raising their fees or increasing the demand for their services—that is, by prescribing more return office visits.[12]

Elective surgery is an example of how demand for services does not equal need. Studies have shown that surgical rates for comparable populations vary with the number of physicians per capita and the types of insurance coverage. This finding indicates that the decision for surgery is not always based on the patient's condition.[13]

An Aging Population

Americans are living longer. For people born in 1979, the average life expectancy is 73.8 years, up from 70.9 years for those born in 1970. When we compare this figure with the average life span of 47.3 in 1900, we see that we are indeed an aging population.[14] It is projected that by 1990, 19 percent of the population will be 65 and older.

Older people utilize more health care services. They experience more chronic diseases, which require frequent and costly care. Heart disease, cancer, hypertension, and chronic lung disease are but some of the chronic health problems facing the elderly.

Nursing home care accounts for an increasing proportion of the nation's total health bill. In 1981, nursing home care represented 9.4 percent of all personal health expenditures, compared with 1.5 percent in 1950.

Medicare, Medicaid, and private insurers are placing more emphasis on home care services and outpatient support programs such as adult day health centers. These services enable many chronically ill elderly to remain at home, thereby avoiding costly hospitalizations.

Other Causes

Additional causes of the rapid growth in health care expenditures include:

- *Lack of Consumer Knowledge.* The mystique of the physician—the awe in which the American public holds doctors and the medical system—prohibits normal purchasing behavior. Lack of advertising also contributes to consumer ignorance.
- *Life-styles.* Diets high in saturated fats and sugars, alcohol and drug consumption, cigarette-smoking, unsafe driving, and our fast-paced environment contribute to today's major health problems.
- *Defensive Medicine.* Malpractice suits and the high cost of malpractice insurance have become major considerations for health care providers. Although the effect of these concerns is difficult to measure, we know that such defensive practices as ordering an X-ray "just in case" have led to a rise in use of services.

■ *Cost of Regulation.* The health industry is regulated more than any other. There are hundreds of government agencies controlling hospitals and nursing homes. Compliance with regulatory controls results in a significant amount of nonproductive spending.

■ *Tax Breaks for Health-Insurance Premiums.* Employer contributions to employee health insurance are tax-exempt. Neither employer nor employee is taxed on what is essentially income. As a result, employers offer the most comprehensive insurance coverage possible in lieu of more wages. The more comprehensive the coverage, the more health services are utilized.

IS IT WORTH IT?

Do rising health care costs mean a healthier population? All indications are that the answer is no. Health status is influenced by factors other than the amount of health services used. Nutrition, housing, sanitary conditions, and behavior all affect the likelihood of contracting disease and the ability to recover once ill.

Health services, as we know them, have little to do with health; they are directed primarily toward illness. In other words, the emphasis in this country is on treatment rather than on prevention of illness. Certainly for some diseases such as appendicitis, bacterial pneumonia, or bleeding ulcers, medical treatment will directly affect the outcome—to the point of saving a life. For other diseases—influenza, coronary artery disease, and some types of cancer—the value of treatment is questionable.

Despite the amount of money we spend for health care, America is not the healthiest nation in the world. The infant mortality rate and life expectancy are two generally accepted measures of national health levels. Table 3-1 shows that in 1978 the United States ranked eleventh and twelfth respectively among seventeen selected industrialized countries in these measures. It is difficult to determine whether differences are due to the effectiveness of health care delivery or environmental and socioeconomic differences. Many attribute such unfavorable comparisons to the lack of a uniform health care system in the United States similar to that in countries such as England, where the government provides national health care, and Canada, where the government pays for national health insurance.

Medicine has made massive contributions to the prevention and cure of acute illnesses such as smallpox, polio, and acute rheu-

Table 3-1
INFANT MORTALITY RATES AND MALE LIFE EXPECTANCY IN YEARS: SELECTED COUNTRIES, 1978

Country	Infant Deaths Per 1,000 Live Births	Country	Male Life Expectancy (Years)
Sweden	7.8	Japan	73.2
Japan	8.4	Sweden	72.5
Switzerland	8.6	Netherlands	72.0
Denmark*	8.9	Switzerland	72.0
Netherlands	9.6	Denmark	71.7
France	10.6	Israel	71.6
Canada	12.4	England and	
Australia	12.5	Wales†	70.2
England and		Canada	70.5
Wales	13.1	Australia	70.0
German		France	69.9
Democratic		Italy	69.8
Republic	13.2	United States	69.5
United States	13.8	New Zealand	69.4
New Zealand	14.2	German Federal	
German Federal		Republic	69.2
Republic	14.7	Ireland	69.0
Austria	15.0	German	
Ireland	15.6	Democratic	
Israel	17.2	Republic	68.9
Italy	17.7	Austria	68.4

Source: U.S. Department of Health and Human Services, Public Health Service, *Health— United States 1982* (Hyattsville, Md.: National Center for Health Statistics, December 1982).

*Data for Canada, Ireland, Italy, Australia, and New Zealand refer to 1977; data for Denmark and France are provisional.

†Data for Ireland and Italy refer to 1975; data for France, German Democratic Republic, and New Zealand refer to 1976; data for Canada, England and Wales, and Australia refer to 1977.

matic fever. Thus, we have seen a twenty-six-year increase in life expectancy since the turn of the century. However, closer review of the data shows that for persons at age forty, life expectancy has increased relatively little, and for those at age seventy-five, barely at all.[15] This finding indicates that the impact of health care on longevity decreases with age.

Chronic diseases have replaced acute diseases. Heart disease, hypertension leading to stroke, and cancer are the three leading causes of death. Since they have been resistant to cure, a large portion of the health care dollar is spent in managing these diseases and delaying resultant death and disability. Until cures are found, there will be little appreciable increase in life expectancy. Questions regarding quality of life, cost and benefit comparisons, and social welfare priorities emerge and are always left unanswered.

ATTEMPTS TO CONTROL HEALTH CARE COSTS

Government Controls: Past Efforts

The skyrocketing cost of health care has been a public policy issue for some time. Consequently, private and public organizations have made different attempts to control health costs.

Over the years, voluntary cost containment programs have been established by the American Hospital Association (AHA), the AMA, and other health associations in order to prevent the need for mandatory controls. But these attempts have not been effective. The following are the major efforts by government to regulate health care costs in the 1970s:

1. *Price Controls.* Between 1971 and 1974, hospitals were required to respond to price controls established by Nixon's economic stabilization program. Price and wage freezes and ceilings were initiated, but there were many exceptions and many difficulties. The net result was questionable, at best. No clear evidence exists that price controls are an effective means of controlling costs.

2. *Professional Standards Review Organization.* In 1974, Public Law 92-603 was enacted. It established more than two hundred professional standards review organizations (PSROs) across the country. The premise of PSROs is that physicians review other physicians (peer review). Independent of hospitals, these physicians' organizations review the hospital care provided to Medicare and Medicaid patients in a designated area by examining patients' charts in order to determine whether they are ill enough to require hospitalization. The costs of operating PSROs, however, often equal the gain made in decreasing hospital stays. For this reason, PSROs are being phased out. Although funded for $143 million in 1981, they received only $72 million in 1982.

3. *Health Planning.* In 1974, Congress passed the Health Plan-

ning Act. It required each state to establish certificate of need (CON) legislation and statewide planning structures. Hospitals were required to obtain approval through the CON process for construction and equipment purchases over a specified dollar amount. Local regulatory bodies called health systems agencies (HSAs), made up of consumers and provider representatives, either granted or denied approval of hospital requests. The hope was that these agencies could "plan" health care on an areawide basis. CON failed dismally for many reasons, including cost. In addition to the costs of maintaining the statewide structures, hospitals spent enormous amounts of money in order to comply with the regulations. The Reagan administration phased out HSAs in 1982.

Generally, the three attempts by government to control health care costs failed for the same reason. None of them addressed the underlying lack of market incentives—incentives for physicians and hospitals to provide care efficiently and incentives for consumers to use the most economically attractive services. Without these incentives, no appreciable change can be made. In the next section, we will look at alternative health delivery systems which are designed to change incentives.

ALTERNATIVE DELIVERY SYSTEMS

With the passage of the Health Maintenance Organization Act of 1973, the federal government demonstrated its support of alternative health delivery methods. A health maintenance organization (HMO) is the major alternative to traditional health insurance. HMOs provide direct care to members through their own facilities and physicians or arrange for care by contracting with other health care providers such as hospitals. The most important characteristic of HMOs is that health services are provided on a prepaid or capitation basis rather than by the traditional fee-for-service method described earlier. Therefore, the HMO receives the same payment per member regardless of the number of services provided to the patient. When the cost of care exceeds that prepayment, the HMO must provide the care at a loss. At the same time, the HMO retains any portion of the prepayment which is left over. It is easy to see that incentives to provide only necessary services in the most efficient manner are built into the system.

Apparently the incentives work. Studies have shown that when compared to traditional fee-for-service delivery systems, HMOs provide care at a total cost savings of between 10 percent and 40 percent.[16] The lower cost can be attributed primarily to less hospitalization and lower out-of-pocket expenses to enrollees.[17]

HMOs are not new. The largest, the Kaiser Foundation Health Plan, began during the 1930s and currently serves four million members in nine regions in the United States. Other well-established HMOs, such as the Health Insurance Plan of greater New York and the Harvard Community Health Plan in Boston, have been operating for more than twenty years.

Enrollment in HMOs is steadily increasing. Between 1977 and 1981, HMO membership increased from 6.3 million to 10.3 million. Currently, about two hundred fifty HMOs offer health-service plans to fifty thousand businesses and organizations.[18]

In recent years, other forms of health delivery systems have emerged. For example, there are individual practice associations (IPAs). They are similar to HMOs, but in IPAs participating physicians maintain their fee-for-service practices except with those patients enrolled in the plan. Although enrollees pay a fixed fee, the physicians are paid by the plan for each service provided. However, most IPAs have provisions for physician members to be rewarded for savings and penalized for deficits—thus ensuring proper incentives to keep costs down.

An even more recent form of health plan is the preferred provider organization (PPO). Members of PPOs may obtain their medical care from any physician or hospital, but they are offered significant savings for selecting designated providers noted for their efficiency.

These alternative health delivery systems are a reflection of the direction in which health care is moving—*competition.*

COMPETITION—THE ANSWER?

Overall Trends

During the 1970s, "national health insurance" was proclaimed to be the solution to health care problems in the United States. It was thought that an organized system, federally regulated and providing equal access for all, would best serve this country's health needs. Support for national health insurance, however, faded away about the time the Reagan administration took office. In its place, competition has emerged as the panacea.

The concept of competition in health care has been around for a number of years but did not become a moving force until the 1980s. In 1981, the Omnibus Budget Reconciliation Act clearly stated the procompetitive position of the Reagan administration—to decrease government regulation and to reduce federal health spending. Since that time, legislative changes have reinforced this position.[19]

How Competition Works

First, competitive health care reform changes the incentives of both providers and consumers. The failure to modify existing economic incentives, as we have said, caused the failure of previous attempts to contain health costs.

Figure 3-3 shows how competition is intended to affect both providers and consumers. There are six conditions necessary to provide free market forces. On the side of providers, these are (1) deregulation, (2) elimination of cost reimbursement, and (3) limits on available public funds. On the side of consumers, they are (1) consumer choice, (2) cost-sharing by consumers, and (3) tax credit reform. All are subjects for recent and future legislation and policy changes. Each is briefly described below.

1. *Deregulation.* There will be a decrease in government-mandated price controls and other regulations governing the quality and quantity of services. Reliance on market forces will determine prices. Both federal and state legislation are moving in this direction.

2. *Elimination of Cost Reimbursement.* Prepaid and capitation fee systems of financing health care will become more widespread. In September 1982, President Reagan signed into law a measure that directs the Department of Health and Human Services (DHHS) to develop a prospective payment system for Medicare patients. Beginning in 1983, hospitals were paid a set dollar amount for each patient stay according to diagnosis. This is a major change from the current system of cost reimbursement for services rendered. Individual states have also instituted measures to change reimbursement practices. For instance, in 1983, California began to pay for the care of MediCal (Medicaid in California) patients on a contracted basis with selected hospitals for predetermined daily rates.

Figure 3-3 COMPETITION IN HEALTH CARE

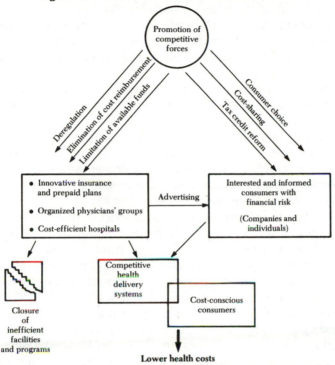

3. *Limits on Available Public Funds.* Federal and state governments will no longer pay the bills submitted to them by providers. Public health spending is being cut. Providers, particularly hospitals, will assume greater financial risk.
4. *Consumer Choice.* In order for competition to exist, consumers must have a choice of providers and health plans. They
   can thus choose the one which would benefit them the most
   and for the least cost. For optimal influences on prices and
   performance of providers, the majority of consumers should
   be able to enroll in their chosen plans on an annual basis.
5. *Cost-Sharing.* Some economists propose that cost-sharing in
   the form of higher deductibles and copayments would increase cost-consciousness among consumers. Some plans do
   exist in which the consumer accepts more financial risk when
   selecting more expensive services. Tax credit reform represents a form of cost-sharing.
6. *Tax Credit Reform.* The Reagan administration is considering

proposals that would require employees to pay taxes on at least part of their health benefits. We have noted that since all health insurance benefits are currently tax-exempt, employers offer comprehensive plans in lieu of higher wages. This, of course, encourages excessive demand for health services.

As shown in Figure 3-3, the impact of these conditions will cause insurers, hospitals, and physicians to organize in innovative ways to provide care efficiently and effectively. At the same time, consumers will be forced to become more cost-conscious as regards health care—choosing those plans and providers which offer the most comprehensive package of services for the lowest price. As in other industries, providers who are unable to compete successfully will have to close their doors.

Advertising also will become an important part of the health care system. In order for consumers to be made aware of available options, health plans and organizations must provide information about their services. Only when consumers know the differences between services offered by competing providers and the prices of each are they able to make rational decisions.

Historically, of course, advertising in the health field has been frowned upon by the general public and adamantly opposed by the medical community. However, in 1978, the Federal Trade Commission lifted barriers to physician advertising. In addition, the AMA has restated its policy. It now responds to consumer demand for more information regarding physician prices and quality of services. It is now not unusual to see a TV commercial which describes the convenience, comprehensive services, and low cost of a health clinic.

Arguments Against Competition

Everyone does not agree that the problems in health care can be explained in terms of marketplace criteria. Critics maintain that because health care is different from other goods and services, the usual assumptions about supply, demand, and price cannot be made.

Why is health care so different? Some conclude that the imbalance now existing in the amount of information available to the patient and provider precludes traditional market behavior. Also, it is agreed that the demand for health care is often governed by factors other than price. For instance, a person who is having an acute appendicitis attack does not wait until prices come down or shop around for the lowest-priced surgeon. Although in the proposed competitive models consumer choice occurs in the selection of prepaid health plans prior to an episode of acute illness, the basis for this argument remains nevertheless.

Probably the most complex and controversial concern regarding competition in health care centers on the physician's role. Should decisions about patient welfare be influenced by economic considerations? Will financial self-interest on the part of physicians affect the way medical care is delivered? Clearly, the concern that both the quality and quantity of health care will be lowered by the promotion of competition deserves careful consideration.

A final and related argument against a competitive system of health care is that competition will result in a two-class health care system—with the aged and the poor in the bottom class. Critics predict that price and ability to pay will become important factors in obtaining health care, thereby placing the higher-risk consumers—the poor and aged—at a distinct disadvantage. This is quite a change in policy from 1965, when Medicare and Medicaid were introduced in the interest of equity of health care for the old and poor.

SUMMING UP

The rapidly rising cost of health care has become an economic and social and therefore political issue of paramount importance. Recognition of this fact has generated much speculation as to the causes of the crisis and a great deal of uncertainty as to the best solutions. It is evident, however, that we as a nation can no longer afford to offer a "blank check" for health care. A new era in health care delivery is beginning.

As we have seen, the health care industry appears to be moving in the direction of increased competition. Although it is not clear to what extent the Reagan administration will proceed with pro-competition legislation, the impact of the competitive movement is apparent. We are seeing increasing numbers of alternative delivery systems and major changes in governmental and private insurance reimbursement methods.

The potential repercussions from decreased public responsibility for health care and increased competition are uncertain, but there is a danger of limited access to health care for those who cannot afford the most or the best. The questions, What is adequate care? Who shall receive it? and Who shall pay? will not be answered immediately or without a political struggle.

Regardless of the political decisions to be made, we as consumers must become more knowledgeable about the health care system. In the future, even more than today, we will be required to make decisions about what our individual health needs are and how best to meet them.

NOTES

1. Robert M. Gibson and David R. Waldo, "National Health Expenditures 1981," *Health Care Financing Review* 4 (September 1982), 1.
2. Rita Ricardo-Campbell, *The Economics and Politics of Health* (Chapel Hill: University of North Carolina Press, 1982), p. 4.
3. Charles H. White and Larkin E. Morse, *Hospital Fact Book, 1980* (Sacramento: California Hospital Association, 1980), p. 24.
4. Ibid., p. 16.
5. Gibson and Waldo, "National Health Expenditures," p. 1.
6. Thomas C. Chambers and Alfred R. Stern, "The Staggering Cost of Prolonging Life," *Business Week*, February 23, 1981, pp. 19–20.
7. "The Heart of the Future," *San Francisco Chronicle*, December 6, 1982.
8. Arnold S. Relman, "CAT Scanners—Conferring 'The Greatest Benefit on Mankind,'" *New England Journal of Medicine* 301 (November 8, 1979), 1062.
9. Alain C. Enthoven, *Health Plan—The Only Practical Solution to the Soaring Cost of Medical Care* (Philippines: Addison-Wesley, 1980), p. 17.
10. Christine E. Bishop, "Health Employment and the Nation's Health," in Philip R. Lee, Nancy Brown, and Ida VSW Red, eds., *The Nation's Health* (San Francisco: Boyd and Fraser, 1981), p. 205.
11. Enthoven, *Health Plan*, p. 27.
12. "Why More Doctors Won't Mean Lower Bills," *Business Week*, May 1, 1981, pp. 130–131.
13. Paul J. Feldstein, *Health Care Economics* (New York: Wiley, 1979), p. 88.
14. Ricardo-Campbell, *Economics and Politics of Health*, pp. 224–225.
15. James F. Fries, "Aging, Natural Death, and the Compression of Morbidity," *New England Journal of Medicine* 303 (July 17, 1980), 131.
16. "The Spiraling Costs of Health Care—RX: Competition," *Business Week*, February 8, 1982, p. 62.
17. Feldstein, *Health Care Economics*, p. 291.
18. "The Spiraling Costs of Health Care," p. 62.
19. Paul J. Sanazaro, "Some Economic and Human Aspects of Cost Control in Patient Care," *Western Journal of Medicine* 137 (August 1982), 127.

GLOSSARY

Blue Cross plan: A private, nonprofit, tax-exempt health service prepayment organization providing coverage primarily for hospital services. Historically, the plans were largely the creation of the hospital industry and were designed to provide hospitals with a stable source of revenues, although formal association between the Blue Cross and the AHA ended in 1972. A Blue Cross plan must be a nonprofit community-service organization with a governing body including a majority of public representatives.

Capitation fee: A single, fixed monthly payment to a physician or group of physicians based on the number of persons the medical group serves. A fixed rate is paid per person regardless of actual utilization.

Certificate of need (CON): A certificate issued by a governmental body to an individual or organization, proposing to construct or modify a health facility or offer a new or different health service, which recognizes that such a facility or service when available will be needed by those for whom it is intended. Where a certificate is required (for instance, for all proposals which will involve more than a minimum capital investment or change in bed capacity), it is a condition of licensure of the facility or service, and is intended to control expansion of facilities and services in the public interest by preventing excessive or duplicating development of facilities and services.

Commercial health insurance carrier: A private, for-profit insurance company which sells health insurance as part of a varied insurance program. Health insurance is usually a small portion of the insurance sold. Companies in this category include Aetna, Cal-Western, and Firemen's Fund.

Computerized axial tomography (CAT) scanning: A new radiologic technique that uses a computer to combine numerous X-rays taken from various angles into a single picture of the part of the body being examined. There are two types of scanners: head scanners and whole-body scanners.

Consumer: One who may receive or is receiving health services. While all people at times consume health services, a consumer, as the term is used in health legislation and programs, is usually someone who is not associated in any direct or indirect way with the provision of health services.

Defensive medicine: The prescribing by physicians of a variety of tests and treatments which are not really needed in order to protect themselves against the possibility of a malpractice suit.

Fee-for-service: The method of charging whereby a physician or other health practitioner bills for each encounter or service rendered. This is the method of billing employed by the majority of physicians, and contrasts with work performed under salary, per capita, or prepayment systems.

Health care delivery system: All of the services, functions, and resources in a geographic area whose primary purpose is to affect the state of health of the population.

Health insurance: A generic term applying to all types of insurance indemnifying or reimbursing for costs of hospital and medical care or lost income arising from an illness or injury. Often called accident and health insurance or disability insurance.

Health maintenance organization (HMO): A term specifically defined in the Health Maintenance Organization Act of 1973 (Public Law 93-222) as a legal entity or organized system of health care that provides directly or arranges for a comprehensive range of basic and supplemental health care services to a voluntarily enrolled population in a geographic area on a primarily prepaid and fixed periodic basis. The term is sometimes used loosely to denote any organized prepaid system when in fact it is defined under federal law.

Health planning: Planning concerned with improving health, whether undertaken comprehensively for a whole community or for a particular population, type of health service, or health program.

Hill-Burton: A program of federal support for construction of hospitals and other health facilities. In return for this federal money, hospitals incur an obligation to furnish a certain amount of free services to low-income individuals and must provide services to the community including Medicaid/Medi-Cal and Medicare recipients.

Home health care: Health services rendered to an individual as needed in the home. Such services are provided to aged, disabled, sick, or convalescent people who do not need institutional care. The services may be provided by a visiting nurse association (VNA), home health agency, hospital, or other organized community group.

Medicaid: Provides certain kinds of medical services for those receiving cash assistance as well as for those deemed medically indigent. A federally financed program matched by the states and administered by the states under Title XIX of the Social Security Act.

Medicare: A federally financed program under Title XVIII of the Social Security Act which mainly provides health insurance for those over sixty-five. It also covers persons eligible for Social Security disability payments and for certain individuals who need kidney dialysis or transplantation.

Nursing Home: Institutions other than hospitals providing levels of maintenance and personal and nursing services to persons unable to care for themselves.

Professional standards review organizations (PSROs): Federally funded organizations charged with comprehensive and ongoing quality review of services provided under the Medicare, Medicaid, and Maternal and Child Health programs. They are usually sponsored by local medical societies or foundations. The purpose of this review is to determine for purposes of reimbursement under these programs whether services are medically necessary; provided in accordance with professional criteria, norms, and standards; and in the case of institutional services, rendered in an appropriate setting.

Third party payer: An organization, public or private, that pays or insures health or medical expenses on behalf of beneficiaries or recipients (e.g., Blue Cross and Blue Shield, commercial insurance companies, Medicare and Medicaid).

Usual, customary, and reasonable reimbursement (UCR): Health insurance
  plans that pay a physician's full charge if it does not exceed the usual
  charge; does not exceed the amount customarily charged for the service by other physicians in the area (often defined as the 90th or 95th
  percentile of all charges in the community); or is otherwise reasonable.
  In this context, usual and customary charges are similar but not identi-
  cal to customary care. Most private health insurance plans, except for
  a few Blue Shield plans, use the UCR approach.
Utilization review: A control method to ensure proper use of health care
  resources by providing for the regular review of such operational features as admission of patients, length of stay, services performed, and
  referrals.

SUGGESTED READINGS

Eastaugh, Steven R., *Medical Economics and Health Finance.* Boston: Au-
  burn House, 1981.
Enthoven, Alain C. *Health Plan—The Only Practical Solution to the Soar-
  ing Cost of Medical Care.* Philippines: Addison-Wesley, 1980.
Fuchs, Victor R. *Who Shall Live?* New York: Basic Books, 1974.
Hamilton, Patricia A. *Health Care Consumerism.* St. Louis: C. V. Mosby
  Company, 1982.
Johnson, Everett A., and Johnson, Richard L. *Hospitals in Transition.* Rock-
  ville, Maryland: Aspen Systems Corporation, 1982.
Luft, Harold S. *Health Maintenance Organizations: Dimensions of Perfor-
  mance.* New York: John Wiley & Sons, 1981.

Glossary Source: California Health Facilities Commission, *Consumer Guide to
Health Care Costs* (Sacramento: CHFC, 1980).

4

Toxic Wastes: A Sleeping Giant

What are the dilemmas of environmentalism?

Can we afford to clean up the environment? If so, who should pay the cost?

What are the problems of defining hazardous waste materials?

What role should government play in protecting the environment? Has the government's role changed over time?

What are likely to be the environmental policies of the 1980s?

In an average day most Americans wake up to the sound of an alarm clock made from plastic. We brush our teeth with toothpaste containing various chemicals and wash with manufactured soap. For breakfast, we fry eggs in a chemically treated pan and then wash the pan with a man-made detergent. Many parts of our modern kitchen are preformed in a plastics factory, and our floor is covered with glued-on fabricated sheets of vinyl. For lunch we wrap a sandwich in a disposable plastic bag, and in the evening we may listen to records made from yet another chemical process.

Between thirty and forty years ago, the United States embarked on a course in which industrial processes and the production of food additives, fuels, fabrics, construction materials, fertilizers, drugs, and pesticides became heavily dependent on complex chemicals (see Figure 4-1). Synthetic fibers and plastics were developed, and petroleum was cracked into by-products.

Between 1942 and 1962, plastics production alone grew from 500 million to 7.8 billion pounds, and the United States supplied nearly 40 percent of all the world's chemicals. Adding to the momentum was World War II, during which vast federal funds were allocated for corporate research laboratories. These laboratories provided a capital and technical base from which, after the war

Figure 4-1 ANNUAL PRODUCTION OF SYNTHETIC ORGANIC CHEMICALS, 1920–1978

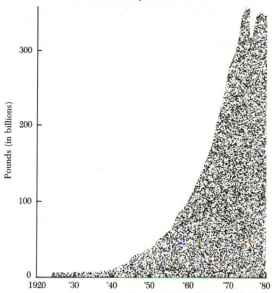

Source: Council on Environmental Quality, *Contamination of Ground Water by Toxic Organic Chemicals* (Washington, D.C.: Government Printing Office, 1981).

ended, factories were able to greatly expand. In their infancy, the chemical trade and other industries were able to burn their residues into the air, allow them to drain into lakes and tributaries, dump them at sea, or simply flush them into municipal sewers. The number of factories and the quantities of waste from factories, farms, homes, and mining activities increased at a frantic pace. Yet the technology for treating unwanted by-products remained as primitive as when the boom first began. There were no profits to be made from destroying the waste products of industrial society; money was to be made only from hurriedly manufacturing the products.[1] Figure 4-2 illustrates the sources and disposal of waste materials in the environment.

Finally, legislation was passed to prevent wanton despoliation of surface water and air. After the 1960s, laws required factories to scrub airbound particulates from smokestacks and extract large quantities of toxic sludge from liquid waste. It was then necessary to dispose of these wastes, along with the precipitates from distillers and furnaces, by other means. As a result, hazardous wastes were pumped into drums and tank cars and hauled to unused corners of plant properties or to offsite trenches and garbage dumps, with-

**Figure 4-2 SOURCES AND DISPOSAL OF WASTE MATERIALS
IN THE ENVIRONMENT**

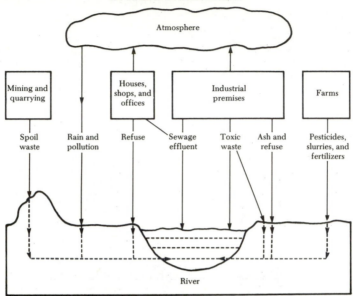

out the interference of governmental regulation. There they began
to accumulate to the point where pockets of buried refuse dominated large sections of every industrial landscape.

Many forms of industrial garbage were generated, but it was
the category of "hazardous waste" that soon constituted a new environmental dilemma.[2] Hazardous waste promises to be the major
environmental problem of the 1980s and beyond. American industry produced about 126 billion pounds of toxic wastes in 1981,
enough to fill the mammoth New Orleans Superdome from floor
to ceiling once every day (see Figure 4-3). Traditionally, only 10
percent of this waste has been disposed of safely, according to the
Environmental Protection Agency (EPA).

The hazardous waste problem has been called "the sleeping
giant of the decade." But although it is becoming the environmental issue of the 1980s, we know very little about this hidden and
awakening giant.

ENVIRONMENTAL DILEMMAS

It is helpful to keep in mind that every environmental issue forces
us to face certain dilemmas.[3] The first involves the Doomsday
prophets.

Figure 4-3 U.S. SOURCES OF HAZARDOUS WASTE

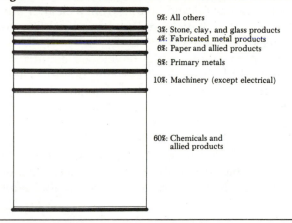

9%: All others

3%: Stone, clay, and glass products
4%: Fabricated metal products
6%: Paper and allied products

8%: Primary metals

10%: Machinery (except electrical)

60%: Chemicals and
    allied products

Source: Council on Environmental Quality, *Eleventh Annual Report to Congress* (Washington, D.C.: Government Printing Office, 1981).

"The real environmental issue is survival. The industrial society is destroying the world!" So say Doomsday prophets. "Governments ought to stop the rush to destruction before it's too late; probably it's too late anyway," they warn.

Doomsayers have always been vocal, readily attaching themselves to the fashionable issues of their day. Are such prophets necessary? They are adept at stirring the populace out of cozy, complacent attitudes, but in so doing they usually provoke overreaction in those they claim to be saving. Like Aesop's character, they cry wolf too often. Throughout history, they have been confounded and had their causes eroded by human ingenuity.

Survival is of course a very real issue. We humans have had to carve out our niche on earth. We have been an endangered species until recent times (and still are in some parts of the world). We continue to be predators as well as beneficiaries of nature's largesse. And environmental hazards have always been present. It is in this context that the warnings of Doomsday have to be placed. Humans are ever searching for new goals. Will we opt for short-term gains or accept the more difficult constraints of far-sighted actions?

Underlying environmental dilemmas is the fact that so much is written about the problems and so little about possible solutions. Solutions *are* possible. They are generally known, in outline at least. But, remarkably, the institutional mechanisms to phase them into the human framework are often primitive.

Environmental problems do not disappear at the wave of a

wand. Solutions always cost something in time, effort, and money. Will those who clamor for and benefit from a cleaner environment with potable water, sanitation, and ecological stability vehemently oppose paying their share of the cost?

In an evolutionary sense, the developed countries are at the start of what might be called a "recycling phase." Their concerns are mainly with waging war on dirty air, polluted water, noise, congestion, outmoded housing, and local shortages of energy. In contrast, developing countries are in various stages of aspiring to this "pinnacle of success"—another dilemma!

Governments, aided by every human and technical resource available to them, have to resolve such dilemmas. It is their function to arrive at politically and economically acceptable solutions. This is never an easy job.

Love Canal: The Symbol of a New Problem

The symbol of the new environmental health danger is known by the oddly incongruous name of Love Canal. The Niagara Falls, New York, community of Love Canal is the site of a long-forgotten chemical dump—a graveyard for toxic wastes. More than two hundred families were evacuated from the area because dozens of chemicals had seeped into their basements, into a creek, and even into the land on which a school was built. The community became a virtual ghost town in 1978 after President Carter declared it the first man-made environmental disaster.

But Love Canal was not an isolated case. At the end of the 1970s, horror stories about thousands of oozing chemical dumps began appearing on the front pages of newspapers throughout the country. Water supplies were pronounced undrinkable as underground wells that had been pure for centuries suddenly were found to be contaminated by chemicals.[4]

How Far-Reaching Is the Problem?

Approximately 70 percent of the nation's hazardous wastes are generated in the Middle Atlantic, Great Lakes, and Gulf Coast regions. A 1978 EPA draft report showed New York, Pennsylvania, Michigan, Ohio, Indiana, and New Jersey highest on the list of toxic landfills, with California, Texas, and Louisiana not far behind. Another EPA breakdown listed California as having the most industrial storage, treatment, and disposal sites (2,985), while still other lists have included Illinois and Tennessee in the various "top tens." Missouri, Florida, Massachusetts, South Carolina, Wisconsin, Georgia, Connecticut, North Carolina, Kentucky, Colorado, Alabama, Oregon, Washington, Virginia, and West Virginia belonged to the second highest category of producers. States with the lowest amounts were in the far Midwest and Rocky Mountain regions as well as in some sectors of upper New England. But no state is devoid of landfill problems.

All dumpsites have the potential to harm the environment and those who live in it. Groundwater contamination, surface runoff into waterways, air pollution via evaporation of chemicals and wind erosion, poisoning upon direct contact, fouling of the food chain, and fires and explosions are the most frequent disruptions. The examples are easy to find. In May 1977, a Delaware dumpsite accepting both municipal and hazardous wastes reportedly threatened a groundwater supply for forty thousand households. Nearby, in the grimy industrial town of Chester, Pennsylvania, in September 1978, water supplies to six hundred households were shut down because an unlined lagoon was leaking lithium, a metallic element apparently capable of causing mothers to bear deformed young. In Belmont, California, in June 1978, eighteen people were hospitalized, fifteen hundred evacuated, and two firemen permanently disabled with lung disease and brain damage when an old cylinder containing waste fumigants spewed its contents into the air. The deaths of twenty-two cattle in Franklin County, North Carolina, were traced to a trash heap containing calcium arsenate. In Batesville, Mississippi, three children were hospitalized for respiratory damage and coma as a result of exposure to the insecticide methyl parathion, which had been poured on the shoulder of a road. Even New York City, despite a population density that precludes a large number of dumps, had a surprising number of problems. At College Point, Queens, there was a 350,000-gallon pond laden with PCBs that tended to catch fire, sending smoke near Shea Stadium. In the same borough, the water supplier for five hundred thousand residents was forced to close four of its seventy-seven wells because of toxic infiltration, and in yet another instance, a sewage treatment plant on Jamaica Bay blew up as a result of solvents and explosives thrown into sewers. Meanwhile on Staten Island, New York, a three-thousand-acre city dump ("Fresh Kill") was found to be largely uncovered, and a depository called the Chelsea Terminal dump was in need of serious cleanup.[5]

Synergism

It is not enough to be concerned about the possible effects of hazardous wastes by themselves. We must also ask what happens when they are mixed together. It is well known that two chemicals, upon combination, can create a total effect greater than the sum of their separate effects. This phenomenon is known as *synergism.* Hydrogen peroxide in amounts above 1.5 parts per million, combined with 1 part per million of ozone, was found to be lethal to some animals, whereas the peroxide by itself produced only slightly toxic effects at nearly two hundred times that concentration. One chemical may inhibit the production of a nerve-protecting enzyme, making it simpler work for a second material, with a history of attacking the nerve cells, to do its damage. Bacteria may also work on wastes to make them more lethal, and mixtures can transform stable compounds into ones that explode.

Danger to Water Supplies

Probably the most dangerous consequence of the improper dumping of toxic wastes is contamination of underground water supplies (Figure 4-4).[6] The level of pollution of lake water is determined largely by the quality of feeder streams, disposal of nearby wastes, land use practices, soil erosion, and runoff of fertilizers and pesticides from farmlands and gardens. Airborne pollutants can also affect lake water quality. Half the nation depends on groundwater for drinking. Once an underground reservoir is contaminated, it can take centuries for the danger to disappear.

Problems develop when landfills leak or bulldozers disrupt long-forgotten waste sites. One EPA study found that 90 percent of the landfills in the eastern half of the United States were leaking toxic substances into groundwater.

For quite some time, it has been common practice for waste producers to collect chemical residues in containers and bury or dump them in empty fields, abandoned mines, or rivers. Illegal dumping at night adds to the problem, and even legal disposal by companies on their own property affords no safety unless pollutants are fixed firmly in place. When rainfall percolates through a landfill, it removes the soluble components from the waste, producing a grossly polluted liquid called *leachate.* This leachate can spread as far as a mile, and it may last for years. In 1979, EPA's Office of Solid

Figure 4-4 LAKE-WATER IMPAIRMENT, 1978

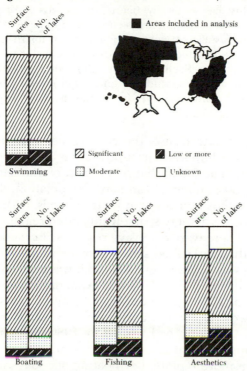

Source: Council on Environmental Quality, *Environmental Quality, 1981,* 12th Annual Report, pp. 56–57, 1982.

Waste estimated that an average landfill site, about seventeen acres in size, produces 4.6 million gallons of leachate a year after ten inches of rainfall.

Once it finds its way underground, leachate is nearly impossible to retrieve. The chemicals, shielded from the atmosphere, are not subject to the photolytic degradation of the sun, nor do they readily evaporate. Instead they cling tenaciously to the particles of soil or remain in aquifers that stay in the same locations for great lengths of time. When the groundwater does move, it quickly filters into surface bodies of water, or finds its way into the kitchen sink.

Despite the importance of groundwater pollution, President Carter in 1978 produced an extensive water policy message without addressing the issue. In criticizing the omission, the United States comptroller general said,

The relationship between disposal practices and the effects on ground-water quality has generally been ignored. Land disposal sites for wastes are often located in areas considered to have little or no value for other uses; sufficient concern is not given for the type of soil on which they are situated or their proximity to water resources, particularly groundwater. Such improper siting, coupled with limited state enforcement of other standards and requirements, has resulted in groundwater contamination in some heavily populated areas throughout the country.

Unlike the White House, the comptroller general's office was well aware of how important groundwater is to the populace. A survey by the office had found that 80 percent of municipal water systems, serving 30 percent of the actual population, depended entirely upon groundwater brought up from wells, with an additional ten million families in more sparsely inhabited regions relying upon private wells. There were extensive reserves of groundwater in the nation, more than 180 billion acre-feet of it within a half-mile down, but much of it was not recoverable, and it was unevenly distributed across the land. Moreover, its use was exponentially increasing each decade, creating shortages in the High Plains of Texas and dry portions farther west. In 1950, Americans used about thirty-five billion gallons a day; the figure had tripled by 1980.

As the supply of water dwindles, the spread of contaminants increases even more rapidly. Permeating our soils as never before are great quantities of solvent materials laced with benzene, chloroform, carbon tetrachloride, and most ubiquitous, trichloroethylene. Carbon tetrachloride, a simple molecule, is a potent carcinogen. Benzene, which is used in countless industrial processes, has been found to cause chromosomal damage at levels of less than ten parts per million. Sufficient carbon tetrachloride creates massive discharges of epinephrine from the sympathetic nerves. This chemical overwhelms the liver, leading to cirrhosis and damage to the central portions of its lobules. Internal irritations and scars may be followed by fatal growths of cancer; in experimental mice, rats, and hamsters, the administration of these agents has initiated malignant tumors.

The effects of long-term exposure to small amounts of solvents, pest killers, and plasticizers through groundwater contamination (or by other means) have not yet been fully studied, and perhaps they never will be, for scientists cannot experiment on human beings as they do on rats. Yet our folly in waste disposal has begun inadvertently to create an enormous laboratory that engulfs both cities and states, casting large numbers of people, without their knowledge, in the role of guinea pigs.

PROBLEMS IN DEFINING HAZARDOUS WASTES

We will see that it is difficult to establish just and effective hazardous waste regulations, in part because it is hard to study and therefore define precisely which materials should be considered hazardous.

A Common Definition

A generally accepted definition of hazardous waste is: any by-product that poses a substantial present or potential threat to plants, animals, and humans because it is harmful and nondegradable and may be biologically magnified (accumulating in the fat instead of being excreted).[9] Examples of hazardous waste include filter cakes, organic tars, and other compounds from the manufacture of pharmaceuticals; waste solvents containing halogenated hydrocarbons; residuals or raw materials from paint manufacture; dust from air-pollution equipment; still bottoms culled from pesticidal units; and lead-tank sediments from petroleum refineries. Other sources include paper mills, metal fabricators, glass and stone producers, and machinery use. In short, hazardous wastes are either flammable, explosive, corrosive, or toxic.

But it is one thing to give a definition to an object and quite another to translate that definition into political and economic policies. As we might expect, there are intelligent people with well-argued opinions on both ends of the spectrum. At one extreme are those who believe human activities should generate no pollutants; *they advocate very strict government regulations.* At the other extreme are those who believe industry can and should take responsibility for protecting the public; *they are opposed to any government regulation of any industry.*

Obviously, some balance between these two extreme positions is preferable, and therein lies the problem. The best regulations would protect human health and the environment while imposing the minimum economic hardship on industry and thus the national economy. Unfortunately, as we have seen, no one fully understands the possible long-term adverse health effects of many chemicals. Indeed, only recently has environmental contamination been recognized as a problem worthy of intensive scientific study.

Certainly some hazardous wastes have properties that are easy to recognize—for example, ignitability, corrosivity, reactivity, and acute toxicity—making their definition and regulation relatively uncontroversial. But chronically toxic chemicals are harder to identify and thus are the subject of considerable controversy. Chronically toxic compounds can take fifteen or twenty years or longer to produce adverse health effects. Because everyone is exposed to a wide variety of chemicals for many years, it is difficult to identify cause-and-effect relationships. Although epidemiological studies (studies that deal with the incidence, distribution, and control of disease), bioassays (the determination of the relative strength of a substance), and other research efforts provide some insight, our understanding of the scientific principles of chronic toxicology is in its infancy and is inadequate to clear up regulatory disputes.

Defining and identifying acutely toxic chemicals can also be a problem because virtually all substances become toxic at sufficiently high doses. Some chemicals produce death in microgram doses and are considered extremely hazardous or toxic. Others are essentially harmless, and may result in a toxic response only at doses over several grams. But most chemicals fall between those two extremes, posing the question of where on such a scale we make the (perhaps arbitrary) switch from "toxic" to "safe."

There is also the problem of synergism, mentioned earlier. The fact is that laboratory tests generally focus on a single compound, but compounds almost always exist in mixtures, and there is growing evidence of synergisms between them. Thus, the health impacts of the mixture may be totally unlike those of the individual components. For example, we may determine that a compound is harmless, but in combination with another chemical (perhaps also harmless), this compound may become highly toxic. Since we do not understand how these interactions occur, we need to examine not only an enormous number of chemicals but also all possible combinations—a formidable task. Because most standard laboratory studies use nonhuman subjects and high chemical doses, another troublesome question is how reliably we can extrapolate the results to people.

Constant changes in the EPA's official list of hazardous wastes are evidence of the problems of definition (as well as political and economic pressures) in this area. In May 1980, that list contained about three hundred chemicals and eighty waste streams. There have been almost daily additions to the list as more toxicological evidence is gathered about specific compounds or groups. Not surprisingly, many substances have also been deleted, since the EPA created the list under substantial public pressure and in many cases without sound scientific data. Given that situation, the tendency was to include any waste streams that aroused the slightest suspicion. Whenever research uncovers an unnecessary item on the list, however, industry claims "overregulation."

RCRA: THE FEDERAL RESPONSE

The effort to develop sound waste-management policies has proved controversial and complex. In an attempt to develop a comprehensive plan to handle the toxic waste problem, Congress passed the Resource Conservation and Recovery Act (RCRA) of 1976. When the RCRA is fully implemented, it will provide federal standards on toxic waste disposal. The RCRA gives the EPA overall responsibility for setting hazardous waste regulations and assigns individual states responsibility for developing specific hazardous waste programs. However, for reasons already given, these tasks have been difficult.

The RCRA eventually will mandate the design of a system to eliminate open dumping, to inventory waste sites, to regulate how landfills are constructed and monitored, to require private funding for long-term care of the dumpsites, to send grants to rural communities to improve solid waste management programs, and to institute a permit or "manifest" system whereby chemical material is recorded "from cradle to grave." Persons owning or operating facilities for the treatment of hazardous substances will be required to obtain permits that list composition, quantities, and the rate of disposal of such rubbish as well as dump locations. (Exempt from this requirement are farmers, retailers, and any concern producing less than one thousand kilograms of hazardous waste per month, a statute that raised controversy among environmentalists, who pointed out that even small quantities have been known to pose health hazards.) Within five years of the dump inventory, to be carried out by the states and localities, all open sites will be closed or upgraded according to new strictures devised at the EPA. RCRA also created the Office of Solid Waste Management Programs within the agency and authorized the EPA to seek court declarations of dangerous situations as "imminent hazards" and to force industries to pay the price of cleaning them up.

There were many defects in the RCRA, both in its design and in the way in which the EPA implemented the new legislation. One inherent fault was that the RCRA dealt mainly with active or future dumps, ignoring abandoned sites for which the generating company or waste hauler was no longer responsible. "There is no disagreement that inactive sites are a public menace," protested Leslie Dach, a scientist for the Environmental Defense Fund. "Yet protection of the public from the hazards associated with these facilities has been neglected by EPA. The main reason they don't want to look at them is the bill." There was also the problem of timing. When the comptroller general's office reviewed the RCRA in 1978, it predicted that "the improvements mandated will not be accomplished within the legislative time-frames." Indeed, where by law the EPA was supposed to issue specific regulations within eighteen months of President Ford's signing into law the RCRA, partial implementation did not come before 1980 and the full law will not be implemented for years to come. Meanwhile, waste haulers and small landfill owners who would not be able to afford to operate under the RCRA restrictions were hurriedly piling in waste to beat the deadline, thereby creating more problems for future generations. Because of the delays, at least 160 billion pounds of additional hazardous waste found their way into substandard settings.

The first and perhaps most important regulations the EPA had to devise were those in Section 3001 of the RCRA, concerning the definition of those wastes to be considered "hazardous." It was the design of this definition that caused the most internal dissension and helped delay implementation. Ignitable, corrosive, reactive, or toxic chemicals were to be included, as determined by a series of laboratory tests. The required tests, detailed in a March 1978 draft of the regulation, were extensive. They covered a broad range of effects that included the capability of compounds to cause mutagenesis (genetic changes) in living organisms. The draft went through a "working group," then through a "steering committee" and a "red-border review," and finally on to the administrator. The process took so long the EPA was sued by the state of Illinois and the Environmental Defense Fund for delinquency in attacking what the plaintiffs saw as an immediate crisis.

By the time the Section 3001 regulations were printed in the Federal Register (along with Section 3002, which concerns testing for toxicants in the wastes of generators and haulers), there had been a substantial reduction in the range of compounds considered hazardous and in the obligations of industry to fund such testing. The agency had decided to cut down the scope of the regulations, ostensibly because there were not enough test results available for many compounds and because complete testing of every waste stream would be prohibitively expensive for government and industry alike. No longer were mutagenic chemicals necessarily listed under the heading of "hazardous waste," and originally missing from the section were such notorious toxicants as C-56, Mirex, Kepone (which destroyed fishing in the James River in Virginia), one waste known to contain dioxin, residues from the manufacture of endrin and heptachlor (two suspected carcinogens), and a dye intermediate, o-anisidine, which had caused tumors in more than 90 percent of the animals tested.

Cost Is a Consideration

It would be a mistake to think that the EPA or any government official had conducted a conspiracy to endanger the health of citizens living near chemical receptacles. As Steffen Plehn, deputy assistant administrator for solid waste in the Carter administration, argued rather forthrightly, economics was a heavy consideration. When asked at a Boston press conference if the regulations had been diluted a bit too much, he told reporters that environmental needs must be balanced "with other social and economic needs." For example, the requirement that companies monitor their facilities for forty years had been reduced at one juncture to twenty years as a result of its estimated cost of $800 million a year—more than four times what industry was then expending on treatment of hazardous wastes. Those figures were debatable—current costs seemed to have been underestimated—but Plehn's statement showed clearly that the EPA's main concern was the presidential budget. The simple reality was that the office of EPA administrator was very nearly a cabinet position, filled largely at the pleasure of the president and the Office of Management and Budget.

The agency's own budget acted as a severe constraint as well. For fiscal year 1979, it had been appropriated $1.2 billion; only $25.2 million went to the branch overseeing hazardous waste management, and of that, substantially more than half went into efforts at implementing the RCRA. Land pollution efforts were granted only 3 percent of the agency's resources, while 10 percent, respectively, went toward preserving water and air.

Had the entire annual budget for the EPA been sunk into the division of hazardous waste management, there would still have been huge shortfalls. The agency's consultant, Fred C. Hart Associates, estimated that even the temporary containment of one nonnuclear chemical landfill would cost $3.6 billion, while a permanent solution would rise to $25.6 billion. This meant that if there were, as the EPA originally estimated, 1,100 chemical landfills constituting "significant problem sites" (excluding those containing radioactive wastes), it would cost more than $26 billion to rectify the situation on a long-term basis. Hart, however, calculated that there were more like 1,703 significant depositories, which would have raised the cost to approximately $44 billion. Not all would have to be funded by the taxpayer. It was estimated that in perhaps half of the cases, specific industries could afford the costs; and at 26 percent of the sites, some form of remedial action had already been taken (although any costs to industry would undoubtedly be passed on in the form of higher prices for products). But at best the cost to government threatened to be far beyond any possible allocation.

Superfund: Paying for the Cleanup

With these considerations in mind, President Carter, who had called the presence of toxic substances in the environment "one of the grimmest discoveries of the modern era," asked Congress on June 13, 1979, to create legislation that would impose fees on industries to clean up both hazardous waste and oil spills. Congress responded in December 1980 by passing the Comprehensive Environmental Response Act, which established a trust fund to pay for such cleanups.[10] Responsibility for administering these monies, known as the Superfund, was given to the EPA (see Box 4-1). The $1.6 billion fund was intended to finance cleanup of leaks into the environment of hazardous wastes when no responsible party could be identified or when the responsible party refused or was unable to pay. The bill gave the federal government the authority and money to act in emergencies to clean up chemical spills or dumps that threatened public health or the environment. The government could then sue those who caused the damages—if they could be found—to recoup the cleanup costs.

Part of the fund (87.5 percent) was to be financed by a tax on oil and specified chemicals; the remaining 12.5 percent was to come from regular appropriation of funds by Congress.

The chemical industry's major concern over the new legislation focused on the sticky question of legal liability. The Carter administration originally had wanted a "strict, joint and several liability" policy to be applied to chemical accidents. Strict liability would have made most parties involved in the disposal process— generators, disposers, haulers—open to damage suits regardless of

Box 4-1
TRACKING THE EPA'S "SEWERGATE"

The EPA has been a controversial agency since its inception, but the most recent attack against the agency is the most serious in its twelve-year history. In the eye of the storm lies the Superfund. The controversy over that fund—spiced with charges of "sweetheart deals" between the EPA and business, embarrassing memos, missing appointment calendars, and the shredding of sensitive documents—resulted in the resignation of top-level EPA officials, including the director, Anne Gorsuch (later Anne Burford). A timetable of the volatile case follows:

August 1978—The Niagara Falls, N.Y., community of Love Canal is declared a disaster area. Leaking toxins there focus national attention on the problem of abandoned chemical waste dumps.

December 1980—Congress creates the $1.6-billion Superfund to help pay costs of cleaning up hazardous waste dumps.

July 1981—Superfund comes under its first criticism when subcommittees in both the House and Senate question delays in projects. Later that month, the EPA earmarks $4 million to clean up Love Canal.

October 1981—EPA releases list of the 115 worst dump sites.

February 1982—Rita Lavelle is named EPA Superfund chief.

April 2, 1982—Representative John Dingell (D-Mich.) says an EPA aide revealed enforcement strategy to a dump-case defendant.

June 1982—EPA employee Hugh Kaufman charges that the agency tried to silence his criticism of the toxic waste cleanup effort.

October 1982—Representative James Florio (D-N.J.) charges that too many Superfund requests are being rejected by the EPA.

November 1982—A House subcommittee subpoenas 700,000 documents on hazardous wastes as part of a Superfund inquiry.

December 2, 1982—EPA administrator Anne Gorsuch refuses to hand over documents requested by the House Public Works and Transportation Committee.

December 16, 1982—Lavelle denies at a congressional hearing that she ordered an investigation of Kaufman and wanted to fire him.

December 16, 1982—Gorsuch is cited for contempt of Congress for withholding requested documents and materials.

January 4, 1983—Paper shredders are brought to the EPA, and some unspecified hazardous waste documents are destroyed.

February 2, 1983—Gorsuch asks the attorney general's office to investigate possible improper business contacts by Lavelle.

February 4, 1983—Gorsuch asks Lavelle to resign. Lavelle refuses.

February 6, 1983—President Reagan fires Lavelle. A guard is posted at her office to prevent her from taking documents.

February 12, 1983—Lavelle claims she is being made a scapegoat by the Reagan administration.

February 14, 1983—The EPA negotiates a settlement with Kaufman, agreeing not to interfere with his right to talk about the controversy.

February 15, 1983—Gorsuch defends the EPA budget at a Senate hearing and claims attacks on her are politically motivated.

February 16, 1983—President Reagan tells a news conference of a Justice Department investigation of possible wrongdoing in the EPA. He indicates he will turn over subpoenaed documents to Congress.

February 17, 1983—A White House spokesman explains that Reagan meant that he will not turn over disputed documents to Congress unless the Justice Department advises him to do so.

February 17, 1983—Lavelle for the second time fails to appear before House investigators.

March 9, 1983—EPA Director Anne Burford resigns under pressure by the White House. John Hernandez is named acting director by President Reagan.

March 16, 1983—John Hernandez is accused of altering an EPA report which was critical of Dow Chemical Company when he was deputy administrator under Anne Burford.

May 19, 1983—William Ruckelshaus is confirmed by the Senate as the new EPA Director.

---

negligence or compliance with contemporary waste disposal standards. Joint and several liability would have made any participant liable in an action, regardless of the extent of participation. Within Congress, supporters of a tough law backed a proposal that in effect would have established a new "toxic tort law" which departed from traditional theories of regulation and common law. Instead of being required to furnish direct proof that a substance caused injury, plaintiffs would merely have to provide evidence of statistical probability—that they were exposed to a known or suspected carcinogen and that they developed cancer.

These concepts of liability were not adopted. The final bill provided that those who own or operate waste disposal sites, produce wastes, or transport them are liable for all cleanup costs and for up to $50 million for each incident of damage to government-owned natural resources. Injured persons would receive no compensation and would have to seek redress through litigation in state courts, an expensive and time-consuming process that critics of the liability portions of the bill said effectively precluded many victims from being compensated. One version of the bill would have allowed victims direct access to federal courts to seek damages, but that was not in the final bill.

The final measure did not cover oil spills, as President Carter had proposed, and it contained weaker liability provisions than the Justice Department had sought to impose on persons who leak or dump chemicals.

Some legislators and environmentalists are concerned with EPA administration of the Superfund thus far. Many are upset that the EPA missed the June 1981 deadline for developing a National Contingency Plan, slated to be the cornerstone of the Superfund response actions. Furthermore, the agency has not completed a uniform scheme for states to rank sites they identify as threatening. And emergency actions taken thus far have focused mostly on preventing further leaching of hazardous materials from existing waste sites into groundwater; little actual hazardous waste removal and treatment have occurred. There is also much speculation that Superfund money will not be sufficient for cleanup, with administration of the program taking most of the funds.

Certainly, the passage of the legislation did not mean the issue of cleanup costs and compensation to victims was settled. Advocates of a strong law were disappointed with many aspects of the final bill, particularly the sections on liability of companies that dispose of hazardous wastes.

The Sierra Club, a major environmental group, said it would lobby in later Congresses for more benefits for victims. The Superfund itself called for a number of studies, including one dealing with the adequacy of existing common law to provide redress for people harmed by the release of hazardous substances. For most persons suffering losses, the primary avenue of redress is through claims against the polluter. This process is often difficult to follow. The actual losses must be determined, the polluter identified, and the relationship between the pollutant and damages proven. Delays during litigation are often long and can force settlement that may not be fair to victims. In addition, total damages may exceed the polluter's ability to pay.

The real cost of waste cleanup is another major issue that is expected to come before Congress in future years. There are indications that a lot more money will have to come from somewhere. We have already learned that Fred C. Hart Associates have estimated the cost to be anywhere from $3.6 billion to $44 billion, depending upon the number of waste sites and whether a short- or long-term solution is applied. The Council on Environmental Quality has estimated the cost at between $28.4 billion and $55 billion.

Using the Courts to Stall

In his book *Zero-Sum Society*, Lester Thurów argues that the American political system is suffering a degree of paralysis because most groups, including minority groups, have learned to use the political system (most notably the courts) to delay the costs of decisions which are against their interests. As Thurow points out, to delay an action is often to win, in effect.

> They [groups] have discovered that it is relatively easy with our legal system and a little militancy to delay anything for a very long period of time. To be able to delay a program is often to be able to kill it. Legal and administrative costs rise, but the delays and uncertainties are even more important. When the costs of delays and uncertainties are added into their calculations, both government and private industry often find it pays to cancel projects that would otherwise be profitable. Costs are simply higher than benefits.[11]

Although Thurow is in this instance referring to the increased political power of minority groups to delay the actions of government and industry, the idea nevertheless applies to economically powerful corporations working against the actions of environmental groups and government regulatory agencies. And in either case, the result too often is inaction, or paralysis.

This is what happened many times during the 1970s. As pollution control regulations were issued, industry countered with a steady wave of lawsuits designed to delay their implementation. In most cases, it cost a company less in legal fees to stall than it would have cost to correct the problem. Perpetual delay was, as supply-siders like to say, "cost-effective." A favorite perpetual-delay argument of corporate lawyers involves "scientific certainty." It goes like this: Unless science can say with absolute certainty that one level of pollution is distinctly worse than another, standards can't be valid. If, for instance, a factory's sulfur-discharge limit is set at 100 tons per day, the company sues demanding incontrovertible proof that 101 tons of sulfur per day will cause health hazards but 99 tons will not.

As we have already learned, such proof is impossible to obtain. This is, in fact, the crux of the hazardous waste regulation problem: we do not have enough solid scientific information to identify with certainty the "right" level of regulation.

Because it is impossible to establish *with certainty* the ideal level of pollution control, the EPA should have conceded early on that standards would contain an arbitrary element. After all, most social judgments are arbitrary to some extent—why is it legal to drive fifty-four miles per hour but not fifty-six? Is fifty-six drastically faster than fifty-four? Why can businessmen deduct travel expenses on their way to the company's hunting lodge for a "working weekend" but not on their way to the office to improve production? Unfortunately, early in the 1970s, the EPA sent its people back to the laboratory in a futile attempt to develop standards that would be truly certain. This led to a problem known around the agency as "paralysis by analysis"—there was so much complex and slightly differing information that policymakers couldn't make up their minds what to do. Instead, they did nothing.

Other Problems with the EPA

There are other reasons the EPA is to blame for some of its problems with industry. Much of the time it did not treat business with sensitivity, and the agency's regulations were at times needlessly complex. EPA regulations based on the Clean Air Act, for instance, split the country into no fewer than 239 regions with different standards and procedures.

The agency also showed a fondness for expensive high-tech gimmickry. A good example can be found in its administration of the Clean Water Act, the second of its three major missions (air, water, and chemicals). The EPA began by trying to regulate the estimated fifty thousand industrial facilities discharging pollutants directly into rivers and streams. This effort was generally successful, although former EPA assistant administrator William Drayton believes some ten thousand sources of direct pollution remain.

But when industry was stopped from dumping pollutants directly into the water supply, it had to find somewhere else to turn. Some responsible companies chose to pay a little more and send their chemical wastes to one of the country's handful of secure, well-managed disposal sites and treatment facilities. Others dumped their wastes illegally, on farmers' fields or into the same old rivers at times when no one was looking. (Pollutant discharge at 3 A.M.—when all good inspectors are home in bed—became common for some factories.) Still others turned to municipal sewer systems as disposal mechanisms. Soon forty thousand industrial facilities were discharging wastes into sewers that fed some twenty thousand municipal treatment plants—which in turn eventually dumped their by-products into a river or stream.

The EPA faced two basic choices. It could prevent industry from pumping any dangerous and tricky chemicals into the sewers, specifying instead that such wastes be "pretreated" at their point of creation. Or it could attempt to fund the construction of waste-water treatment plants so sophisticated they could handle anything. It chose the latter course.

That decision is now widely considered disastrous. First, it posed a technological problem almost beyond solution. When chemicals are at their point of creation, they are usually in fairly concentrated forms. Equally important, their nature is known to the manufacturer. Once a few gallons of toxin have been mixed with a few hundred million gallons of municipal water, the concentration falls so low that it is difficult to detect, let alone deal with; no machine, no matter how capable, can do it on a reliable basis. Other substances, especially heavy metals like cadmium, prance right through every kind of treatment equipment. So this decision meant in effect that instead of industry, the EPA and local public works departments would become the villains; chemicals would reach the river as a result of being discharged from treatment plants.

Many institutional forces favored this arrangement. Industry was pleased because it transferred the problem to publicly owned and financed treatment plants (many of them built at federal expense). The EPA seemed to like it because it gave the agency a huge empire of expensive, complicated projects to finance and supervise. In January 1981, after years of dawdling, the agency finally came to its senses and proposed a new arrangement under which industry would be required to treat its hazardous wastes on-site, keeping them out of sewers. Naturally industry howled at the thought of assuming an expense that had until then been shouldered primarily by taxpayers. But the new system, by using a cheaper and more reliable means of chemical management, promised to lower pollution control costs to society as a whole.

However, just after the pretreatment regulation was published, EPA director Anne Gorsuch suspended it. In the name of the free market, a publicly subsidized (and generally ineffective) means of industrial waste treatment continues.

Environmentalism: An Economic Issue

We often think of the issue of environmentalism as a battle between ethical and economic values. It is not. It is a thoroughly economic issue in which a particular segment of society (upper- and upper-middle–income people) wants some economic goods and services (a clean environment) that cannot be achieved without collective action. Therefore, it has to persuade the rest of society that it is important to have a clean environment and impose rules and regulations that force others to produce a clean environment—at a cost.

Environmentalism is closely linked with changes in the distribution of income. If we look at the countries that are interested in environmentalism, or at the individuals who support the movement within each country, we are struck by the extent to which environmentalism is an interest of the upper middle class. Poor countries and poor individuals simply aren't interested. This is not surprising. As our incomes rise, we are likely to shift our focus of demand for more goods and services. Initially, we are only interested in physiological survival. Food constitutes our main demand. As we grow even wealthier, our demands shift toward roomier housing and higher-quality food. At still higher income levels, demands rise for services. To get services we start to eat out in restaurants more and at home less. To avoid the drudgery of household work, we mechanize household operations, and wives go off to find more interesting work outside of the home.[12]

Suppose now that a family has reached an economic level where it can afford good food, fine housing, vacations, consumer durables, and all of those goods and services that represent the American dream. What is there left that can mar its economic happiness? Up to this point each family member can individually buy a rising real standard of living. But now the family runs into environmental pollution. If the air is dirty or noisy, the water polluted, and the land despoiled, there is a roadblock in its way to a higher real standard of living. The family cannot achieve a higher real standard of living unless something can be done about environmental conditions. Environmentalism is a demand for more goods and services (clean air, water, and so forth) that does not differ from other consumption demands except that it can only be achieved collectively. In any geographic region, we either all breathe clean air or none of us breathe clean air.

This is why we can think of environmentalism as a natural product of a rising real standard of living. We have simply reached the point where, for many Americans, the next item on the acquisitive agenda is a cleaner environment. If they can achieve it, it will make all of the other goods and services (boats, summer homes, and so forth) more enjoyable. A clean environment may also enable them to live longer to enjoy the benefits of their high incomes.

One of the difficulties in legislating for a clean environment is that we are not used to thinking of it as a normal economic commodity. Environmental conditions have been excluded from our traditional measures of economic output for two reasons. Since they cannot be sold in private markets, it is difficult to determine exactly what they are worth. And in the past, they may have had no price tag. If the water is clean, no one would be willing to pay for clean water—it is already free. But neither of these reasons alters the fact that clean water is an economic good just as much as the private boat that sails upon it. Given the relative supplies and demands for a clean environment, environmental goods now have a positive price. They are a part of economic growth. They have not yet been included in our measures of GNP, except on an experimental basis, but this reflects measurement problems in calculating the GNP and not the economic merit of including them.

Herein lies a major difficulty in the discussion of any environmental problem. Since a clean environment is evaluated differently by different income classes, the comparison of costs and benefits will also differ markedly. Different groups can look at exactly the same costs and exactly the same improvements in the quality of the environment and disagree as to whether the costs exceed the benefits. Since we have to share a common environment with a common set of costs, environmental expenditures inevitably end up raising the real income of income classes who have a clean environment next on their acquisitive agenda, and they lower the real income of those who have to help pay for a clean environment but do not place a high value on it.

Everyone Has a Different Cost-Benefit Ratio

Because environmentalism *is* a question of economics, and not one of ethics, we should not expect to find an absolute right or wrong answer to the problem. Unfortunately, arguments over pollution control too often exhibit the fallacy of all or nothing. Some people seem to feel that the environment should be restored to pre-industrial purity (which, incidentally, was not all that pure). Others apparently agree with the mayor of a small midwestern city who once told a citizens' group: "If you want the town to grow, it's got to stink." Neither viewpoint is acceptable.

Though waste and pollution problems are too big to be eliminated, they can be alleviated if we produce fewer goods (or a different mix of goods), recycle more of what has been produced, or change the form of wastes or the manner of their disposal. But we must remember that these alternatives are subject to economic evaluation. In principle, pollution is at an optimal level when the cost of additional reduction would exceed the benefits. If a dollar spent on an upstream mill can save downstream water users at least a dollar, it should do so—from society's point of view.

However, as we might expect, until recently upstream mills were profoundly disinclined to spend anything to relieve downstream distress. They were accustomed to regarding the waste disposal capacity of the stream as a free good. But wastes discharged upstream can impose costs of one kind or another downstream. Such costs are labeled, among other things, spillovers, side effects, external diseconomies, disamenities, and externalities.[13]

Like any other investments, outlays for environmental improvement can be evaluated by standard cost-benefit analysis.[14] Where capital outlays are required, as would usually be the case, the basic budgeting procedure is to forecast, for each year of the project's life, the probable benefits (damages avoided) minus the operating costs. Since it is a truism that a dollar earned next year is worth less than a dollar in hand, these net benefit levels must be discounted to their present value. Normally this is done by multiplying each year's net benefits by a discount factor based upon the estimated "opportunity cost" of capital—that is, what could have been earned if the funds had been used differently.

In assessing the benefits and costs of pollution control projects, government inevitably finds itself in a statistical scissors. Those that will have to pay for environmental improvements, such as businesses and municipalities, tend to inflate costs and deflate benefits. Those who particularly want the improvements—recreationists, let us say—can be counted on to do the reverse.

Many economists are convinced that of the two biases, the recreationists' happens to be the right one. Respectable project analyses, they argue, are typically biased in favor of rejection because costs are overstated and benefit levels understated. Overstatement of costs is traceable to the human tendency to travel familiar roads. When project analysts talk about abating water pollution, for example, they usually mean constructing plants for secondary or tertiary treatment of effluents. But in some parts of the country, it would be much cheaper not to treat waste water at all, but simply pipe it to storage lagoons for settling. Eventually the waste water could be used for irrigation. In other areas, costs can be greatly reduced by supplementing waste treatment with modification of productive inputs, changes in production processes, artificial aeration of streams, augmentation of low stream flow by planned releases from reservoirs, and storage of wastes for eventual discharge during periods of high flow.

It isn't important for our purposes that we understand how each of these methods work; rather, it is important to know that when project analysts fail to scan the full range of technological options—and they usually do fail—they are bound to come up with an outsize price tag. The costs side of our equation is usually inaccurate as well because of the first dilemma described in the opening pages of this chapter: people opt for short-term goals rather than long-term ones. Consequently, we tend not to consider the very much higher costs of cleanup and restitution facing us down the road.

The benefits of environmental improvement, on the other hand, tend to be understated because whole categories of damages are generally tossed out of the calculation. The researcher usually concentrates on measuring physical damages. (This is difficult because the relationships between quantity of pollutants and resultant damage are both complex and highly variable.) Researchers will make little or no attempt to quantify nonphysical damages—such as the impairment of human effectiveness or well-being resulting from air pollution, or the loss of recreation and aesthetic values resulting from water pollution.

Regardless of the difficulty of developing reliable estimates of both costs and benefits, the fact remains that to carry out an adequate economic analysis of any undertaking to improve environmental quality, analysts must relate benefits to costs. More precisely, they must estimate the specific dollar value of benefits to be derived from a given additional expenditure. This is made all the more difficult when we consider that environmental quality is a *public benefit,* while the *cost* of environmental cleanup is many times a *private one.*

Hazardous Waste Policies for the Eighties

In January 1970, President Nixon in his State of the Union address declared the goal of the seventies to be "a new quality of life in America." The enthusiasm with which his remarks were met led Assistant Director of the U.S. Bureau of the Budget (now called Office of Management and Budget, OMB) Maurice Mann to note: "For once, Madison Avenue and Pennsylvania Avenue and Main Street are singing the same song—Environment, I love you—the way you used to be."

If "a new quality of life in America" was Nixon's goal for the seventies, what is Reagan's goal for the eighties? One important goal is to *deregulate,* "to get government off the backs of the American people."[15] This includes what is perhaps the most pervasive of all regulatory functions: environmental protection.

Although President Reagan believed he had received a mandate for deregulation in the 1980 election, it appears there is not widespread support for deregulation in the area of environmental protection. As the pollster Louis Harris said after a June 1982 survey, "The American people's desire to battle pollution is one of the most overwhelming and clearest we have ever recorded in our twenty-five years of surveying public opinion."

The contradiction between such support and the Reagan administration's assault on environmental programs has generated a great deal of conflict on Capitol Hill. And though the battle rages in half a dozen agencies, from the Interior Department to the Occupational Safety and Health Administration, the most conspicuous struggle took place at the Environmental Protection Agency. While congressionally authorized hazardous waste and toxic chemical programs were doubling the agency's workload, the EPA administrator, Anne Gorsuch (later Anne Burford), before she was forced to resign in March 1983, intended to cut spending by at least 40 percent in 1983 and perhaps by as much as 60 percent by fiscal 1984, according to EPA sources. Since the EPA under President Carter operated more efficiently, with fewer employees per workload, than most other agencies in Washington, Gorsuch's claim that she could do twice as much with half the money astonished many environmentalists. As one of them put it: "These people aren't going to regulate until they see dead bodies."

Because resources are now so limited, large groups of chemicals are being exempted from the regulatory process. Meanwhile, Gorsuch reversed recommendations to regulate formaldehyde and diethylhexyl phthalate, both proven carcinogens in animals to which a great many workers are exposed. Nor had anything been done as of mid 1983 about several pesticides that the previous administration was on the verge of regulating. Instead, the EPA administrator and her staff talked about agreements with industry to deal voluntarily with pesticides and with the testing of new chemicals before they are put on the market. As the EPA backs off, the chemical industry is projecting an annual growth of 5 to 9 percent—a rate that could double human exposure to toxic chemicals in ten years. We must wait to learn what William Ruckelshaus, Anne Burford's successor as EPA administrator, will do in this area.

In July 1982, the EPA announced that it was suspending the requirement that industries generating hazardous wastes report each year on what happens to those wastes (the "cradle-to-grave" policy). It proposed instead to take an annual survey of 10 percent of the companies involved. Agency officials said the change would permit a more efficient accumulation of information, as required by the 1976 RCRA, while imposing a lesser burden on chemical companies and other waste generators. It would also save the government money through reduction of paperwork. But environmentalists and other critics within and without the agency said that the change of rules would make it impossible to monitor hazardous wastes.

Gorsuch also slowed use of the Superfund and moved to allow construction of hazardous waste facilities other than landfills (although in July 1982 she announced plans to lift the ban on containerized liquids in landfills, only to reinstate it three weeks later under public pressure). She also supported expansion of existing landfills by 50 percent, without regulations to control emissions into the environment. All of this adds up to a significant delay of the nation's readiness to deal with hazardous wastes. According to many, this delay is bound to be expensive.

In 1981, EPA officials insisted in sworn testimony before congressional committees that their budget cuts would not undermine the agency's work. But when they petitioned the U.S. District Court in Washington to delay or void parts of a five-year-old agreement mandating many of the water-quality efforts, their legal brief admitted that budget cuts made implementation impossible.

Seeking to justify the rollback in environmental protection spending, the Reagan administration cites the cost of environmental regulation both to industry and to government. But let us put the matter in perspective. The entire proposed EPA operating budget for 1982 was less than $1 billion; Gorsuch's cuts achieved a saving of only $2.68 per American. The OSHA budget is but $206 million, that of the Office of Surface Mining less than $200 million, and that of the Mine Safety and Health Administration only $150 million. In 1982, these four agencies cost the taxpayer less than half the price of one new aircraft carrier—or 0.7 percent of the proposed defense budget. As for the cost to industry, EPA studies under Carter showed that environmental regulation drove up the costs of American products only about 0.3 percent per year while increasing overall employment and stimulating technological innovation. Under Reagan, the figure has been revised to 0.6 percent, though the employment stimulus is still judged to be strong, accounting for four hundred thousand jobs in 1981.

Is Government Regulation Always Best?

Government regulation is only one (although an important one) of many methods for controlling environmental quality.[16] There are in fact several more creative options available. For example, one of the simplest methods of environmental protection is a requirement that industries carry insurance against accidents. This requirement forces the insurance industry to set premiums after examining the risks of an operation, thus creating powerful incentives for business to minimize environmental hazards. Another way to help industry police itself might be the installation of worker and consumer representatives on corporate boards of directors. And in a few cases—particularly those involving pollutants that are easy to measure—taxation may work better than regulation. Even the National Wildlife Federation, though it is a longtime supporter of traditional regulatory efforts, advocates an "acid rain tax" on sulfur emissions.

Unfortunately, Reagan appears as loath to encourage such innovative efforts as he is to preserve more traditional controls. He wants simply to lighten the burden on business, a goal, we will recall, that is consistently justified by cost-benefit analyses that inflate costs and ignore benefits. The real tragedy is that the environment will not bounce back as soon as federal spending resumes. Once a hazardous waste dump leaks, the damage is done. Once an aquifer is contaminated, we have probably lost it forever. And once a cancer cell begins to grow, modern medicine is often helpless. Right now we stand to lose a decade of progress in the newborn science of environmental protection, and the full weight of that loss is impossible to calculate.

SUMMING UP

The chemical industry has acknowledged that problems of safe waste disposal do exist, and that past practices have been deficient. But the industry also claims that a "chemophobia" has overtaken the country and could lead to staggering costs for cleanup beyond efforts that are reasonably necessary for public health.

Advocates of stronger controls respond that chemical contamination is a critical issue. It cannot be avoided in an industrial society where people demand more potent medicines, more types of plastics, and stronger pesticides. They argue that large sums of money must be expended for cleanup and that strict laws must be passed to make companies producing hazardous wastes liable for financial damages if those wastes harm humans.

There is little doubt that health problems associated with chemical waste have increased since World War II. There remains some question, however, about the relationship between hazardous substances and human health, even when the substances are known to produce illness in test animals. Even so, Congress has begun to accept the view that a relationship does exist. It has dealt with that link by passing such legislation as the Resource Conservation and Recovery Act of 1976 and the 1980 Superfund law.

There is also agreement that hazardous waste disposal is one of the most serious environmental problems faced by this country. There is also consensus that protecting human health and the environment from the effects of toxic chemicals is a complex undertaking. A vast number of chemicals touch the everyday lives of nearly all Americans. Only a small percentage of these chemicals pose threats to humans and the environment, but some can cause serious problems.

The Reagan administration's philosophy of reducing federal regulation of business and federal spending may hamper efforts to clean hazardous wastes, by reducing the role of the EPA and other agencies and giving states greater authority to identify and deal with contamination caused by dangerous dumpsites.

Returning authority and responsibility back to the states may sound fine until we think it through. The EPA was created in 1970—with broad bipartisan support—precisely because most states had abdicated their responsibility for environmental control. No prize is offered for guessing the states' response to this latest development. There is no reason to expect them to willingly take on the expense of environmental cleanup and control at a time when they too are strapped for money.

Some people think the only satisfactory answer is some significant changes in the life-styles and habits of Americans and the industries they operate. But because dozens of chemicals suspected of being hazardous play a role in the way Americans live and work, changes will be extraordinarily difficult to accomplish. The most pessimistic observers believe that basic change will occur only after a major environmental or health disaster directly attributable to a widely used chemical.

NOTES

1. For a discussion of the production and disposal of chemicals in this country, see Michael H. Brown, *Laying Waste: The Poisoning of America by Toxic Chemicals* (New York: Pantheon, 1980); John H. Duffus, *Environmental Toxicology* (New York: John Wiley, 1980); Ralph Nader and Ronald Brownstein, *Who's Poisoning America: Corporate Polluters in the Chemical Age* (San Francisco: Sierra Club, 1981); and Nancy J. Sell, *Industrial Pollution Control: Issue and Techniques* (New York: Van Nostrand Reinhold, 1981).
2. See, among others, Tom Alexander, "The Hazardous-Waste Nightmare," *Current,* 223 (June 1980), 25–33.
3. For an interesting discussion of the many dilemmas confronting us when deciding environmental policies, see George Marsh, *Man and Nature or, Physical Geography as Modified by Human Action* (Cambridge, Mass.: Harvard University Press, 1864); J. Maddox, *The Doomsday Syndrome* (London: Macmillan, 1971); and United Nations, *Report on the United Nations Conference on the Human Enviroment,* no. E.73.II.A.14, Stockholm, June 1972.
5. For additional examples, see *Environment and Health* (Washington, D.C.: Congressional Quarterly, 1981), p. 28.
6. See especially, Rachel Carson, *Silent Spring* (Greenwich, Conn.: Fawcett, 1962). Also see Carol Keough, *Water Fit to Drink* (Emmaus, Pa.: Rodale Press, 1980).
7. Toxic Substances Strategy Committee, *Toxic Chemicals and Public Protection: A Report to the President* (Washington, D.C.: Government Printing Office, 1980).
8. Environmental Protection Agency, *Movement of Hazardous Substances* (Washington, D.C.: Office of Research and Development, 1979).
9. H. M. Dix, *Environmental Pollution: Atmosphere, Land, Water, and Noise* (New York: John Wiley, 1981), p. 6.
10. *Environment and Health,* p. 38.
11. Lester Thurow, *The Zero-Sum Society* (New York: Basic Books, 1980), p. 13.
12. Abraham Maslow, *Motivation and Personality* (New York: Harper & Row, 1954), and *Toward a Psychology of Being* (New York: Van Nostrand, 1962).
13. Externalities can be reduced (never eliminated) by many different means, including environmental standards, taxes, charges, subsidies, and generalized pressure. Each stratgegy results in a different mix of industrial, municipal, and federal expenditures for environmental quality.
14. *Environment and Health,* pp. 127–129.
15. Ibid.
16. For a discussion of alternatives to environmental protection in addition to those listed here, see Regina Axelrod, ed., *Environment, Energy, Public Policy: Toward a Rational Future* (Lexington, Mass.: Lexington Books, 1981).

GLOSSARY

Environmental Protection Agency (EPA): Agency of the Federal government empowered to monitor and enforce laws passed by Congress that are designed to protect the environment.

Hazardous waste: Any by-product that poses a substantial present or potential threat to plants, animals, or humans because it is harmful or nondegradable, or because it may be biologically magnified.

Love Canal: A community in Niagara Falls, New York, site of a toxic chemi-

cal waste dump that was declared the first man-made environmental
disaster by President Carter in 1978. Since then, the term "Love
Canal" has come to symbolize the problem of environmental contamination by the dumping of the toxic wastes.

Resource Conservation and Recovery Act (RCRA): Legislation passed by
Congress in 1976 that grants the EPA overall responsibility for setting
hazardous waste regulations and assigns individual states responsibility
for developing specific hazardous waste programs.

Superfund: Shorthand for the Comprehensive Environmental Response
Act, legislation passed by Congress in 1980 that established a trust fund
for the cleanup of hazardous waste dump sites.

Synergism: Phenomenon in which the combination of two or more chemicals creates a total effect greater than the sum of their separate parts.

SUGGESTED READINGS

American Chemical Society. *Cleaning Our Environment, The Chemical
Basis for Action.* Washington, D.C.: ACS, 1969.

Axelrod, Regina S., ed. *Environment, Energy, Public Policy: Toward a Rational Future.* Lexington, Mass.: Lexington Books, 1981.

Brown, Michael H. *Laying Waste: The Poisoning of America by Toxic
Chemicals.* New York: Pantheon, 1980.

Carson, Rachel. *Silent Spring.* Greenwich, Conn.: Fawcett, 1962.

Courrier, Kathleen. *Life After '80: Environmental Choices We Can Live
With.* Andover, Mass.: Brick House Publishing, 1980.

Epstein, Samuel S. *The Politics of Cancer.* San Francisco: Sierra Club
Books, 1978.

Fuller, John G. *The Poison That Fell from the Sky.* New York: Random
House, 1977.

Keough, Carol. *Water Fit to Drink.* Emmaus, Pa.: Rodale Press, 1980.

Marcus, Alfred A. *Promise and Performance: Choosing and Implementing
an Environmental Policy.* Westport, Conn.: Greenwood, 1980.

Siebert, Horst. *Economics of the Environment.* Lexington, Mass.: Lexington, 1981.

Turner, James S. *The Chemical Feast.* New York: Grossman, 1970.

5
The Rise and Fall of Cities

What are the perils now facing American cities?

What are the major causes of these problems?

Why do the problems of eastern and midwestern cities differ from those of western and southwestern cities?

Are the suburbs immune from the problems of our urban centers?

What has been the federal response to the problems of urban America?

A front-page headline in the *New York Times* of March 23, 1975, stated: "Urban Crisis of the 1960s Is Over, Ford Aides Say"—a statement that flew in the face of reality. Several months later, New York Mayor Abraham D. Beame disclosed that the city was on the verge of bankruptcy, and it took an appropriation of $2.3 billion in loans and loan guarantees to New York, passed by Congress in December of that year, to prevent the city's default (see Box 5-1). New York State likewise came across with financial aid, leaving the state in the city's former position of facing monthly encounters with impending economic disaster.

If New York's close encounter with default caught the country off-guard, its situation played up the plight of several of the nation's largest metropolitan centers. The 1980 census reveals that the suburbs and newer cities in the South and West continue to be the mainstay of metropolitan growth. Economically, the central cities continue to lose out to other sections of the metropolitan community. The *Population Bulletin* reported that during the 1960s, approximately 70 percent of the total increase in employment and 95 percent of the increase in manufacturing occurred in large metropolitan areas outside the central city.[1] The 1980 census indicates

Box 5-1
WHY NEW YORK WENT BROKE

Like many Northeastern cities, New York has undergone a dramatic immigration of poor and low-income people since mid-century—especially of Puerto Ricans and rural blacks. As these people migrated to the city, they needed help from its welfare, health, education, and housing agencies. During the 1960s, militant community organizations put increasing pressure on city agencies to meet these needs better. In responding to these demands, New York City saw its budgets soar during the 1960s. The number of city workers grew rapidly, and salaries increased much faster than salaries of workers in private enterprise. Even more important, fringe benefits such as pensions increased liberally. Many city employees were able to retire in their early forties with pension benefits equal to half their last year's salaries.

New York's tax revenues did not rise fast enough to cover all these expenditures. To make up the deficit between revenue and expenditure, the city got into the practice of borrowing short-term money by issuing municipal notes in order to make interest payments on its long-term obligations. By 1975, the city was running a deficit of $800 million, and the debt repayment totaled $1.6 billion per year. New York was unable to make these payments in 1975 without borrowing more short-term money. However, the fact that the city was in danger of defaulting on its bond payments made its credit rating drop, and investors were unwilling to buy new city bonds or short-term notes.

that the decade of the 1970s was no different for the central cities of the Northeast and North Central regions.

These economic problems have been further aggravated by the increasing numbers of urban families on relief. New York's near financial disaster was not helped by the fact that one out of every seven people in the city was on welfare, a sizable jump over the one out of every sixteen reported in 1965. Even if the states and the federal government eventually assume more of the costs of welfare, which of course is not likely under the Reagan administration, cities must still contend with their swelling municipal payrolls and pension costs.

Politically, the cities find themselves in a minority status with respect to their state and national governments. The suburbs rather than the cities have gained the greatest representation by virtue of the Supreme Court's legislative-reapportionment decisions in the early 1960s, and it is the suburbs, not the cities, that are sending more representatives to Congress. The same is true for the newer metropolitan areas of the South and West. Following the 1980 census, reapportionment in the House of Representatives required a shift of seventeen seats. Of the ten states required to surrender seats, only one, South Dakota, was a western state.

Also, many of the long-range prospects for the cities are tied to the general state of our economy. Again, the 1980 census shows cities in the Northeast and North Central regions as particularly hard-pressed because of the changes that have taken place within their metropolitan areas. A study completed by the Brookings Institution in 1975 did rate twelve out of fifty-eight central cities surveyed as being better off than their suburbs with regard to employment, welfare, crowded housing, poverty, and income and educational level of the populace. However, of the twelve cities (including Houston, Phoenix, and Dallas), eleven were located in the southern and western portions of the country.[2]

NEW YORK CITY RAISES SOME QUESTIONS

When New York City's financial plight became known, people began to ask some obvious questions: Which cities would be next? Who was to blame for New York's problems? Were they caused by poor management and big spending habits? People also wanted to know: Are central cities alive and well generally? Even if so, is the clock ticking toward a rude awakening? And whatever became of the urban problems of the 1960s and the profusion of remedial programs they spawned?

This chapter is about these and related questions. It is about finance, housing, crime, transportation, and other problems of the cities. It is also about the role of government—what government has done and what it can do in affecting the forces which shape cities and urban conditions. To provide a backdrop for this discussion, we turn first to some of the major trends shaping our urban society.

DEMOGRAPHIC TRENDS AFFECTING THE CITIES

To understand the fiscal situation of our large central cities, we must examine two trends of the 1970s: the accelerating migration of people and jobs from the central cities to small towns and suburbs, and the movement of households and employment from most of the Northeast and North Central states to the South and West. We have already mentioned both these trends in passing, but they deserve a closer look.

Some General Trends

The U.S. population rose in the 1970s by 23.2 million—numerically the third-largest growth ever recorded in a single decade.[3] Even so, the gain added up to only 11.4 percent, the lowest in American annals except for the Depression years.

A striking reversal occurred during the 1970s in one of the nation's best-established population trends. For many decades prior to 1970, the population of metropolitan areas—the larger cities with their suburbs—typically grew more rapidly than that of their nonmetropolitan surroundings. For example, in the 1960s, the metropolitan counties as defined in 1980 increased by 17 percent, compared with only 4 percent for nonmetropolitan counties (Table 5-1). In contrast, preliminary 1980 census data show that since 1970, the metropolitan areas have grown by only 9.5 percent, compared with a 15-percent increase for nonmetropolitan areas and 11 percent for the country as a whole.[4]

The movement of people to nonmetropolitan areas is based on a number of factors:

■ Relocation of industries, businesses, services, and educational institutions to once-remote areas. Early in the decade, industry began following people to the suburbs, allowing an increasing number of Americans to live in formerly rural areas and commute to suburbs rather than cities.

■ Increasing ease of long-distance commuting.

■ Growth of retirement and recreational communities in rural areas.

■ Renewal of mining.

The United States, however, continues to be largely a metropolitan nation; in 1980, 165 million people, 73 percent of the total population, lived in officially defined standard metropolitan statistical areas (SMSAs). During the 1970s, two-thirds of the nation's population growth (14.3 million out of a total of 22.2 million) occurred in metropolitan areas. During the 1960s, however, the same metropolitan areas accounted for 92 percent of the nation's growth.

Growth rates since 1970 have been lowest in the largest metropolitan areas. The New York SMSA, the largest of all, experienced a loss of more than nine hundred thousand persons between 1970 and 1980. Of the six other metropolitan areas with a 1970 population of more than three million, Philadelphia, Detroit, and Boston each had a small loss while Chicago had a small gain. Only the Los Angeles and San Francisco SMSAs grew significantly during this pe-

Table 5-1

POPULATION OF SPECIFIED GROUPS OF METROPOLITAN AND NONMETROPOLITAN COUNTIES: 1960, 1970, AND 1980 CENSUSES

Population in thousands

Metropolitan Areas, Nonmetropolitan Counties, and Regions	Counties and County Equivalents	Land Area (square miles)	Population			Change		Percent Change	
			1980 Census (prelim-inary)	1970 Census[1]	1960 Census[2]	1970–80	1960–70	1970–80	1960–70
UNITED STATES	3,143	3,536,853	225,479	203,302	179,311	22,177	23,991	10.9	13.4
Metropolitan[3]	678	532,222	165,183	150,883	128,841	14,300	22,042	9.5	17.1
Over 3,000,000	65	61,377	53,707	52,861	45,766	845	7,096	1.6	15.5
1,000,000 to 3,000,000	144	82,706	44,007	39,341	32,403	4,667	6,938	11.9	21.4
500,000 to 1,000,000	119	80,557	25,054	22,548	19,386	2,506	3,162	11.1	16.3
250,000 to 500,000	143	126,827	21,335	18,262	15,838	3,072	2,424	16.8	15.3
Less than 250,000	207	180,755	21,080	17,870	15,448	3,210	2,422	18.0	15.7
Nonmetropolitan counties by commuting to metropolitan areas[4]	2,465	3,004,631	60,296	52,419	50,470	7,877	1,950	15.0	3.9
30 percent or more	48	23,331	1,755	1,346	1,110	409	236	30.4	21.3
20 to 29 percent	143	74,821	3,533	3,037	2,897	496	140	16.3	4.8
10 to 19 percent	344	258,998	10,873	9,370	8,796	1,503	574	16.0	6.5
5 to 9 percent	318	231,422	10,217	8,899	8,435	1,318	464	14.8	5.5

Table 5-1 (Cont.)

Metropolitan Areas, Nonmetropolitan Counties, and Regions	Counties and County Equivalents	Land Area (square miles)	Population			Change		Percent Change	
			1980 Census (preliminary)	1970 Census[1]	1960 Census[2]	1970–80	1960–70	1970–80	1960–70
3 to 4 percent	232	178,888	5,709	4,989	4,817	720	172	14.4	3.6
Less than 3 percent	1,380	2,237,171	28,209	24,778	24,414	3,431	363	13.8	1.5
NORTHEAST	217	163,271	49,002	49,061	44,678	−58	4,383	−0.1	9.8
Metropolitan	101	55,214	41,599	42,481	38,609	−882	3,871	−2.1	10.0
Over 3,000,000	35	11,897	24,662	25,739	23,250	−1,077	2,488	−4.2	10.7
1,000,000 to 3,000,000	9	6,166	4,554	4,786	4,560	−232	226	−4.8	5.0
500,000 to 1,000,000	29	16,271	7,322	7,206	6,453	116	753	1.6	11.7
250,000 to 500,000	16	12,732	3,140	2,970	2,760	169	210	5.7	7.6
Less than 250,000	12	8,148	1,922	1,780	1,587	142	193	8.0	12.2
Nonmetropolitan counties by commuting to metropolitan areas	116	108,057	7,404	6,580	6,069	824	511	12.5	8.4
30 percent or more	4	2,518	704	500	331	204	168	40.8	50.8
20 to 29 percent	10	5,939	661	618	599	43	19	7.0	3.2
10 to 19 percent	25	15,495	1,963	1,757	1,613	206	145	11.7	9.0

5 to 9 percent	25	21,815	1,679	1,544	1,455	135	89	8.7	6.1
3 to 4 percent	12	11,628	470	405	385	64	20	15.9	5.2
Less than 3 percent	40	50,662	1,927	1,755	1,685	172	70	9.8	4.2
NORTH CENTRAL	1,056	751,823	58,668	56,590	51,619	2,078	4,971	3.7	9.6
Metropolitan	197	121,604	41,016	40,126	35,473	890	4,653	2.2	13.1
Over 3,000,000	15	9,283	12,302	12,277	10,917	25	1,361	0.2	12.5
1,000,000 to 3,000,000	56	25,216	13,809	13,716	12,031	93	1,685	0.7	14.0
500,000 to 1,000,000	20	9,590	3,986	3,874	3,393	112	481	2.9	14.2
250,000 to 500,000	37	26,956	4,792	4,536	4,055	257	480	5.7	11.8
Less than 250,000	69	50,559	6,127	5,723	5,077	404	646	7.1	12.7
Nonmetropolitan counties by commuting to metropolitan areas	859	630,219	17,652	16,464	16,146	1,188	318	7.2	2.0
30 percent or more	19	9,316	610	516	470	93	46	18.1	9.8
20 to 29 percent	44	22,310	964	868	829	95	39	10.9	4.7
10 to 19 percent	111	63,837	3,537	3,237	3,039	300	197	9.3	6.5
5 to 9 percent	103	63,472	2,997	2,770	2,665	226	106	8.2	4.0
3 to 4 percent	68	47,938	1,655	1,575	1,565	81	9	5.1	0.6
Less than 3 percent	514	423,346	7,891	7,498	7,578	392	−79	5.2	−1.0
SOUTH	1,425	873,723	74,813	62,813	54,961	12,000	7,852	19.1	14.3
Metropolitan	312	182,009	48,302	40,088	32,808	8,214	7,280	20.5	22.2
Over 3,000,000[5]	2	800	459	439	356	20	83	4.5	23.4
1,000,000 to 3,000,000	64	32,859	18,850	15,397	11,593	3,452	3,804	22.4	32.8
500,000 to 1,000,000	61	32,946	9,526	8,357	7,174	1,169	1,182	14.0	16.5
250,000 to 500,000	81	45,115	10,066	8,212	6,999	1,854	1,213	22.6	17.3
Less than 250,000	104	70,291	9,402	7,683	6,685	1,720	998	22.4	14.9

Table 5-1 (Cont.)

Metropolitan Areas, Nonmetropolitan Counties, and Regions	Counties and County Equivalents	Land Area (square miles)	Population			Change		Percent Change	
			1980 Census (preliminary)	1970 Census[1]	1960 Census[2]	1970–80	1960–70	1970–80	1960–70
Nonmetropolitan counties by commuting to metropolitan areas	1,113	691,713	26,511	22,725	22,153	3,786	572	16.7	2.6
30 percent or more	24	10,893	437	326	306	111	21	33.9	6.8
20 to 29 percent	87	45,467	1,846	1,506	1,434	340	72	22.6	5.0
10 to 19 percent	188	104,924	4,804	4,024	3,851	781	172	19.4	4.5
5 to 9 percent	160	93,993	3,993	3,448	3,343	545	106	15.8	3.2
3 to 4 percent	133	79,534	3,140	2,680	2,604	461	76	17.2	2.9
Less than 3 percent	521	356,902	12,291	10,742	10,616	1,549	126	14.4	1.2
WEST	445	1,748,036	42,995	34,838	28,053	8,157	6,785	23.4	24.2
Metropolitan	68	173,396	34,265	28,188	21,951	6,077	6,237	21.6	28.4
Over 3,000,000	13	39,398	16,284	14,407	11,243	1,877	3,163	13.0	28.1
1,000,000 to 3,000,000	15	18,465	6,795	5,441	4,219	1,354	1,223	24.9	29.0
500,000 to 1,000,000	9	21,750	4,220	3,111	2,366	1,109	745	35.6	31.5
250,000 to 500,000	9	42,024	3,338	2,545	2,024	793	520	31.2	25.7
Less than 250,000	22	51,758	3,629	2,684	2,099	944	585	35.2	27.9
Nonmetropolitan counties by commuting to metropolitan areas	377	1,574,641	8,730	6,650	6,102	2,080	548	31.3	9.0
30 percent or more	1	603	5	4	3	1	1	23.4	40.4
20 to 29 percent	2	1,105	63	45	35	17	10	38.9	27.7
10 to 19 percent	20	74,742	569	353	293	217	60	61.4	20.5
5 to 9 percent	30	52,142	1,549	1,137	973	412	164	36.3	16.9

| 3 to 4 percent | 19 | 39,788 | 444 | 329 | 262 | 114 | 67 | 34.6 | 25.6 |
| Less than 3 percent | 305 | 1,406,262 | 6,101 | 4,782 | 4,537 | 1,318 | 246 | 27.6 | 5.4 |

Source: Population Profile of the United States: 1980, Series P-20, No. 363, U.S. Department of Commerce, Bureau of the Census, p. 12.

[1]Includes officially recognized corrections to 1970 census counts.

[2]Adjusted to exclude 12,520 persons erroneously reported in Fairfax County, Va. (Washington, D.C.–Md.–Va. SMSA).

[3]Standard Metropolitan Statistical Areas (SMSAs) or, where defined, Standard Consolidated Statistical Areas (SCSAs) and county equivalents of SMSAs in New England (NECMAs); as defined by the Office of Federal Statistical Policy and Standards, Dec. 31, 1979. Size classification based on 1970 population of each SCSA, NECMA, or SMSA as defined in 1979.

[4]Classification based on 1970 census data on percent of workers reporting place of work who commuted to metropolitan territory as defined in 1979 (see footnote 3).

[5]Represents portion of Philadelphia–Wilmington–Trenton SCSA in the South (New Castle County, Del., and Cecil County, Md.).

Table 5-2

POPULATION OF STATES BY REGION: 1980, 1970, AND 1960 CENSUSES

	Census			Percent Change	
	1980	1970*	1960	1970–80	1960–70
United States	226,504,825	203,302,031	179,310,655	11.4	13.4
Regions:					
Northeast	49,136,667	49,060,514	44,677,819	0.2	9.8
North Central	58,853,804	56,590,294	51,619,139	4.0	9.6
South	75,349,155	62,812,980	54,960,595	20.0	14.3
West	43,165,199	34,838,243	28,053,104	23.9	24.2

Source: Population Profile of the United States: 1980, Series P-20, No. 363, U.S. Department of Commerce, Bureau of the Census, p. 11.

*Data for 1970 and 1960 include corrections to published counts.

riod (14.6 and 9.5 percent, respectively). Together, these seven very large areas had a net growth of only 1.6 percent in the 1970s, compared with a net growth rate of 15.5 percent for the same areas in the 1960s.[5]

The South was the only region in which metropolitan areas as a group grew faster than nonmetropolitan areas during the 1970s (see Table 5-1). Metropolitan areas in the South and West grew substantially (19.1 and 23.4 percent, respectively).

This is not surprising when you consider that of the twenty-three-million increase in the U.S. population between 1970 and 1980, almost ten million (42 percent) occurred in the states of California, Texas, and Florida, each of which gained more than three million people. The states with the fastest rates of population growth during the decade were all in the West or the South (see Table 5-2 on p. 145 and Figure 5-1).

Nonmetropolitan growth rates in the 1970s generally exceeded metropolitan growth rates in the manufacturing-belt states of the Northeast and Midwest; in Virginia, Kentucky, Tennessee, and Florida; and on the Pacific Coast. In the manufacturing-belt states, where a high proportion of the population lives in metropolitan areas, metropolitan growth rates were low; however, non-metropolitan areas showed considerable increases in several of these states, reflecting migration from the nearby urban centers. On the Pacific Coast, the metropolitan areas showed moderate to rapid growth while nonmetropolitan areas grew rapidly. In fast-growing Florida, there was rapid growth in almost all counties but at a higher rate in nonmetropolitan counties than in metropolitan areas.

Table 5-1 also groups nonmetropolitan counties according to the intensity of their commuting ties to metropolitan areas. The counties with the closest commuting ties (20 percent or more in 1970) had higher growth rates in both the 1960s and 1970s than the more remote counties with weaker commuting ties. This indicates that a portion of nonmetropolitan population growth in both periods was due to suburban development beyond the official SMSA boundaries. Perhaps one fourth or one third of nonmetropolitan growth in the 1970s can be attributed to this kind of outer suburban development. However, since 1970, the gap in growth rates between the different nonmetropolitan categories has narrowed. Even those counties far removed from direct metropolitan influence are now growing more rapidly than metropolitan areas or than the nation as a whole.

Most important to our discussion of cities is that central cities

Figure 5-1 PERCENT CHANGE IN POPULATION BY STATE, 1970 TO 1980

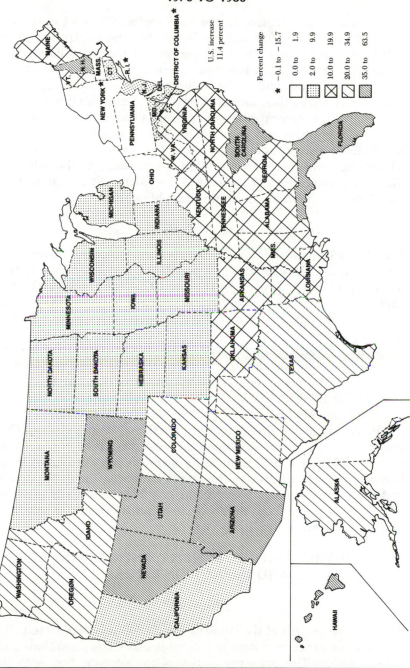

Source: *Population Profile of the United States: 1980,* Series P-20, No. 363, U.S. Dept. of Commerce, Bureau of the Census, p. 5.

lost population (particularly in the Northeast and North Central regions). Preliminary 1980 data indicate that the central cities of SMSAs as a group lost about 0.5 percent of their population between 1970 and 1980. A few central cities had large annexations during the decade, and without the population added by these boundary changes, the loss would have been considerably greater. Many individual central cities, of course, had substantial gains during the decade; this was particularly true of smaller cities in the South and the West, as already noted. The portions of the SMSAs outside the central cities (generally corresponding to the suburbs) showed a gain of about 17 percent in the 1970s, a little higher than the 15-percent increase of nonmetropolitan areas.

Racial Shifts

The census Current Population Survey data indicate a continuing increase in the black central-city population and a decrease in the white population. However, by the late 1970s, the rising black population was essentially due to natural increase, and black migration was no longer contributing much, if any, net population gain to central cities.

While overall suburban growth slowed down considerably during the 1970s, the survey data indicate that the black population in the suburbs grew at an increasingly rapid rate during the latter years of the 1970s.

The relatively high rate of growth of nonmetropolitan areas in the 1970s was largely due to increases in the white population. The black population in nonmetropolitan areas did not change greatly between 1970 and 1980, indicating a continuing outmigration of blacks from rural counties in the South. However, the data suggest that these outmigrants are now going chiefly to metropolitan areas in the South or the West rather than to northern urban areas, as many did in earlier decades.

SUBURBIA AND THE SUNBELT: THEIR MEANING AND IMPACT ON CITIES

Suburbia

The massive growth of the suburbs since 1945 was due principally to the continuance of generally favorable economic conditions and federal policy. The mass prosperity of the postwar era, with its higher pay and shorter working hours, made it possible for many workers, both working class and white collar, to live farther from their jobs than ever before. The fact that median real income had more than doubled between 1950 and 1975 enabled the majority of American families to afford serviceable cars and to own homes. Suburbanization has been encouraged by the federal government which, through the Federal Housing Administration and GI Bill of Rights, has underwritten the low-interest mortgages of millions of home buyers. The government has also contributed to suburban growth through the construction of thousands of miles of highway which have made additional localities accessible to commuters.

In moving out of the city, the suburbanite sought to retain urban economic and cultural advantages while avoiding the city's afflictions and resisting its way of life. The suburbs were cleaner, quieter, and safer than the city. It should also be noted that many of the new suburbanites fled from their old central-city neighborhoods because the poor and blacks had moved into them. Like those who had earlier fled from the immigrants, the middle-income migrants of the postwar era were moving partly because of their prejudices and exaggerated fears, but also because of the genuine problems which inevitably accompany the arrival of impoverished newcomers.

The appeal of the suburbs also reflects the powerful antiurban strain in American thought, an offshoot of the agrarian tradition of Thomas Jefferson, who viewed cities as inevitably harmful to the moral and political health of the Republic. A 1980 Harris Poll of attitudes toward cities, for example, clearly indicates that most Americans believe cities offer the best cultural activities, jobs, and health care but the worst housing, public schools, and crime. They may be pleasant to visit, but not to live in. "The suburbanite," writes Janet Roebuck, "makes his own compromise between the rural dreams of Thoreau and the urban realities of IBM."[6]

Decentralization of Business

The growth of residential suburbs has been accompanied and encouraged by the increasing decentralization of economic life. In the nineteenth century, major commercial and industrial firms in the central cities were of necessity anchored near the railroad terminal and the ocean or river docks. Whereas the technology and transport of the nineteenth century had promoted the centralization of business and industry, the technological trends of the twentieth century have promoted their dispersion. Thus, the thorough utilization of the telephone has made it possible for business to be conducted with far less personal contact than in the past. Similarly, the growing use of the truck for commercial transport and the airplane for long-distance travel have reduced the dependence of business upon central cities, which can now be bypassed by trucks and which are sometimes farther from the airport than are some of the suburbs.

The dispersion of manufacturing has been followed in turn by the decentralization of wholesaling and retail trade. Thanks to the automotive revolution, it is no longer essential for a wholesale merchant to locate in the central city; by 1970, more than a quarter of the jobs in wholesale trade were located in the suburbs.

Retailing was revolutionized by the emergence of the large-scale shopping center in the 1930s. These centers are located in either the outer districts of the central cities or in the suburbs beyond and have parking space for hundreds and sometimes thousands of cars. Many of these centers now include restaurants, movie theaters, and even churches. By 1983, there were 23,304 shopping centers in the nation, and they had succeeded in diverting a large and growing share of metropolitan retail business from the downtown merchants of the central cities. In that year, shopping centers had more than half of the retail trade in twenty-three of the nation's major metropolitan areas.

The economic activities that have tended to remain longest within the central cities are those connected with business management and with the service sector of the economy. In these areas, centrality and the face-to-face contact it permits are still important. The concentration of corporate management and of such service industries as banking and communications is reflected in the high-density commercial activity traditionally found in the central business districts of the large cities. In the twelve leading centers of business administration, office space increased by 44 percent between 1950 and 1970. In addition, gross floor space in Manhattan's central business district increased from 128 million to 226 million square feet.

Despite the office-building boom in the central cities, the suburbs and satellites in many of the older centers of the East and Middle West have absorbed a growing share of both the managerial and service functions within their respective SMSAs since World War II. Suburban office parks in places like Carlton (outside St. Louis) or Greenwich, Connecticut, are luring major corporate offices away from the central cities. New York City in the 1970s lost financial firms to New Jersey and corporate headquarters to suburbs in Westchester, Long Island, and Connecticut.

Why the Exodus?

This exodus has occurred for a number of reasons. Undoubtedly, the high taxes and severe social problems of the contemporary central city have played a role. More important has been the high cost of central-city space in comparison to space in the suburbs. Another significant influence on the decision to move has been the desire of company officials to work closer to where they live, so that they can spend more time with their families and avoid a daily round-trip journey that in some instances took as long as four hours. Furthermore, by the 1970s new developments in communications and computer technology were beginning to make it less necessary for many companies to be near the financial, legal, and cultural resources on which they had traditionally relied.

In general, many central cities, especially in the East and Middle West, have been losing jobs while the suburbs have been gaining them. By 1980, the metropolitan suburbs had surpassed their central cities as sources of employment. By then too, more than twice as many suburbanites were working in the suburbs as were commuting to central cities, and there was also a swelling tide of reverse commuters, proceeding from central-city homes to suburban jobs.

To some extent, even culture, which has traditionally been concentrated in the big cities, has been decentralized. Concert halls have been built in places like San Rafael outside of San Francisco, and many small cities have their own symphony orchestras. Theaters have proliferated in suburbia, as have a wide variety of restaurants and even singles' bars. Professional sports also have been suburbanized with the construction of major-league athletic stadiums in such places as Pontiac, Michigan; Bloomington, Minnesota; Hackensack, New Jersey; and Foxboro, Massachusetts.

With their continued growth and development, many suburbs have ceased to function merely as "bedrooms" for central cities and have come increasingly to resemble the cities from which they sprang. In the suburbs, as in the outermost central-city areas, commercial and industrial areas are now to be found interspersed with residential districts. By the 1970s, high-rise office and apartment buildings had begun to emerge in the suburbs. "Suburbia," wrote Louis Masotti in 1973, "is clearly no longer just a family place."[7]

The fact that central cities must continue to provide services both to residents *and* visiting suburbanites while at the same time losing needed tax revenues to the fleeing middle- and upper-middle-class whites and commercial and industrial firms makes for a bleak picture indeed!

We might expect that with fewer people to serve, cities would find it less costly to provide the same level of services. In the long run, outmigration from the older cities may have this effect of lowering average service costs (although this is questionable when we consider that the people left behind require more public assistance than the average population).[8] But in the meantime, as noted, the outmigration has been responsible for a good part of the cities' fiscal predicament.

The dilemma confronted by the older cities is that few of the costs associated with urban growth are easily reversible into economies of diminution. Once a city's road, sewer, and water networks have been constructed to serve a given population, the cost of maintaining these networks does not decline significantly when the population shrinks. On the contrary, as the city ages, it becomes more costly to keep in repair (see Box 5-2). Similarly, when households abandon the central city, the need for police and fire services does not decline in proportion to population. Instead, abandoned homes become the focus for vandalism and crime, pose fire hazards, and ultimately must be razed at city expense.

The Sunbelt

The other major population trend, in addition to the exodus to small towns and suburbs, is the dramatic urban and metropolitan growth in the so-called Sunbelt, the southern and southwestern areas stretching from Virginia to central California. The growth of the Sunbelt metropolises is part of a long-term shift of population *and* power toward the South and West that is fraught with important consequences for the future.

Already it seems clear that population shifts of the 1970s will deeply affect how Americans live, buy, work, and play in years to come. The rise of regional power points to greater payrolls and financial authority in erstwhile hinterlands and more decentralizing of business operations, industrial plants, and market strategy.

Clearest of all is the recent population shifts which altered the

Box 5-2
YEARS OVERTAKING CITY'S BONES

A major water main breaks and the intersection of Light and Lombard streets becomes a river, snarling traffic for days and costing close to $100,000 to repair.

A large section of the Russell Street Bridge buckles, and city officials spend about a year repairing the damage, detouring and delaying traffic at one of Baltimore's major entry points.

A storm drain at the corner of Chester and Eager streets collapses, leaving a gaping cavern "you could put a Mack truck in," according to one city official, and a repair bill of several hundred thousand dollars.

While these cases apply to the City of Baltimore, we could as easily give similar examples for most every major older city in this country. The water main, the bridge and the storm drain are all part of the city's infrastructure, and the message they carry is that the city's—and America's—infrastructure is falling apart: neglected, decaying and, in some cases, obsolete.

Experts speculate that the cost of making all needed repairs is as high as $3 trillion across the nation . . . [yet] public reaction to such an expenditure is not nearly as admiring as the one for a more visible project such as a swimming pool or a park.

Another problem is placing responsibility for mishaps caused by an aging infrastructure. For example, in May 1982, Amtrak workers discovered a crack in a section of the 109-year-old tunnel, which runs under Upton, Bolton Hill, and other sections of Baltimore. Owned by Amtrak, the tunnel was closed to train traffic for about a day—bringing traffic along one of the country's major north-south train routes to a standstill.

In the meantime, four homes over the tunnel began to crumble, and city officials condemned the houses. After three months of investigation by the city, Amtrak and representatives of the Federal Railway Administration, the answer was that no concrete determination could be made on what caused the tunnel to shift and the houses to crumble.

The Wilson Street incident is the kind that makes people take notice of the problems an old, decaying city foundation can cause. It left four families in temporary housing for almost three months. And it left them in limbo—unable to prove that the destruction to their homes was the result of any one particular factor.

In the end, the city, Amtrak and the Federal Railway Administration agreed to relocate the Upton families in new homes owned by the city, and to split the cost of the relocation and to reimburse the residents for money they spent when they were forced to abandon their homes. They also agreed that none of them would admit liability for the incident.

Source: Mark Miller, "Age is Overtaking Pipes, Bridges," *News American,* August 21, 1982.

balance of power in U.S. politics. Seventeen seats in the House of Representatives shifted from states that lost residents to those that gained with reapportionment—the determination of each state's number of seats was based on its 1980 population. New York lost five House seats; Illinois, Ohio, and Pennsylvania, two each; and Indiana, Massachusetts, Michigan, Missouri, New Jersey, and South Dakota, one each. The biggest winner was Florida, which picked up four seats. Texas gained three, California two, and Arizona, Colorado, Nevada, New Mexico, Oregon, Tennessee, Utah, and Washington, one each. In other words, along with the capital investment and industrial growth have gone people, votes, and power.

Of course, we shouldn't forget that finance and corporate headquarters remain, for the most part, concentrated in the Northeast and North Central regions. Indeed, despite the serious decay that has struck portions of the inner cities of these venerable regions, "the North remains dominant on all measures of economic performance and has lost ground to the South in relative terms only." But the *vitality* of urban America—measured by corporate investment as opposed to disinvestment—has shifted to the Sunbelt cities:

> The emerging interregional disinvestment pattern has favored the West and later the South at the expense of the Northeast and Midwest. Between 1960 and 1979, the capital stock in the South grew twice as fast as that in the Northeast. Between 1966 and 1979, the industrial Northeast and Midwest lost nearly 800,000 manufacturing jobs, while national expansion added 2.3 million total jobs elsewhere. For every 100 manufacturing jobs created by new plants in the North, 111 were lost to some form of disinvestment. In the South, 80 manufacturing jobs were lost for every 100 added through new capital investment.[9]

Much of the urban population growth in the South and to a lesser extent in the West is due to annexation of neighboring communities. A major reason for the extensive annexations by the newer metropolitan centers in the South was their eagerness to avoid the predicament of cities farther to the north and east, such as Newark and Cleveland, that are surrounded on all sides by prosperous and well-populated communities that are rather hostile toward them and indifferent to their problems. Consequently, new southern and western cities have sought to annex their suburbs while the latter were themselves still too small and poor to provide a full array of services and were therefore usually amenable to the idea. Finally, such cities as Houston, Texas, and Charlotte, North Carolina, have been aided in their expansion by the laws of their respective states which deny to suburban residents any say as to whether their communities shall be annexed by nearby cities.

DECLINE OF THE OLDER CITIES

Although the declining cities of the Northeast and North Central regions remain the nation's greatest centers of culture, finance, and business management, it is within them, and especially in their oldest neighborhoods, that we find today's urban problems at their worst. A major source of these problems lies in the fact that cities have continued to function as magnets for the poor and unskilled, principally blacks from the South and the Caribbean and Spanish-speaking immigrants from Latin America. Such newcomers increase the need for public services at a time when the tax base is declining because of the departure of business and the middle class for the suburbs and for other regions as described above. From 1970 to 1974, notes George Sternlieb, the income of those moving into central cities was in aggregate nearly $30 billion less than the income of those moving out.[10] "Twenty years down the road," said a Cleveland official in 1971, "it is perfectly conceivable that the city will be just one great big poorhouse."[11]

Caught between rising social needs and falling tax revenues, the cities have been forced to choose between bleak alternatives. They must either cut back on services, a course likely to injure the well-being of the poor, or raise taxes, which is likely to add to the city's problems by speeding the departure of business and the middle class. It was precisely these conditions which brought New York City to the fiscal crisis of 1975 in which the city was forced into additional borrowing, higher taxation, and extensive cutbacks in services.

Problems of Housing

A key aspect of the urban condition, now as in the past, is the shortage of adequate housing for low-income families. The migration to the suburbs of middle- and moderate-income families after 1945 alleviated the problem somewhat by creating millions of inner-city vacancies which then became available for rental to others. At the same time, however, many formerly livable areas in the central cities were themselves becoming slums. From 1960 to 1965, the proportion of all Los Angeles housing that was classified as "substandard" rose from 18 to 35 percent. In New York City, the number of slum dwelling units increased from 475,000 in 1960 to roughly 800,000 by 1968.

Many factors have caused this deterioration. Probably the most important reason is the inadequate earnings of the unskilled. Poverty necessitates overcrowding, which in turn promotes decay and blight. The process has been furthered by the advanced age of much of the housing. As of 1970, nearly half of the nation's housing stock had been built before 1929. Congestion and decay have also been encouraged by federally subsidized urban renewal, which from 1949 to 1967 demolished over a million housing units, at least some of it livable, while providing only a little more than half a million units of public housing. Frequently, owners have been unwilling to make repairs, which might reduce their profits. Finally, the antisocial conduct of a minority among the poor, perhaps embittered by the way society has treated it, has also been a factor at times in the creation of slums, as may be seen by the rapid deterioration of some public-housing projects.

The population is rapidly declining in the most impoverished districts of the nation's older big cities as building after building deteriorates and is scrapped by its owner. Hundreds of apartment buildings, row houses, and even private homes have been abandoned each year in New York City, Philadelphia, Detroit, Chicago, St. Louis, and other cities. Landlords abandon buildings in order to escape from the property taxes and the mortgage payments. With no heat and no repairs, the regular tenants soon depart, leaving the building to be occupied by vagrant and criminal elements until torn down by the city. "Some blighted areas," Kenneth Jackson has remarked, "are left to the rats, and some are devoid even of rodents."[12]

Gentrifying the Ghetto

Although, as we have noted, more people are moving out of cities today than are moving in, popular accounts of a back-to-the-city movement have some truth to them. As was the case during the 1960s, the 1970s saw revitalization of some inner-city neighborhoods (known as *gentrification*) in many of the nation's largest cities. Even though the extent of this revitalization is not yet documented, the manner in which it has occurred is a noteworthy break from the past.

In contrast to the federal urban-renewal programs we have described, much of the housing activity during the 1970s, whether through government programs or the private market, involved renovation of existing structures. Nationwide, expenditures for additions and alterations to existing residences doubled in only four years during the mid-1970s.

The return to the city is due not only to disenchantment with the green dream of suburbia or a sudden passion for town houses. There is also a deeper, perhaps subconscious feeling that there is no more escape, that the time has come to stay put, to make the best of the America we have. There is no other.

We have been a nation on the run. We all wanted to breathe free and that meant moving on, westward and upward. It did not seem to matter if we made a mess. It would soon be left behind. A mess left behind was progress. We believed that progress was perpetual, affluence kept flowing, and man could be perfected.

But now the continent is conquered. We have run out of "West"; we are running out of riches; and we are being forced to recognize that there are limits to economic growth and collective upward mobility. We must change our habits of waste. The affluent society will have to become a conserving society.

So it seems that urban renewal is giving way to urban rehabilitation. The bulldozer is being replaced by hammer, trowel, and paintbrush. The government's urban-renewal program concentrated on the central business district. The citizens' spontaneous rehabilitation efforts began in the neighborhoods.

The back-to-the-city trend does not necessarily spell good for everyone, however. Historically, as we have seen, housing has filtered down to lower-income households as it is vacated voluntarily by higher-income households moving on to better homes. Everyone gained. But now, in some areas, older housing which previously filtered down to lower-income people has begun to percolate back up to higher-income families. Unlike filtering, such percolation leads to displacement—forced moves by lower-income families, often to less desirable or more expensive dwellings.

Because it is such a distinct break from the past, and because frequently blacks are displaced by whites, it does not take many of these moves to arouse public interest. The changes are all the more visible because, both for economic and psychological reasons akin to blockbusting, but in reverse, they tend to concentrate in one neighborhood at a time.

As measured by either numbers of people or their socioeconomic status, however, there is little evidence of a nationwide back-to-the-city movement.[13] Recalling our demographic trends, we know that for every person who moved into a central city during the 1970s, nearly two left. But the fact remains that some of the nation's cities did experience dramatic demographic change during the 1970s. The explanation is that the change has been largely internal to the cities and has taken place at the neighborhood level.[14] Back-to-the-city is the demographic misnomer of the decade. Back-to-selected-neighborhoods would be a much more accurate label.

Crime

Since the 1960s, crime, especially violent crime, has become the problem of greatest concern to most residents of the major cities. Between 1960 and 1974, according to the FBI, the national rate of violent crime nearly tripled, while that for property crime increased two and one-half times. Crime in general, and violent crime in particular, tends to occur disproportionately in big cities. Thus, in 1974, roughly 30 percent of all reported crimes of violence took place in the six cities with populations of over a million, although their residents comprised only 10 percent of the national population. With the crime rate soaring upward, central-city residents, especially the elderly, tend to remain home at night rather than run the risk of being mugged, robbed, or worse.

The Suburbs Are Not Immune

While social conditions are on the whole better in the suburbs, these areas have increasingly been afflicted with the same maladies as the cities. Hardest hit have been the oldest suburban communities, which are usually those nearest the central cities. Since 1950, the rate of taxation has been rising spectacularly in many suburbs, in some cases doubling and tripling in the course of a single decade. In some of the older suburbs, as in their central cities, population has declined, weakening the tax base. In 1969, the total of suburban residents with incomes below the poverty line was about two-thirds of that for the central cities. Housing blight has also emerged in the suburbs, where it usually takes the form of rundown cottages and shacks. Moreover, suburban crime rates have been climbing far more rapidly of late than have those of the central cities. During the 1960s, according to FBI crime reports, the rate of serious crime increased 50 percent faster in the suburbs than in the central cities. There was not a significant change in this trend through the 1970s.

ENVIRONMENTAL PROBLEMS

Since World War II, metropolitan areas have also been beset by environmental and physical problems, one of which is the problem of water supply. The nation increased its consumption of water by roughly 50 percent in the 1960s, primarily to meet the expanding requirements of industry. Although municipalities require only about 6 percent of the nation's water supply, many cities and towns have suffered shortages on occasion. Many cities have been compelled to go even farther afield for their water. Thus, San Francisco extended its reservoir system from twenty-five miles outside of the city in the early 1930s to a distance of one hundred fifty miles by 1964. Perhaps the best example is Los Angeles which, with hardly any rainfall of its own, obtains some of its water from over three hundred miles away.

The problem of water supply has been complicated by the growing burden of pollution (see chapter 4). Seepage from the septic tanks used in many suburbs has often contaminated local streams. Some rivers and lakes are so dirty that people can no longer safely swim in them. By 1965, Lake Erie, after decades of serving as the receptacle for the wastes of twelve American and three Canadian cities, was approaching the point at which it would no longer be able to support life. In 1965, Michigan, Indiana, Ohio, Pennsylvania, and New York joined with the Public Health Service in launching a long-term program for the cleansing of Lake Erie.

Another severe problem is air pollution. It has been claimed that merely to breathe the air in New York City is as damaging to health as smoking two packs of cigarettes a day. Pollution in certain cities, notably New York and Los Angeles, sometimes becomes intolerable as a result of what is called a temperature inversion, in which warm air rises above the layer of cold air, thereby trapping the remaining warm air below. Since the now unmoving air is polluted, many people become ill. In New York City, an inversion in 1953 killed at least 170 people, and another inversion ten years later caused about 400 deaths.

It wasn't until the 1960s that a substantial segment of the public became aroused and a powerful environmentalist movement began to emerge. The relative affluence of most Americans had made many of them less willing than in the past to sacrifice the environment in the interests of economic growth. However, with the current recession and limited economic growth, it appears many of us are willing once again to sacrifice at least some environmental quality for better economic times.

To be sure, environmental controversies are often highly complex, with at least some merit on both sides of the issue. Government agencies that deal with these issues have the thankless and difficult task of reconciling the requirements of economic growth with the promotion of a healthy environment. The EPA and other environmental agencies have been the target of simultaneous attacks—accused by business of doing too much, thereby injuring the economy, and by environmentalists of doing too little, and thus failing to protect the public. Although environmental officials have often retreated, or been forced to retreat, by elected officials (particularly under the Reagan administration), their efforts during the 1970s resulted in somewhat cleaner air and water for many of the nation's metropolitan areas.

TRAFFIC AND TRANSIT

In the post–World War II era, certain metropolitan problems have been severely worsened by the widespread use of the automobile, which by the 1970s accounted in urban areas for approximately 90 percent of all travel and over 80 percent of all trips to work (see Box 5-3). These vehicles contribute significantly to the noise and to the pollution of the central cities. Their worst effects are the traffic jams which daily clog many of the nation's highways and central business districts, some of which were originally laid out in the era of the horse. Traffic congestion not only causes the annual loss of billions of dollars but also inflicts much wear and tear upon commuters.

Cities have made intermittent efforts to accommodate the automobile. Starting in the 1920s, they have widened their streets and have established sophisticated systems of traffic control, such as timed traffic lights. Through traffic has been expedited and linked to local streets by means of tunnels, overpasses, and underpasses, many of them constructed with federal funds. In order to clear a path for traffic, restrictions have been placed on parking in the street. At the same time, city governments have added to available parking through municipal garages and parking lots.

There has been a decline in the ridership on public systems of transportation, due in part to the growing use of the automobile, that has left them financially undermined. This, in combination with rising labor and other costs, has forced the transit lines to raise

Box 5-3
THE HIGHWAY-DOMINATED TRANSPORTATION SYSTEM

Government surrender to the automobile was achieved by the same large corporate coalition that gave birth to bus conversions and created the highway lobby that informally developed national transportation policy. The highway lobby was created in 1932 by Alfred Sloan, Jr., president of General Motors. It linked government agencies and bureaucrats with oil, auto, and transportation firms and trade associations. Through lobbying, campaign contributions, and the influence of corporate representatives in government, highway building was insulated fiscally and politically from opposition.

But highway construction also spawned a political organizing effort on an extraordinary scale. Local, state, and federal highway officials, private construction firms, truckers, construction-material suppliers, gas-station owners, car-insurance salesmen, and auto users created a political coalition that grew with each new highway appropriation. Auto-related employment, in accordance with Sloan's design, became evenly distributed across the country.

Although the changing economic realities of the past decade make the highway-dominated transportation system and the absence of balanced transportation irrational economically, environmentally, and socially, the highway lobby still dominates transportation by political means.

Every federal administration since the sixties pledged a rebirth of mass transit that never occurred. The Reagan administration's wholesale abandonment of mass transit simply ends the political charade. Political rhetoric praising transit began only in response to neighborhoods and transit consumers who mobilized against the highway-building and protested the budgetary neglect of mass transportation. Federal transportation policies, from Nixon to Carter, pursued the promise of urban mobility without competing with automobiles—a contradictory and impossible task. People movers and electrical sidewalks were supported instead of subways, buses, and van pools as alternatives to streetcars and railroads.

---

fares and skimp on maintenance, thereby losing still more of their riders. Though heavily subsidized by the federal government, as of the 1970s most commuter railroads were in bad shape both physically and financially. The national average of daily users of public transit declined from its all-time peak of over twenty-three million in 1946 to fewer than five million in 1982.

Despite the failings of mass transit, many programs have been adopted at every level of government seeking either to promote public transportation or to discourage the use of private cars. Because of the energy crisis and growing concern over air pollution, in 1974 Congress adopted and the president signed into law a measure providing subsidies to mass transit for six years at a rate of $2 billion per year. The monies were to come from the federal tax on gasoline.

Some critics of the automobile have urged that private passenger cars be barred altogether from major business districts, but this has never been done in any city. Various cities have experimented with some success with shopping malls that can be entered only on foot. To the public, however, traffic jams and carbon-monoxide pollution are of little moment. In a referendum held in the Houston area in 1973, the voters rejected a proposed extension of the city's bus lines by a margin of over three to one. Under the proposed plan, the new buses were to have been paid for by a levy on automobiles, taxing car owners in direct proportion to the size of their vehicles. "We still like cars," explained the mayor of one of Houston's suburbs, "and even more, we like those pickup trucks with the gun-racks."[15]

PROBLEMS IN GOVERNING METROPOLITAN AREAS

Too Many Units of Government?

The failure of city governments to deal effectively with problems like pollution, sanitation, and planning has sometimes been blamed on their *fragmented power base.* Municipal governments have been further handicapped by the fact that many of these problems have become metropolitan in nature and are not confined to a specific locality. Unfortunately, urban governments have enough difficulty in combating their own particular troubles and have little real authority to take bold steps in the area of metropolitan planning and area redevelopment. As a consequence, many city reformers concentrate attention on the search for a viable form of metropolitan government and push the perennial quest for honesty in city government into the background.

While there is some dispute among government experts as to whether the best solution lies in the establishment of metropolitan government—a single-purpose government with authority to govern an entire metropolitan region—there is more agreement over the point that the number of local governments has become burdensome. This contention is hardly new. As early as 1931, the National Municipal League's Committee on Constructive Economy in

State and Local Governments reported that "the United States is cursed with too many local governments."[16]

Experts regard the zealousness with which small units of local government guard their autonomy as one of the major obstructions to effective city and metropolitan action. The modernization of sewage disposal facilities, for example, can be totally ineffective if outlying areas resist participating in any proposed changes. By the same token, industrial suburbs can contribute to the air pollution of their neighboring counties without running the risk of being subject to adequate regulation.

During the last several decades, the number of local governments has continued to grow at a rapid rate. As of 1982, the Census of Governments listed 78,268 units of local governments such as counties, municipalities, townships, school districts, and special districts. Many of these units overlap within the confines of a given metropolitan area. It is ironic that in spite of the existence of all these units of government, there is usually no central body to resolve the more urgent regional questions. If it is conceded that the modern metropolitan community is beset by difficulties that would tax the capacity of even the most efficient type of government, it is also likely that metropolitan fragmentation compounds the problem. As Daniel R. Grant has argued, "The structure of local government is perhaps ten percent of the problem, if a figure must be picked, but it is an important ten percent."[17]

Annexation as One Solution

Efforts have been made to achieve a more efficient governmental organization through annexation or consolidation—the joining of existing governments, such as city and county, into one governmental unit (see Box 5-4). Nevertheless, there is substantial opposition to proposals of this type. Suburbanites fear they will be forced to pay additional taxes to revitalize inner-city areas and will lose control over their schools and their zoning regulations. To local officials, annexation or consolidation means a loss of jobs. Other citizens have misgivings about the dangers of supergovernment. Integrated government would help central cities relieve their financial burden, but residents do not always see it that way. Minority groups, who are now becoming a political force in several large cities, often view these plans as a threat to their hard-fought political ascendancy. Instead, they talk about decentralization and community control.

The legal ramifications with respect to consolidation can be

Box 5-4
PROBLEMS WITH ANNEXATION

The major shortcoming of annexation is that it is too late for this method to have any significant effect in many of our largest metropolitan areas. Most state laws make it impossible for one municipality to annex territory that is within the corporate limits of another. Thus, central cities such as Chicago and Detroit, which are surrounded by incorporated suburbs, are virtually precluded from using annexation. It is not just by chance that cities such as Oklahoma City, Dallas, Houston, and Phoenix, which have followed the most aggressive annexation policies, are located in the newer areas of the West and Southwest where the development of suburbs has not yet surrounded them.

A lack of enabling legislation permitting annexation across county lines in most states, along with the impossibility of annexing across state lines, also limits the usefulness of annexation as a solution to areawide problems. In many cases, small municipalities in fringe areas around larger cities incorporate precisely to head off annexation. There have been other instances where annexation has proceeded on an irrational basis because of competition among cities.

Cities are sometimes criticized for overannexing to stop incorporation or annexation by other cities. After annexations totaling 187 square miles by Kansas City in 1960, a picture in the local paper showed a city police car driving down a country road with grazing cattle along the roadside and a farmer on his tractor in the background. For many, the implication was obvious—this was territory that did not belong in the city. In defense of such action, it can be pointed out that bringing an area into the city before it is built up will ensure that it develops in accordance with the city's planning and zoning laws. Because county planning is often weak, the alternative usually is to wait until an area has developed in willy-nilly fashion before annexing it.

Cities which add large areas through annexation are often criticized by both sides. Residents in the newly annexed area charge that the city will not be able to provide full services, and citizens of the city point out that fringe areas often do not pay sufficient taxes to cover the costs of the services they get, thus forcing taxpayers in the older areas of the city to "subsidize" service costs in the new area.

complicated. In many states, laws affecting county lines cannot become effective unless submitted to a vote of the people in the counties affected. Various states also have requirements providing that a consolidation of two or more counties, or the division or abolition of a county, can only be achieved by a separate referendum held in each of the counties involved. Paradoxically, home-rule charters, which had been won by American municipalities in the late nineteenth and early twentieth centuries after considerable agitation, have been invoked on innumerable occasions to block any attempts at general governmental reorganization. It is interesting to note that the two best-known examples of metropolitan government outside the United States—Greater London and Metropolitan Toronto—were both achieved by an act of Parliament without a popular referendum.

Regional Units

States have encouraged studies of governmental problems in metropolitan areas, often undertaken with the backing of local and national foundations. Beginning in the 1960s, there was a consensus that the states should have some kind of agency for local affairs, and many such agencies were established. States also encouraged the formation of councils of governments (COGs), which usually consist of a council of elected officials from city, town, and county governments. To date, the COGs have not completely justified their existence, for they lack authority to put their proposals into operation. Georgia undertook a more successful endeavor in the mid-1960s. It set up eighteen economic development districts, which function as regional planning and development agencies. State officials distribute federal and state monies through them rather than through Georgia's 159 county governments. These special districts have eliminated waste and duplication of services and have provided for the orderly growth and development of the areas involved.

Another dramatic attempt to solve urban problems was the formation of the Urban Development Corporation in New York State in 1968. The UDC was formed in response to repeated defeats of housing bond issues and the failure of local government officials to make effective use of existing housing programs. A superagency, the UDC was designed to take forceful action in the field of housing in substandard areas. It was organized as a public corporation with authority to set aside local laws, ordinances, zoning codes, charters, and construction regulations. The UDC was hailed as a bold experiment, but it soon ran into trouble with respect to some of the construction that it undertook. In February 1975, it defaulted on a loan and on $100 million in bond-anticipation notes. New York State subsequently made efforts to reorganize the corporation, but its default reminded many people of the difficulties involved in finding solutions to problems of this magnitude.

THE FEDERAL RESPONSE: DILEMMAS OF URBAN POLICY

The Kennedy Years

Cities received more attention during the 1960s than at any other time since the Depression as the public suddenly became aware of an urban crisis. The concern started during the administration of John F. Kennedy, whose interest in urban problems intensified when he became aware of the importance of big-city votes in his successful 1960 presidential campaign. The following year, he appointed the President's Committee on Juvenile Delinquency and Youth Crime, which sponsored research and demonstration projects in several cities. It was the first of many federal attempts during the decade to help youngsters in ghetto areas. In January 1962, Kennedy called for the creation of a Department of Housing and Urban Affairs, telling Congress: "We neglect our cities at our peril, for in neglecting them we neglect our nation."[18] The bill creating the department was defeated in the House Rules Committee, partly because Kennedy had linked civil rights to urban affairs by indicating that Robert C. Weaver, a black man, was his choice for the position. The bill was later passed in September 1965 at the urging of President Johnson, who also named Weaver to head the department, now called the Department of Housing and Urban Development (HUD).

The Johnson Years

Lyndon Johnson, who had been a protégé of FDR, seemed determined to outdo his mentor and demonstrate to the public that he was qualified to serve as president in his own right. The product of a boyhood spent on a small farm in the southwestern part of Texas, he may have shared rural America's traditional distrust of cities. Nevertheless, he understood some of the hardships of poverty and, skilled politician that he was, realized the political value of an urban base. In addition, of course, the inner-city riots of the 1960s helped to make the urban predicament a political issue. The result was the greatest burst of legislative activity since the early days of the Roosevelt presidency. Johnson's War on Poverty, part of his Great Society program, emphasized social issues and focused mostly on poor youth, a large portion of whom were black.

The War on Poverty never reached its full potential, as huge sums were diverted from it, beginning in 1967, for the Vietnam

War. The Office of Economic Opportunity (OEO), for example, was revamped by Richard M. Nixon, who was elected president in 1968, although most of its programs remained in operation. In March 1974, Nixon asked Congress to dismantle the OEO; in the previous year, its appropriations had totaled only $1.9 billion, which was approximately the amount funded during Johnson's last year in office.

The Nixon and Ford Years

By the time Nixon became president, it was beginning to look as if the federal government had a talent for spending money on programs of dubious value. The public was left wondering whether there was any way out of the urban crisis. There was certainly no shortage of ideas: people interested in city affairs were having a hard time keeping abreast of developments and the already voluminous writings on the subject. There was also confusion in Washington. Robert Conot reported that during the 1960s, it was not unusual for the staffs of congressional committees to be approached by supposedly knowledgeable people who asked their support for legislation that had already been enacted.[19]

Nixon astutely understood these frustrations and was aware that his presidency coincided with a period in which the United States was rapidly becoming a nation of suburbs. By the mid-1970s, only 15 percent of the nation's population lived in central cities with over five hundred thousand people. With the growth of suburban areas, the problems of the biggest cities were beginning to appear remote to the "silent majority" of Americans. While not ignoring urban America, many of Nixon's policies were designed to appeal to the views of suburbanites. By talking about the need to tone down the powers of the federal government, as he did in his first inaugural address, the president was uttering a sentiment that found an especially warm reception among those not directly involved in the daily turmoil of big-city living. Yet Nixon also lived in a time of increasing agitation over urban problems, and his knowledge of this fact foreshadowed aspects of his policy.

Although his pace was not as frenetic as Johnson's, Nixon manifested a concern for the social ills plaguing the American urban community, at least until the end of 1972. The first official act of his administration, in January 1969, was to establish an Urban Affairs Council. The function of the council was to "advise and assist" the administration on urban matters and to develop a national urban policy. Nixon redirected the focus of the War on Poverty.

Federal monies continued to go to the poor, but no longer was there an emphasis on training programs for youths. Instead, the administration increased expenditures for food stamps and made more funds available for services which sometimes benefited the nonpoor as well, such as Social Security and Medicare.

Other aspects of Nixon's urban program revealed a desire to eliminate some of the red tape that had bogged down so many earlier projects. The president's references to a "New Federalism" (now talked about by President Reagan)—a call for the states and cities to assume more control over matters pertaining directly to their own needs—made him sound like Eisenhower, but he proved himself capable of spending money like Roosevelt and Johnson. The cornerstone of his New Federalism was the State and Local Fiscal Assistance Act (revenue-sharing), passed three weeks before his landslide victory in 1972. This act provided for the distribution of $30.2 billion over a five-year period to state and local governments on the basis of their population, retroactive to January 1, 1972. Two-thirds of the money was given to local governments (counties, cities, and towns) to be used in any or all of nine priority areas: public safety, environmental protection, transportation, recreation, health, libraries, social services, financial assistance to the poor and elderly, and capital expenditures. The remaining one third was for state use, without any restrictions, provided that it was used for legal purposes only. The act specified that there could be no racial, sexual, ethnic, or religious discrimination in the application of these funds.

There were some doubts on both sides about the relative merits of revenue-sharing. Washington feared that most of the money might be spent in such a way as to circumvent the intention of the act. Municipalities and towns feared that the more affluent suburbs would benefit more, while larger cities believed they would find it difficult to obtain funds other than revenue-sharing monies from the federal government. The Urban League also argued that under-counting of black persons in the census (estimated to equal 7.7 percent of the total black population in 1970) was depriving many cities of their fair share of revenue-sharing funds.[20]

In the Housing and Community Development Act of 1974, Congress appropriated $8.4 billion over a three-year period and provided single grants to localities for community-development programs. The housing provisions of the act were set forth in Section 8, and they were designed to replace programs in public housing, urban renewal, and model cities. According to Section 8, the rent of poor families was to be subsidized by the government in three kinds of housing: sound existing housing, rehabilitated housing, and newly constructed developments.

In spite of the government's good intentions in making provisions for housing the poor, Section 8, as implemented, failed to accomplish its purpose. By the end of 1975, only two hundred families had occupied housing under the program, chiefly because investors and financial institutions found it risky to finance new or rehabilitated housing, while landlords offering sound existing housing showed little interest in renting to poor tenants under the terms of the act.

The Carter Years

Nixon's call for a national urban policy still had not been realized by the time Jimmy Carter took office in 1977. Carter therefore created the Urban and Regional Policy Group (URPG) to (1) analyze urban problems, (2) review existing programs, (3) submit new proposals where needed, and (4) reorganize bureaucratic authority for urban policy. The outcome of the Carter proposals can tell us much about the problems of urban policy and about the politics of policy-making.[21]

While the URPG was working on its set of guidelines for an urban policy, a group of academics was organized to draft another document: the 1978 Urban Policy Report. A law passed by Congress in 1970 had ordered that the president submit such a report in March of every even-numbered year. Thus, the URPG was developing one set of proposals to be "showcased" in the State of the Union address in January while a completely separate group was developing another set to be presented in March.

Even though the president wanted the URPG to have some proposals ready by November, it couldn't reach agreement in a few short months, mostly because the committee included people from six major agencies. Instead, it hired a consultant to piece together the various "wish lists" of the agencies, organized into four policy clusters with the following aims:

- To create ample jobs for the urban poor, blacks, and other minorities and strengthen local economies.
- To commit the federal government to act to revitalize the physical environment of urban areas and their neighborhoods.
- To strengthen the capacity of all levels of government and neighborhood groups to meet the needs of people and cities in distress.
- To expand freedom of choice and equity in urban areas.[22]

Unable to act effectively, the URPG stopped meeting. Instead, HUD became coordinator of the effort to develop a new national urban policy within the Carter administration, working with the Domestic Policy Staff in the White House Office. In January 1977, Carter gave the HUD group new guidelines for the biennial Urban Policy Report due in March. The original instructions had been to "tilt" the policy toward the distressed large cities. Now there were to be four emphases. The most important was that the new policy not require any new money. This meant no new programs unless old ones were ended. The second was a focus on neighborhoods. This meant less attention to the economic development of decaying center cities. The third was a strong role for the states. This meant more attention to smaller communities because state politics tend to overrepresent rural and suburban areas. The fourth was a strong role for the private sector. This meant less of a role for the federal agencies and for federal funds.

Unfortunately, the agencies couldn't agree in time for the biennial report to be issued in March 1978 as the law provided. That document wasn't produced until August. Instead, in late March, Carter released a final revised draft of the old URPG report, now retitled "A New Partnership to Conserve America's Communities: A National Urban Policy." Along the way, that old report focusing on decaying cities had become a new urban policy tilted toward smaller, newer communities.

The new report included twenty proposals. Three of the four major ones recommended expansion of existing programs that had been adopted to stimulate the economies of urban areas. The major new proposal was a National Development Bank to provide loan guarantees and mortgage assistance for companies locating in distressed areas. When the report's programs were announced, they appeared designed to help distressed big cities. However, when the programs were "fleshed out" and formally submitted to Congress later that spring, they were broadened to include thousands of small towns.

Even so, the proposals fared badly in Congress. The development bank was never adopted, nor were any of the measures to stimulate the economies of urban areas. One exception was some tax credits for businesses hiring in urban areas. Of the twenty proposals, only ten were enacted, and all of them were amended by Congress before passage. The Carter administration later claimed credit for passage of thirteen of nineteen urban proposals, but it was able to do so only by dropping some of its original items and replacing them with newer, more successful ones, such as desperation loan guarantees for New York City. Eventually, the administration withdrew the development bank proposal.[23]

Meanwhile, the long-awaited biennial Urban Policy Report was finally issued on August 16, 1978. The report itself included little that was new. It could not be said to constitute a fresh national urban policy. While releasing it, however, President Carter also issued new executive orders. The most important required government agencies to locate their offices in center cities rather than in suburbs and to purchase their supplies and material from companies in areas with high unemployment. Even these measures met with resistance from the agencies so ordered. In the two years between the order and Carter's departure, 230 offices were moved back into central business areas across the nation. That's not much considering the many thousands of agency offices, and some— almost 90 percent—were already in central-city locations when the order was issued.

Other policies aimed at helping big cities have also been confusing and unnecessarily complex. The result has been a continuing failure to develop a national urban policy. One expert, Rochelle L. Stanfield, summarized the matter this way:

> Like so many other Carter initiatives, the urban policy was an attempt to please everyone that ended up pleasing no one. It tried with one stroke to satisfy the traditional urban lobby—the big cities, blacks, labor, and Frostbelt states that made up the old Democratic constituency—and to curry favor with the rising new political forces in the small towns, suburbs and Sunbelt states. The result was a diffusion of resources at a time of scarcity when targeting was necessary. Carter had tried to bring consistency and coherency to a de facto urban policy that had been marked by conflict and inconsistency for half a century, but his policy caused greater confusion among urban officials who no longer knew "where they stood" with the administration, heightened tensions with Congress, and raised some problems for the working of the federal system.[24]

WHAT NOW?

The election of Ronald Reagan in part represents a desire for decentralization in urban planning. However, there are still those who favor a national urban policy of the sort the Carter administration attempted but failed to develop.

Just before Reagan took office, the President's Commission for a National Agenda for the Eighties, created by Carter, issued a report that included a section on urban policy. It recommended that the Carter approach be abandoned, concluding that the effort to stop or slow the movement of people and businesses out of the older cities of the Northeast and Midwest toward the Sunbelt was foolish. It urged the government to target its limited resources to reach people in need rather than to build convention centers and hotels that only provide low-paying jobs for the poor in old cities. Better to help the poor move where the good jobs are or will soon be, it claimed, for only by recognizing the depth of the economic problems of our aging cities and allowing them to find new and less grandiose roles can we restore the national economy to real health.[25]

The Economic Recovery Tax Act

Whether or not President Reagan had this report in mind when he signed into law the Economic Recovery Tax Act in August 1981, the report is certain to have a major effect on metropolitan areas by region. The new tax law is the centerpiece of the Reagan administration's program to invigorate the economy (see chapter 1). The business provisions of this 1981 tax act were designed to address three problems believed to underlie economic slowdown: high capital costs, insufficient liquidity, and pessimistic expectations.[26]

Although there is considerable economic debate over the possible consequences of the tax act, it does appear that it will affect metropolitan areas differently for three reasons: (1) Metropolitan areas vary in their attractiveness as sites of production. By enhancing liquidity, tax incentives increase the ability of businesses to migrate to the more attractive areas. (Of course, this mobility is conditioned by a firm's "footlooseness" and organizational structure.) (2) Conditions specific to metropolitan areas may affect the extent to which otherwise similar plants could be eligible for tax incentives. (3) Different metropolises will experience the benefits of tax incentives to different degrees, depending on how the local economy operates to amplify the economic impact of the incentives.

"Footloose" firms (those not bound to particular locations because of resource and/or market availability) can relocate or establish new plants in areas with relatively cheap, plentiful, and productive labor; with inexpensive and available energy; with little unionization, low taxes, and a good business climate. Because, as we have seen, these characteristics vary from place to place, certain areas will grow faster, other things being equal.

Of course, the propensity of firms to move depends also on their organizational structure and liquidity. One study has demonstrated that family-owned businesses tend to be less mobile than larger, publicly-owned firms.[27] Because tax incentives affect patterns of business ownership, they affect the geographical distribution of employment. Another analysis suggests that by increasing cash flow, business incentives accelerate the capital mobility that would have occurred eventually anyway. Specifically, the investment-tax credits and accelerated depreciation allowances encourage firms to write off capital installed in declining cities more quickly and then reward the firms for starting anew. Faced with the question of where to place their capital, firms choose locations in growing rather than declining areas.[28] As a 1977 Rand study put it, "Tax credits, applied without regional targeting, generally represent a subsidy to growth areas . . . at the expense of those areas that are growing more slowly." In short, residents of declining areas could be made relatively worse off.

Urban Enterprise Zones

During the 1980 presidential campaign, Ronald Reagan called for the creation of "urban enterprise zones." Such zones are areas designated for economic improvement, where the location of businesses would be encouraged by certain federal tax incentives. Proponents of the urban-enterprise-zone concept stress that the program is designed to work with and not replace existing federal programs. Opponents believe the zones might threaten such programs.

Varying enterprise-zone bills have been introduced into the Ninety-sixth Congress. Probably the best known and most popular is the proposed Urban Jobs and Enterprise Zone Act (known as the "Kemp-Garcia" bill). Essentially, Kemp-Garcia would establish ten to twenty-five enterprise zones each year for three years. The zones would be designated by local government with the approval of the U.S. Secretary of Housing and Urban Development. They would have to have specific physical and economic characteristics, and the local government would be required to make certain commitments.

Those areas which HUD designates as enterprise zones based upon the severity of their economic distress will qualify for a package of benefits designed to lure job-creating businesses into the inner city. Any business that is willing to take the risk of locating in one of these zones and that will pledge to hire at least 40 percent of its workers from the unemployed labor force will qualify for a lucrative series of federal tax incentives.

By simply locating in the zone itself, business will qualify for some of the incentives, but by employing at least 40 percent of its workers from the unemployed labor force, it will gain additional incentives. And workers who take jobs in the zones will receive a 5-percent break on their personal income taxes up to $1,500 a year.[29]

Since the proposal involves tax law, its legislative future in Congress is expected to be influenced by the debate over the budget and President Reagan's New Federalism.

SUMMING UP

Many Americans—particularly those who live in areas far removed from the turmoil of inner-city life—may be tired of being told about the urban crisis. Such is the public mood today. Perhaps Gorham and Glazer say it best:

> Twenty years ago federal direct intervention in cities was minimal; it reached its height in the late 1960s and has been on the decline since then. Although there are mixed views about the justification and merit of spending more money, practically no voices at the moment are arguing for more substantive federal intervention in city problems . . . This is not to say that there is widespread satisfaction with the state of our cities, only that a smaller percent of the population care about the cities, while even fewer have confidence that the federal government (or any other level of government for that matter) knows how to make things better.[30]

To ignore the cities, however, is also to ignore various aspects of American life that are dynamic, including its problems. In the past, it was the resolution of these problems that sparked the economic development of the country and made possible the spirit of community that enabled the cities to accommodate the diverse groups of people who congregated in them. When cities are viewed from this perspective, we can maintain that the failure to deal with urban problems—rather than the existence of them—bodes ill for the future.

As James E. Peterson of the National Council for Urban Economic Development said in 1976, "If nothing is done to help the cities recover, if present trends continue, the cities will be reservations for dependent people. They won't die; they won't just go away. The federal programs already in place will see to that. They will just fester."[31]

NOTES

1. Editorial Research Reports on the Future of the City, *The Future of the City* (Washington, D.C.: Congressional Quarterly, 1974), p. 7.
2. For a summary of the report, see Richard P. Nathan, "For Cities, No Single Problem or Solution," *New York Times*, August 23, 1975, p. 21.
3. *Population Profile of the United States: 1980*, Series P-20, No. 363, U.S. Department of Commerce, Bureau of the Census, p. 2.
4. Ibid., p. 5.
5. Ibid., p. 6.
6. Janet Roebuck, *The Shaping of Urban Society* (New York: Scribner's, 1974), p. 193.
7. Louis H. Masotti, "Prologue: Suburbia Reconsidered—Myth and Counter-Myth," in Louis H. Masotti and Jeffrey K. Hadden, eds., *The Urbanization of the Suburbs* (New York: New View Points, 1974), p. 19.
8. See, for example, "Contrary to Conventional Wisdom, Cities Are Not Permanent," *Across the Board* XVIII (April 1981), 18–22.
9. President's Commission for a National Agenda for the Eighties, *Urban America in the Eighties* (Washington: U.S. Government Printing Office, 1980), p. 42.
10. George Sternlieb, *New York Times*, February 13, 1976.
11. Jack Rosenthal, *New York Times*, May 30, 1971, repr. in Louis H. Masotti and Jeffrey Hadden, eds., *Suburbia in Transition* (New York: New Viewpoints, 1974), p. 27.
12. Kenneth Jackson, Columbia University, unpublished paper, 1975.
13. *American Demographics, Inc.* 6 (September 1980), 10–11.
14. Ibid.
15. "Why Houston Voters Vetoed Mass Transit," *Business Week*, October 13, 1973, p. 28.
16. Quoted in Thomas H. Reed, ed., *Government in a Depression: Constructive Economy in State and Local Government* (Chicago: University of Chicago Press, 1933), p. 7.
17. Daniel R. Grant, "Urban Needs and State Response: Local Government Reorganization," in Alan K. Campbell, ed., *The States and the Urban Crisis* (Englewood Cliffs, N.J.: Prentice-Hall, 1970), p. 65.
18. Quoted in Blake McKelvey, *The Emergence of Metropolitan America, 1915–1966* (New Brunswick, N.J.: Rutgers University Press, 1968), p. 206.
19. Robert Conot, *American Odyssey: A Unique History of America Told Through the Life of a Great City* (New York: Morrow, 1974), p. 646.
20. Urban League Data Service, "Estimating the 1970 Census Undercount for State and Local Areas," Paper presented at the Annual Conference of the National Urban League, July 23, 1973, Washington, D.C. (Washington, D.C.: National Urban League, 1973).
21. See, for example, Eric L. Stowe, "Defining a National Urban Policy: Bureaucratic Conflict and Shortfall," in Donald B. Rosenthal, ed., *Urban Revitalization* (Beverly Hills, Calif.: Sage, 1980); Harold L. Wolman and Astrid E. Merget, "The Presidency and Policy Formulation: President Carter and the Urban Policy," *Presidential Studies Quarterly* 10 (Summer 1980); 402–415; and Rochelle L. Stanfield, "Toward an Urban Policy with a Small-Town Accent," *Publicis* 8 (Winter 1979), p. 31–43.
22. Myron A. Levine, "The President and National Urban Policy," Paper presented

at the 1979 Annual Meeting of the Northeastern Political Science Association, Newark, N.J., November 9, 1979.

23. Several years later, Carter again proposed it, first as his reelection campaign was getting underway. Once again, Congress refused to pass it.

24. Stanfield, "Toward an Urban Policy," p. 31.

25. See, for example, Timothy B. Clark, "Public Policy Focus," *National Journal* 11, February 21, 1981, p. 322. For a similar argument, see John D. Kosarda, "The Implications of Contemporary Redistribution Trends for National Urban Policy," *Social Science Quarterly* 60 (December 1980), 372–400. The entire issue is devoted to metropolitan and regional change in the United States.

26. Specifically, the act provided for: (1) reduced tax rates for some businesses; (2) decreased "service lives" of plant and equipment for tax purposes ("10-5-3" depreciation); (3) a lengthened carryover period for business operating losses; (4) new tax credits against wage payments for research and development; and (5) the sale of investment tax credits by firms showing no income-tax liability to firms with tax liability (the "net-leasing" provision).

27. John Rees, "Manufacturing Change, Internal Control, and Government Spending in a Growth Region of the U.S.," Paper presented at the 24th North American meeting of the Regional Science Association, New York City, November 1977.

28. George Peterson, *Federal Tax Policy and Urban Development* (Washington, D.C.: Urban Institute, 1976).

29. For a summary of the proposed Kemp-Garcia bill as well as pro and con arguments, see the *Congressional Record* 128 (March 1982), 69–96.

30. William Gorham and Nathan Glazer, eds., *The Urban Predicament* (Washington, D.C.: Urban Institute, 1976), p. 14.

31. Quoted in Rochelle L. Stanfield, "Are Brighter Days Ahead for the Nation's Decaying Cities?" *National Journal*, October 30, 1976, p. 1555.

GLOSSARY

Annexation: The addition of territory to a unit of government. Annexation usually denotes the addition by a city of land adjacent to it, to meet the problems of metropolitan expansion. Procedures for annexation are established by state law and generally require an affirmative vote of both the central city and the area concerned. In a few states, areas may be annexed by action of the city alone through judicial procedures.

City: A municipal corporation, chartered by the state, that is usually larger than a village, town, borough, or other incorporated area. The term is a legal concept, and exactly what constitutes a city is defined by state law. This is generally based on population but may be based on assessed valuation.

City council: The policymaking and, in some instances, administrative board of a city. The structure and powers of city councils vary with the plan of city government. In the weak-mayor and commission plans, the council plays a large role in lawmaking and in the direction and control of administrative departments. In the strong-mayor and council-manager plans, the council's job is largely in the realm of lawmaking, with only general oversight of administration. In all cases, the most important jobs of the council are to pass ordinances that determine public policy, and to exercise control over the purse strings. Other functions, which vary from city to city, may include serving as a board of review for tax assessments, issuing licenses, and making appointments. Members of city councils are elected (on a partisan or nonpartisan basis) from wards or districts, at large, or by a combination of both.

City-county separation: Political separation of the city from the county. Cities are generally part of the county in which they lie and the city residents pay county taxes and receive certain county services. More than thirty cities in Virginia, and the cities of St. Louis, Denver, Baltimore, and San Francisco, are separated from their counties and provide their residents with county services.

Council-manager plan: A form of city government in which the city council appoints a professional administrator or manager to act as the chief executive. With variations from city to city, the essentials of this plan are (1) a small council or commission of five to seven members elected at large on a nonpartisan ballot, with power to make policy and to hire and fire the manager; (2) a professionally trained manager with authority to hire and fire subordinates who is responsible to the council for efficient administration of the city; and (3) a mayor chosen separately or from within the council, but with no executive functions. The council must refrain from bypassing the manager by interfering with subordinates or in the details of administration, and the manager must follow the policies outlined by the council. A merit system for selection of employees is generally used under this plan.

Councils of government: Voluntary organizations of counties and municipalities concerned with areawide problems. About two hundred regional councils have been established, mainly since 1966, under incentives furnished by federal grants. Most are located in metropolitan areas (for example, the South East Michigan Council of Government) and, under authority granted by participating units, undertake such tasks as regional planning, community development, pollution control, water systems, and airport construction. Congress has encouraged this development by requiring such councils to determine the regional effects of programs funded by federal grants. In some cases, the council becomes the "designated agency" through which federal departments, such as the Department of Housing and Urban Development, work in making grants to local communities.

Home rule: The power vested in a local unit of government, usually a city, to draft or change its own charter and to manage its affairs. Home rule limits legislative interference in local affairs. Most states permit some degree of freedom for cities, and increasing numbers are granting it to counties. Home rule may be required or permitted by the state constitution or be granted by the legislature without specific constitutional authorization. Under home rule, the voters choose a commission to draft a charter that may be approved or rejected by the voters. This is in contrast to the granting of charters by the legislature under special acts, general laws, or optional plans. The city under home rule has control over its local problems provided it does not violate the state constitution or general laws of the state.

Mayor: The chief executive and/or the ceremonial leader of a city. The role of the mayor varies with the form of city government. Under the strong-mayor–council plan, the mayor has extensive executive power, including control over appointments and removals of city officials and the veto power. Under a weak-mayor–council plan, the mayor has limited executive powers. The mayor in the commission and manager plans is largely a ceremonial figure.

Metropolitan area: A large city and its surrounding suburbs, which are socially and economically integrated although composed of separate units of government. The term *metropolitan* is derived from the Greek terms *meter* (mother) and *polis* (city). In 1980, the Office of Management and Budget (OMB) identified 288 "standard metropolitan statistical areas" (SMSAs), up from 212 in 1960. These are determined through application of a complex definition set by OMB, which generally includes groups of densely populated cities, suburbs, and counties that are economically and socially integrated. In addition, thirteen areas, typified by New York, Chicago, and Los Angeles, are designated as "standard consolidated areas" because of the very complicated nature of these regions, which combine several contiguous SMSAs.

New Federalism: Desire to increase the involvement of local governments in the administration of domestic programs. Critics of New Federalism believe that it is overly decentralized and that it is not in the nation's best interest to allow state and local agencies the kind of freedom they have under New Federalism principles.

Special district: A unit of local government established to provide a single service. About one-half of the special districts in the United States are for fire protection, soil conservation, water, and drainage. Other common types of special districts provide cemetery, sewer, park, recreation, housing, and mosquito-abatement services. A school district may be classified as a special district, but the Census Bureau and political scientists classify it separately. Special districts are usually created to meet problems that transcend local government boundaries or to bypass taxation and debt restrictions imposed upon local units by state law.

Zoning: The division of a city or other unit of government into districts and the regulation by law of the uses of the land. Zoning is concerned with the nature of buildings (residential, industrial, or commercial), their height and density, and the uses made of particular tracts of land. Zoning laws are enacted under the police power of communities to protect the health, safety, and welfare of the people, and the United

States Supreme Court upheld zoning as a proper exercise of that power in 1926 in *Euclid* v. *Amber Realty Co.* (272 U.S. 365). A zoning board of appeals is usually created to grant exceptions and variances to persons who might suffer undue hardships under a zoning regulation.

SUGGESTED READINGS

Abrams, Charles. *The City Is the Frontier.* New York: Harper & Row, 1967.

Anderson, Martin. *The Federal Bulldozer: A Critical Analysis of Urban Renewal, 1949–1962.* Cambridge, Mass.: MIT Press, 1964.

Banfield, Edward D. *The Unheavenly City: The Nature and Future of Our Urban Crisis.* Boston: Little, Brown, 1970.

———. *The Unheavenly City Revisited: A Revision of the Unheavenly City.* Boston: Little, Brown, 1975.

Bender, Thomas. *Toward an Urban Vision: Ideas and Institutions in Nineteenth Century America.* Lexington: University of Kentucky Press, 1975.

Callow, Alexander B. *American Urban History: An Interpretative Reader with Commentaries.* 2nd ed. New York: Oxford University Press, 1974.

Chudacoff, Howard P. *The Evolution of American Urban Society.* Englewood Cliffs, N.J.: Prentice-Hall, 1975.

Davies, Allen F., ed. *The Age of Asphalt: The Automobile, the Freeway, and the Condition of Metropolitan America.* Philadelphia: Lippincott, 1975.

Harrigan, John. *Political Change in the Metropolis.* Boston: Little, Brown, 1981.

Wilson, James Q., ed. *The Metropolitan Enigma: Inquiries into the Nature and Dimensions of America's "Urban Crisis."* Cambridge, Mass.: Harvard University Press, 1968.

Source: Jack C. Pland and Milton Greenberg, *The American Political Dictionary,* 6th ed. (New York: Holt, Rinehart and Winston, 1982).

6

Crime and the Justice System

How has crime changed in recent years?

Do we expect too much of the American criminal justice system?

Are more police and new police technology the answer to our crime problem? Or are there better methods for helping to make our communities safer?

Why is plea bargaining a necessary part of the criminal justice system? What are its inherent dangers?

How has the public's mood changed with regard to the criminal justice system? What are the likely consequences of this "new mood" for the system in the near future?

Few social problems are more important—or more enduring—than that of criminal violence. Except for race, with which American criminal violence has always been intertwined, it is hard to think of a problem that evokes such intense and often ugly emotions.

Everywhere in the United States, people worry about criminal violence. According to public opinion polls, two Americans in five—in large cities, one in two—are afraid to go out alone at night. Fear is more intense among black Americans than among whites, and among women than among men. The elderly are the most fearful of all; barricaded behind multiple locks, they often go hungry rather than risk the perils of a walk to the market and back.

These fears are based on a harsh reality: since the early 1960s, the United States has been in the grip of a crime wave of epic proportions. According to the Federal Bureau of Investigation's *Uniform Crime Reports,* the chance of being the victim of a major violent crime such as murder, rape, robbery, or aggravated assault nearly tripled between 1960 and 1976; so did the probability of being the victim of a serious property crime, such as burglary, purse-snatching, or auto theft.[1] The wave may have crested—crime rates have been relatively stable since the mid-1970s—but criminal violence remains extraordinarily high. If recent rates continue, at least three Americans in every hundred will be victims of a violent crime this year, and one household in ten will be burglarized.

THE CHANGING NATURE OF CRIME

Not only has the crime rate risen, but also the *nature* of the crimes themselves has changed. Murder, for example, used to be thought of mainly as a crime of passion—an outgrowth of quarrels between husbands and wives, lovers, neighbors, or other relatives and friends. In fact, most murders still involve victims and offenders who know one another, but since the early 1960s, murder at the hand of a stranger has increased nearly twice as fast as murder by relatives, friends, and acquaintances.[2]

The same pattern is true for rape. In 1967, people known to the victim—estranged husbands and lovers, other relatives and friends, and casual acquaintances—were responsible for nearly half the reported rapes. In 1980, two-thirds of all rape victims were attacked by strangers, with such attacks accounting for virtually the entire 140-percent increase in the number of reported rapes since the mid-1960s.

The most disturbing aspect of the growth in "street crime" is the turn toward *viciousness,* as well as violence, on the part of many young criminals. A public defender noted for her legal ability speaks of "a terrifying generation of kids" that emerged during the late 1960s and early 1970s. When she began practicing, adolescents and young men charged with robbery had, at worst, pushed or shoved a pedestrian or storekeeper to steal money or merchandise; members of the new generation kill, maim, and injure without reason or remorse.[3] Even though it would be an exaggeration to call viciousness the rule, clearly it is far from exceptional.

Given the quantitative and qualitative changes in crime, it is more important than ever to understand this central issue of our time. Unfortunately, space doesn't allow us to study every aspect of crime and society. Rather than examine the relationship between social class, race, ethnicity, and crime, we will focus on the effectiveness of the criminal justice system—the police, criminal court, juvenile court, and the prisons—in solving the crime problem.[4] We begin with a more complete summary of crime rates than those already given, as well as a profile of professional and street criminals.

HOW MUCH CRIME IS THERE?

In 1979, more than twelve million serious crimes were reported in the United States. They occurred at the rate of one violent crime every twenty-seven seconds and one property crime every three seconds. One person was murdered every twenty-four minutes, and one person was raped every seven minutes (see Figure 6-1).

The crime rate increases yearly. Major crimes, for example, increased 148 percent in the 1960s.[5] Violent crime increased 180 percent between 1960 and 1971.[6] Between 1970 and 1975, crimes of violence increased 39 percent, as did property crimes. In 1978 alone, murder increased by nearly 10 percent and rape by over 13 percent. Robberies of all types increased dramatically since 1976 (see Table 6-1). There is little doubt that crime is America's biggest growth industry, and an industry whose "costs" are greater than we generally realize.

Serious as these numbers are, studies indicate they may only describe the tip of the iceberg.[7] Estimates are that actual crime is from two to four times greater than FBI figures suggest. A Law En-

Figure 6-1 CRIME CLOCK, 1979

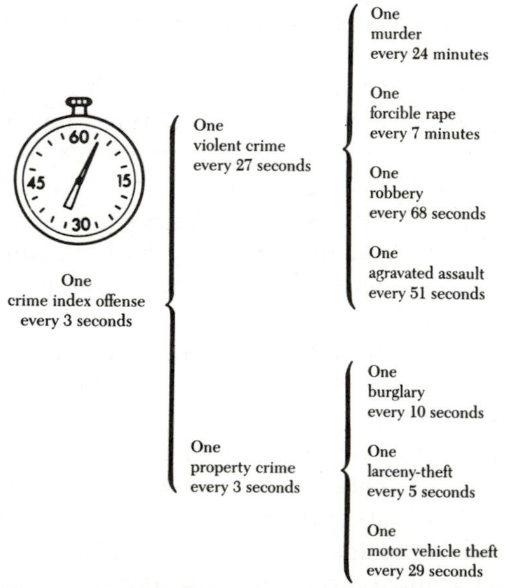

One
murder
every 24 minutes

One
violent crime
every 27 seconds

One
forcible rape
every 7 minutes

One
robbery
every 68 seconds

One
crime index offense
every 3 seconds

One
agravated assault
every 51 seconds

One
burglary
every 10 seconds

One
property crime
every 3 seconds

One
larceny-theft
every 5 seconds

One
motor vehicle theft
every 29 seconds

Source: Federal Bureau of Investigation, *Uniform Crime Reports* (Washington, D.C.: U.S. Government Printing Office, 1979).

Table 6-1
NATIONAL CRIME RATE AND PERCENT CHANGE*

Offense	Number (1980)	% Change Over 1979	% Change Over 1976
Murder	23,044	+7.4	+22.7
Forcible rape	82,088	+8.0	+44.7
Robbery	548,810	+17.5	+30.6
Aggravated assault	654,957	+6.6	+33.4
Burglary	3,759,193	+13.9	+21.7
Larceny-theft	7,112,657	+8.1	+13.4
Motor vehicle theft	1,114,651	+1.6	+16.4

Source: Federal Bureau of Investigation, *Uniform Crime Reports* (Washington, D.C.: U.S. Government Printing Office, 1980).

*Percent by which the rate of crime per 100,000 population changed in 1980 as compared with 1979 and 1976.

forcement Assistance Administration (LEAA) study released in 1977 reported that the actual rate of crime is four times the official rate.[8] Some crimes—such as robbery, rape, and aggravated assault—are severely underreported. For any given city, the study showed that the actual crime rate was from two to five times the reported rate.

White-Collar Crime

So far, the figures given are for crime as we normally perceive it. There is another type of crime which has serious consequences for society but which is generally overlooked (even accepted) by most of us—white-collar crime. White-collar crime includes everything from shoplifting, employee thefts, Medicaid fraud by doctors, and deceptive advertising to illegal campaign contributions, embezzlement, restraint of trade, and other forms of business fraud.

The numbers on white-collar crime are scanty, but data indicate that it is both frequent and expensive. Estimates of its cost range from $100 to $300 billion per year.[9] Even the conservative estimate of $100 billion dwarfs the costs of violent crimes such as larceny, robbery, burglary, and auto theft. These crimes impose a cost on society of about $4 billion a year, a fraction of the cost of white-collar crime. One study estimates that fraudulent car repairs alone cost consumers $9 billion a year, deceptive grocery billing

$14 billion, and lack of competition in the auto industry $16 billion.[10] Banks lose about five times as much to fraud (mostly by their own employees) as to robbers. Organized crime costs society about $20 billion a year and causes a great deal of violent crime.[11]

Shoplifting alone imposes a staggering cost on society. In 1977 its estimated cost, including employee thefts, was $26 billion.[12] Surveillance studies of customers show that about one in ten is a shoplifter, a depressing ratio.[13] Of course, this represents the tip of the iceberg as do the figures on violent and property crimes, since most white-collar thieves are surely not caught. Between 15 and 30 percent of all business failures are caused by financial losses due to employee and customer thefts.[14]

THE SOCIAL AND FINANCIAL COSTS OF CRIME

Many social and economic costs associated with crime are not always considered. For example, where property crimes are concerned, the cost of any criminal "transaction" may drain the resources not only of the intended target but also of insurance companies, credit card companies, police departments, and court systems; a full reckoning of the cost must include such things as repair bills for windows and doors and the price of new locks. When crimes against people are involved, the price paid in fear is never confined solely to the victim.

According to the 1980 Figgie *Report on the Fear of Crime,* 41 percent of Americans surveyed evinced a "high" or "very high" fear of becoming a victim of violent crime, more than 80 times the proportion who will actually be so victimized in any given year.[15] Women are more frightened than men, older people more than younger people, blacks more than whites. Yet relative degrees of fear do not necessarily reflect actual victimization. While blacks do suffer disproportionately from most crimes, women (except for rape) and the elderly (except for purse-snatching) have substantially *lower*-than-average victimization rates.

Fear exacts not only an emotional toll but a toll in freedom. More than 50 percent of Americans surveyed in the Figgie report say that, to avoid attracting attention, they now dress more plainly than they once did. Nine out of 10 do not open their doors unless the caller identifies himself or herself. FBI director William Webster has cited cases of mothers routinely giving young children pocket money so that they might have something to give up if threatened.

WHO ARE THE CRIMINALS?

Age of Population

Most crimes are committed by young people, usually males, under the age of twenty (see Figures 6-2, 6-3). As Northwestern University sociologist Wesley Skogan notes, "Crime is a young man's game." It is therefore tempting to blame the sharp increase in reported crime that began during the 1960s on the "coming of age" of the postwar baby-boom generation.

The truth may not be quite so simple. The 1967 report of President Lyndon Johnson's Commission on Law Enforcement and Administration of Justice puzzled over the fact that the rise in reported crimes was substantially larger than the growth in the size of the crime-prone age groups in the U.S. population.[16] The authors of the report showed, for example, that if the arrest rate for teenagers had been the same in 1965 as it was in 1960, the total number of teenager arrests in 1965 would have come to 536,000. The actual figure was 646,000.

This study shows that changes in the crime rate cannot be simplistically explained by isolating one variable or another. Yet a correlation between rising crime and a rising proportion of young people in the population is too clear to be dismissed. Moreover, mathematical models incorporating rather basic demographic information have proved to be highly accurate in predicting future crime rate trends.[17] Suffice it to say that the current decline in the teenage population probably portends (other factors again held constant) a decline in the crime rate as a whole.

Race and Class

Virtually all recent scholarly studies, regardless of locale or time period, show that arrest rates of blacks for almost every offense are considerably higher than those for whites. For example, in 1981, blacks accounted for 34 percent of all crime even though they only made up 12 percent of the population (see Figure 6-3). (Some exceptions were liquor-law violations, vandalism, and running away from home.) Victimization surveys and victims' descriptions of those who "got away" tell the same story. At the neighborhood level, the volume of crime is strongly correlated with the size of the local black population. The reasons for this link are many and complex, and they have less to do with race per se—or racism—than

Figure 6-2 TOTAL POPULATION AND NUMBER OF PERSONS ARRESTED, 1979

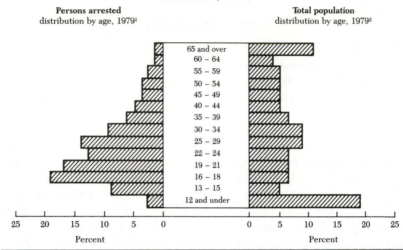

Persons arrested
distribution by age, 1979[1]

Total population
distribution by age, 1979[2]

Source: Federal Bureau of Investigation, *Uniform Crime Reports* (Washington, D.C.: U.S. Government Printing Office, 1979).

Figure 6-3 ARRESTS IN 1981 BY RACE, AGE, AND OFFENSE

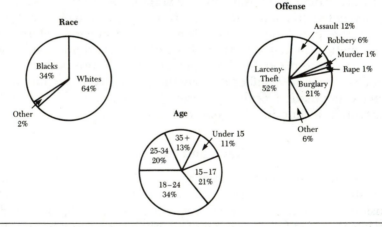

Source: The World Almanac (New York: Newspaper Enterprise Association, 1983), pp. 967–968.

with the conditions in which millions of young blacks are growing up: in poverty, in broken homes, in decaying schools. Such circumstances are "criminogenic" for all groups in the population.

In fact, according to the 1982 *Uniform Crime Reports,* those with minimum education, low income, and lower-class occupations are arrested in numbers far out of proportion to their numbers in the population. In addition, low-income people, *regardless of race,* are often at a disadvantage in the criminal justice system because of such factors as their inability to post bail or to hire an experienced criminal lawyer. The preponderance of black suspects, convicted offenders, and prisoners may be more a function of their class position than of their race. Even so, as Wesley Skogan has remarked, "the fear of crime and concerns about race have become virtually undistinguishable in the minds of many whites."

In the sections that follow, we will analyze the role of the police, criminal and juvenile courts, and prisons. The emphasis is on what these institutions do and do not do, and on what they may reasonably be expected to accomplish. First, we need to ask a related but more general question: Is the criminal justice system capable of solving the crime problem? A brief answer is that it can do more to reduce crime than liberal rhetoric implies, but considerably less than conservatives suggest. But before we begin, let us examine Figure 6-4, which shows how cases in most jurisdictions move through the criminal justice system.

THE JUSTICE SYSTEM: DO WE EXPECT TOO MUCH?

Since the turn of the century, liberals have underestimated the relevance of the criminal justice system and have opposed the search for more effective law enforcement as mere symptom alleviation—the equivalent of putting a Band-Aid on a cancerous sore.

In 1901, Enrico Ferri, an Italian legal scholar who helped develop criminology as an academic discipline, declared that "we have but to look around us in the realities of contemporaneous life to see that the criminal code is far from being a remedy against crime, that it remedies nothing." Ferri concluded that "punishment prevents the criminal for a while from repeating his criminal deed," but added, "it is evident that the punishment is not imposed until after the deed has been done. It is a remedy directed against effects, but it does not touch the causes, the roots, of the evil."

Instead of dealing with symptoms, Ferri argued, we should attack the disease itself: "That which has happened in medicine will happen in criminology." The discovery that malaria is transmitted by mosquitoes led not only to the development of new medicines to cure those already infected, but to the draining of swamps to prevent people from incurring the disease in the first place.[18]

Liberals have been addicted to medical metaphors ever since.

Figure 6-4 THE CRIMINAL JUSTICE SYSTEM AT A GLANCE

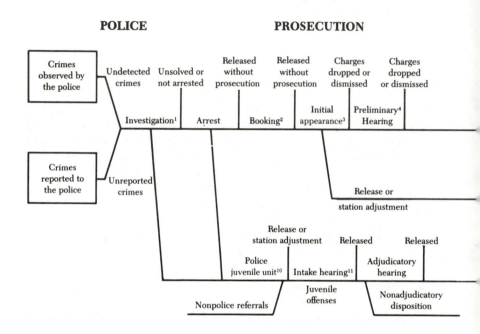

[1]May continue until trial.
[2]Administrative record of arrest. First step at which temporary release on bail may be available.
[3]Before magistrate, commissioner, or justice of peace. Formal notice of charge, advice of rights, bail set. Summary trials for petty offenses usually conducted here without further processing.
[4]Preliminary testing of evidence against defendant. Charge may be reduced. No separate preliminary hearing for misdemeanors in some systems.
[5]Charge filed by prosecutor on basis of information submitted by police or citizens. Alternative to grand jury indictment; often used in felonies, almost always in misdemeanors.
[6]Reviews whether government evidence sufficient to justify trial. Some states have no grand jury system; others seldom use it.

COURTS   **CORRECTIONS**

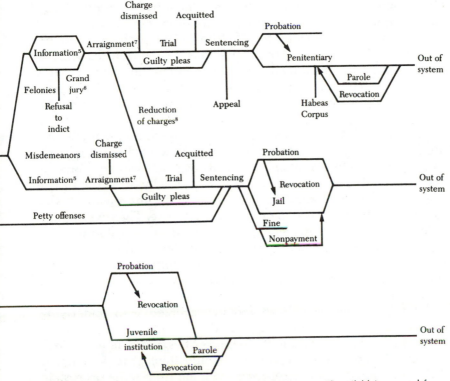

[7]Appearance for plea; defendant elects trial by judge or jury (if available); counsel for indigent usually appointed here in felonies. Often not at all in other cases.

[8]Charge may be reduced at any time prior to trial in return for plea of guilty or for other reasons.

[9]Challenge on constitutional grounds to legality of detention. May be sought at any point in process.

[10]Police often hold informal hearings and dismiss or adjust many cases without further processing.

[11]Probation officer decides desirability of further court action.

[12]Welfare agency, social services, counseling, medical care, etc., for cases where adjudicatory handling is not needed.

Source: Donal E. J. MacNamara, ed., *Annual Editions* (Guilford, Ct.: Duskin Publishing Group, 1982), pp. 4–5.

In dissenting from the 1931 report of the Wickersham Commission (the National Commission on Law Observance and Enforcement), Henry W. Anderson, chairman of its Committee on the Causes of Crime, wrote, "Like eruptions on the human body," criminal acts "are symptoms of more fundamental conditions of personal or social deficiency or imbalance." If "the crime problem is to be solved," Anderson added, "the attack must be made at the sources of the trouble and the remedy must be found in the removal of the causes."[19] It is not a question of either/or; attacking the underlying causes of a problem does not preclude an attempt to alleviate the symptoms.

Even Band-Aids have their uses; no competent or compassionate doctor would leave a festering sore unbandaged or fail to treat some other painful symptom, especially if a cure was not immediately at hand. There is no inherent reason why attempts to cut crime through more effective law enforcement must come at the expense of efforts to cure the underlying disease. The reverse may be closer to the truth. Reluctance to invoke the criminal justice system as a means of reducing crime in the short run may create a backlash against the social and economic reforms that are needed for the long run. We may be seeing this happen with today's call for harsher "law and order" tactics.

But if liberals have been too preoccupied with underlying causes, conservatives have exaggerated the gains that can be wrung from tougher law enforcement. To read critics such as James Q. Wilson and Ernest van den Haag, one would think that the current level of criminal violence represented a fall from some prior state of grace. Their writings imply that once upon a time, before police officers' and judges' hands were tied by the Supreme Court under Chief Justice Warren (which made many decisions in the 1960s protecting the rights of the accused), criminals were easily and quickly apprehended, rapidly tried and convicted, and promptly sent to prison for an appropriate term.[20]

There never was such a time—not in the United States in this century and perhaps not anywhere since the time of Cain and Abel, when criminals were caught and punished by a Higher Judge. As the late Dean Roscoe Pound of Harvard Law School, one of the giants of American jurisprudence, told the American Bar Association in 1906, "Dissatisfaction with the administration of justice is as old as law."

Dissatisfaction was extremely high when Pound spoke because urban crime and violence seemed to be increasing at an explosive rate. Conservatives of that era, as in our own, thought they knew why: courts were unduly concerned with the rights of the accused; hence criminals were not being punished the way they used to be. "It is not too much to say that the administration of the criminal law in this country is a disgrace to our civilization," President (and later Chief Justice) William Howard Taft declared in 1909, "and that the prevalence of crime and fraud, which here is greatly in excess of that in European countries, is due largely to the failure of the law to bring criminals to justice. . . . The trial of a criminal seems like a game of chance, with all the chances in favor of the criminal."[21]

The same charge has been voiced over and over again. In the 1920s, some of the most basic safeguards of criminal procedures did not exist; the police routinely held suspects incommunicado for long periods and extracted confessions through physical and psychological torture, often with the prosecutor's knowledge or participation. Yet police chiefs, prosecutors, and other law enforcement officials complained that their hands were being tied. "There has been too much mollycoddling of the criminal population," Edwin Sims, head of the new Chicago Crime Commission, declared in 1920. A few years later, when a state court excluded a defendant's confession because it had been obtained through use of the third degree, a Chicago police official announced that 95 percent of the department's work would be rendered useless if the decision were allowed to stand. "We are permitted to do less every day," the chief complained. "Pretty soon there won't be a police department."[22]

According to conservatives, we have always been losing "the war on crime," and the remedy has always been the same: to unleash the forces of law and order so that criminals can be quickly caught, convicted, and punished. Like Richard Nixon forty years later, Herbert Hoover campaigned for the presidency in 1928 on a law-and-order platform. "Every student of our law enforcement mechanism knows full well . . . that its procedures unduly favor the criminal . . . and that justice must be more swift and sure," he told the Associated Press a month after he took office. "In our desire to be merciful the pendulum has swung in favor of the prisoner and far away from protection of society."

It would be nice if the real world were as simple as the ideologues of both camps suggest. It is not; if the past teaches us anything, it is that there are no quick and easy solutions to the enduring problem of criminal violence—not through social reform, and not through "law and order." On the contrary, the search for panaceas has often made matters worse. For one thing, the institutions of the criminal justice system are inordinately complex; often their actual operations bear little resemblance to the image that people have of them. Hence, attempts to change the police, courts, and prisons often backfire.

Except in the most general sense, moreover, we know remarkably little about the relationship between what the police, courts, and prisons do, on the one hand, and what criminals do, on the other. We know that punishment deters crime, for example; but we do not know whether *more* punishment, or different *kinds* of punishment, than we now administer will deter crime more effectively. Similarly, the existence of the police undoubtedly leads to less crime than we would have in their absence. But there is no evidence that more police will produce less crime; and the police themselves simply do not know what else to do to bring about a reduction in criminal violence. Nor is there any persuasive evidence that correctional officials know how to rehabilitate criminal offenders.

If we are to have any hope of reducing criminal violence to some more tolerable level, we would be well advised to proceed cautiously, and with modest goals and expectations. We also need to shed our ideological blinders. Crime control is the quintessential political issue, for the administration of the criminal law poses fundamental questions about the relationship between the individual and the power of the state. All of us, therefore, liberals and conservatives alike, approach the subject with intense emotions and preconceptions.

THE POLICE: WHAT THEY DO AND DON'T DO

Americans have ambivalent feelings about the police. They are necessary to our safety, yet they threaten us at the same time. We see them as threatening because by law they are implementers of violent force and have the potential to wield extraordinary power. Of all criminal justice actors, the police are the most powerful, largely because of the great amount of discretion available to them. They can deprive individuals of freedom and under certain circumstances, society permits them to injure and even kill. The police are the most visible, the most pressured, and generally, the most maligned actors in the criminal justice system. They are also the first people we encounter in our map of the system.

Why Aren't They Protecting Us?

We hear more and more people asking, "Why can't the police protect us, instead of just handing out parking tickets? We can't understand why, with all those police officers on the streets, more criminals aren't being caught and our homes and families made to feel safer." The fact is that much of our thinking about the capabilities of the police is shaped by the media's portrayal of them. After all, Kojak always gets his man. So does Columbo; so did Sherlock Holmes, Hercule Poirot, Inspector Maigret, and the other fictional sleuths who have formed our perception of police omnipotence.

Unfortunately, that perception is wide of the mark. There is an enormous gulf between the image and the reality of policing. After the public schools, the police are the best-known agency of government; they are also the least understood—by police officers themselves, as well as by the public. As a result, Americans have come to expect far more of the police than they can possibly deliver.

As Robert diGrazia, the controversial department chief of Montgomery County, Maryland (and former police chief of Boston and St. Louis), told a group of his fellow chiefs, "We are not letting the public in on our era's dirty little secret," namely, "that there is little the police can do" about crime.[23] He may have been exaggerating for rhetorical effect—but not by much. The evidence suggests that traditional remedies simply will not work. For example:

- Short of creating a police state, there is no reason to believe that putting more officers on the street would affect the amount of street crime. The fifty-eight American cities with populations of more than 250,000 average 3.4 officers per 1,000 residents. But individual departments vary in size from 1.7 to 7.0 officers per 1,000 people; there is no observable correlation between the number of police a community has and either the number of crimes that are committed or the proportion of those crimes that are solved. In a controlled experiment conducted in Kansas City, moreover, the Police Foundation found that doubling or tripling the visible police presence had no effect on the number of crimes committed, or on people's feelings of safety.[24]
- New technology does not help, either. Since the mid-1960s, police departments have invested huge sums in computerized telecommunication systems designed to cut the period that elapses between the time a citizen calls the police to report a crime and the time a patrol car arrives at the scene. But cutting

a police department's response time does little good when, as researchers recently discovered, crime victims wait twenty minutes before they call. The emphasis on mobility and rapid response time has kept police officers locked up inside their patrol cars and reduced person-to-person contact between the police and citizens, thereby hampering police officers' ability to prevent or solve crimes.[25]

■ Repealing the so-called exclusionary rule—a rule of evidence which makes illegally acquired evidence inadmissible—would not make the police any more effective in their "war" against crime.[26] Despite loud and frequent complaints, the police have not been handcuffed by the rulings of the Warren Court. Except for minor drug offenses, there is no evidence to suggest that the police make fewer arrests or that prosecutors secure fewer convictions because of Supreme Court decisions safeguarding the rights of the accused. On the contrary, the evidence runs the other way.

Other Police Functions

Although police derive their self-image from playing cops and robbers, their other functions are every bit as important and actually predate their role in crime control.[27] Like lawyers and judges, police are in the business of resolving conflicts—in particular, conflicts that threaten to breach the peace and disturb public order.

Maintaining order remains a major police responsibility; the great majority of the calls patrol officers receive involve breaches of the peace or requests for help rather than reports of crimes in the usual sense of the term.[28] In poor neighborhoods, in particular, police spend large amounts of time responding to "family" (or domestic) disputes—arguments and fights between relatives, lovers, friends, and acquaintances. These calls are the most dangerous kind of police work. In violent disputes among friends or lovers, one of the parties often acts in irrational and unpredictable ways. When officers arrive, moreover, disputants, including the one who called for help, sometimes unite and turn on them as the common enemy.

To be effective in situations of this sort, a patrol officer needs three sets of qualities not normally found in the same person: great subtlety and sophistication in understanding and dealing with people; unusual verbal facility; and the willingness and ability to use physical force—to fight with no holds barred, and to kill if necessary.

The police are called upon to provide a wide variety of social services as well. They rush accident victims to the hospital; bring alcoholics indoors on a winter's night; break into a locked house or apartment to see whether an elderly occupant is dead or ill; persuade a mentally ill person who has barricaded himself in his apartment to return to the hospital; or administer emergency first-aid to a heart attack victim, or someone who has taken a drug overdose, while waiting for the ambulance to come. Police also get cats down from trees, chauffeur dignitaries around town, rescue the drowning, talk suicidal people out of killing themselves, direct traffic, and provide advice and help to the sick and elderly as well as to otherwise healthy people who simply cannot cope with some pressing problem.

Thus, keeping the peace, settling private disputes, and helping sick and bewildered people are as much "real police work" as arresting criminals or riding a patrol car in an effort to prevent crime. And these various roles are not in conflict. For all their macho image, the police are heavily—in some ways, almost totally—dependent on the people being policed. Because they rarely come upon a crime in progress, police depend on members of the public for knowledge that a crime has been committed; they are equally dependent on victims, witnesses, and other informants for knowledge of who offenders are and where they might be found. To exaggerate just a bit, the police can solve a crime if someone tells them who committed it; if no one tells them, they do not know what to do. (When police officers catch an offender on their own, it is more likely to be the result of chance, or the criminal's incompetence, than of their own investigative efforts.[29])

The closer police are to the people on their beats, the more people they know and the more those people trust them, the greater their chances of reducing crime. Police cannot solve a crime if they do not know it has been committed—and the majority of Americans do *not* report the crimes in which they are the victims.[30] Those who do report a crime usually do not do so immediately, thereby giving the offender (and perhaps potential witnesses) time to get away. "Most communities are underutilizing their police departments," San Jose's Chief McNamara argues. "Members of the public have a critical role to play in crime control," he adds; "they are far more likely to play that role if the cop is someone they know and like, instead of his being a brusque aloof stranger."[31] But a police officer is not likely to become someone people know and like by playing cops and robbers all the time. It is when police play Florence Nightingale, to use Egon Bittner's metaphor—when they see themselves as being in the business of providing a wide range of services to the community—that they are able to nurture the relationship they need.

In short, improving police-community relationships is not a goal that can be achieved through a public relations campaign, nor is it a task to be delegated to a specialized staff division; it is what policing is all about. Yet, consciously or not, almost everything about the way most police departments are organized and run is designed to discourage close relationships with the people being policed. The New York City Police Department is generally considered a model of enlightened police-community relations, but until Commissioner Robert McGuire repealed the rule shortly after taking office in January 1978, the department had forbidden patrolmen from holding "unnecessary conversations" with members of the general public.

More effective policing will not be possible without a radical change in the way the police conceive of their jobs and an equally radical change in the way police departments are organized and run.

Can We Reduce Criminal Violence?

We have already discovered that the principal resource for the police is the information received from citizens. Therefore, the first imperative is to remove the obstacles to close police-community relationships.

In addition to community involvement, police officers need to rely more on the information and expertise of their fellow officers. In other words, in the most basic sense of the term, police departments are information-processing organizations; but they have never thought of themselves that way. Almost everything about the way most departments are organized and run serves to inhibit the flow of information and expertise from the community to the police and from one officer to another. Thus, departments use only a minute fraction of the knowledge that is at their disposal.

But the police must also recognize their own limitations; they must change their conception of their role from that of a law enforcement agency, dedicated to catching robbers, to that of a public service agency, devoted to close relationships with and assistance to the people and communities being policed. "Assigning the police full responsibility for the maintenance of order, the prevention of crime and the apprehension of criminals constitutes far too great a burden on far too few," the authors of the Kansas City Preventive Patrol Experiment report have written. "Primary responsibility rests with families, the community and its individual members. The police can only facilitate and assist members of the community in the maintenance of order, and no more."[32]

Finally, serious research and experimentation on policing are barely fifteen years old; their main contribution has been to destroy the assumptions on which most police activity has been based—to demonstrate the extent of our ignorance about what the police can, and cannot, do to reduce crime and improve domestic tranquility. What is needed is not more hardware, communications equipment, or personnel, but more research and experimentation. In the meantime, we—police officials, government leaders, citizens—would do well to abandon our quixotic faith that there is a police solution to the problem of criminal violence.

JUDGES AND THE COURTS

Judges are by tradition and trappings the embodiment of justice. Dressed in black robes and seated high above everyone else in court, judges are imposing, even intimidating. They are supposed to be: they have great power over people's lives, and increasingly, they use it.

But who are the judges? They are former lawyers and former politicians. Most commonly, they are lawyers who knew politicians. Some rise above their own human limitations, but more do not. Mostly, they are ordinary men and women, coping fitfully with the failings of others, the endless procession of broken promises and brutal acts that are the daily business of the courts.

The power and responsibility of judges has increased considerably with the litigation explosion in the United States. Tocqueville's observation that there is "hardly a political question which does not sooner or later turn into a judicial one" has never been truer. This is so not only in the U.S. Supreme Court, which is expected to be the final arbiter of the law, but in courts all over the country. By reading their own views into broadly worded statutes and vaguely defined constitutional rights, judges have assumed—some say usurped—unaccustomed roles. Increasingly, judges, state and federal, can be found ordering government boards and agencies to obey the law. When the boards balk, as they often do, judges end up running school boards, welfare agencies, mental hospitals, and prisons. A judge in Boston, for example, placed sixty-seven public housing projects into receivership under court control because they had been mismanaged by the Boston housing authority. Such decisions often require judges to rule on specific questions like garbage removal from tenements, proper bus routes for school children, and minimum hot water temperatures for prison inmates.

Judges are quick to assert that they are simply enforcing the laws and the Constitution. "Judges, unlike Presidents, Congressmen and lawyers, cannot generate their own business," says Federal Judge Prentice Marshall, who halted discriminatory hiring and promotion practices in the Chicago police department despite Mayor Richard Daley's vow to fight the decision. Whether by default or design, the judiciary increasingly has the last word on important social questions.

The Criminal Court

Criminal courts are on trial, charged with failing to protect the American people against criminal violence. Some critics attribute the failure to a gross shortage of resources which forces prosecutors and judges to indulge in plea bargaining, offering serious criminals a mild penalty in return for a guilty plea. Others put the blame on the Warren Court's concern for the rights of the accused; in their view, the "exclusionary rule" and other procedural requirements force judges to acquit, and prosecutors to release, large numbers of patently guilty offenders. Still others believe the major flaw to be the arbitrary and capricious nature of criminal sentencing, which leads to wide disparities in the punishments meted out to offenders guilty of the same crime. Let's look at these charges to see what truth there is in them.

Plea Bargaining: Contrary to popular impression, plea bargaining is not a recent innovation, nor is it the product of heavy caseloads; it has been the dominant means of settling criminal cases for the last century. It was, in fact, the subject of heated debate during the 1920s, when there was great public clamor over criminal violence. Most of the contemporary arguments against plea bargaining were made then, and most of the recent proposals for doing away with plea bargaining were tried and found wanting. Moreover, research by the political scientist Raymond Moley, who helped direct a number of state and local crime commissions during the 1920s, demonstrated that plea bargaining was not new then, either. On the contrary, Moley discovered that negotiated pleas had replaced jury trials as the principal means of settling criminal cases as early as the second third of the nineteenth century.[33] If plea bargaining is a fall from grace, the fall occurred over a century ago.

Clearly, plea bargaining stems from causes more deeply rooted in the judicial process than court congestion. To be sure, heavy backlogs and inadequate trial facilities may distort the plea-bargaining process. To keep the assembly line moving, prosecutors sometimes recommend, and judges impose, more lenient sentences than they think desirable; this happens far less often than critics allege.[34] More important, jailed defendants who assert their innocence and who might be acquitted are sometimes forced to choose between pleading guilty and gaining their freedom and pleading not guilty and remaining in jail to await trial. There can be no excuse for plea bargaining under circumstances of that sort. But what is indefensible is not plea bargaining as such, but a bail system that makes defendants' liberty contingent on the financial resources at their disposal, and court congestion that keeps defendants in jail for months on end, awaiting trial.

Eliminating plea bargaining would be undesirable even if it were possible. Proponents of abolition assume that the question to be resolved in a criminal case is always simple and clear-cut: Are defendants guilty or not guilty of committing the crime with which they are charged? If the answer is Not Guilty, defendants should be freed; if it is Guilty, they should receive the "proper" punishment for the offense. To convict defendants of any lesser charge, in this view, or to sentence them to any lesser punishment, is a perversion of justice.

It is a curious notion of justice to tie it so completely to the prosecutor's uncontrolled discretionary decision about the crime with which an offender will be charged. Opponents of plea bargaining attribute an objectivity to the charging decision that most prosecutors would be loath to claim; as Professor Arnold Enker has written, the opponents of plea bargaining seem to assume that there is "an objective truth existing in a realm of objective historical fact" that can best be ascertained through a jury trial. But the "truth" of an offense usually is neither objective nor absolute; it is embodied in the way "the facts" are interpreted and in the significance attached to them, as much as in the facts themselves.[35]

In the great majority of criminal cases, "the facts" are not in dispute. What is at issue—what needs to be adjudicated—is the significance that should be attached to the facts. Decisions about the seriousness of the offense and the degree of the offender's culpability involve complex and often highly subjective judgments about such factors as premeditation, intent, force, credibility, negligence, threat, recklessness, and harm. What is being adjudicated is not guilt or innocence, but the punishment the offender deserves.[36]

When the facts *are* in dispute—when there is reasonable doubt that defendants committed the crime with which they are charged—a jury trial is the most appropriate means of adjudication. Whether defendants choose to go to trial depends on their (and their attorneys') assessments of the risks that may be involved. Although the potential gain of complete acquittal is large, the price of defeat may be just as large. If defendants are convicted of the highest charge against them, or if the judge is in the habit of imposing stiffer sentences on defendants who insist on a trial than on defendants who plead guilty to the same offense, conviction at trial may bring a long prison sentence.

Certainly it is essential that defendants be free to exercise their rights to a jury trial. A number of legal scholars argue that plea bargaining denies defendants that freedom by penalizing them for exercising it. When defendants convicted at a jury trial receive stiffer sentences than they would have drawn had they pleaded guilty, they are paying a price for having gone to trial; in effect, the state is punishing them for exercising their constitutional rights.[37]

Procedural Rights: The most popular explanation for the courts' ineffectiveness in "putting away" criminals is that the Warren Court put too much emphasis on the rights of defendants. This concern is not new, however. "Our dangers do not lie in too little tenderness to the accused," Judge Learned Hand wrote in 1923. "Our procedure has been always haunted by the ghost of the innocent man convicted. It is an unreal dream. What we need to fear is the archaic formalism and watery sentiment that obstructs, delays, and defeats the prosecution of crime."

You will recall that arguments of this sort are rooted in ideological preferences rather than in empirical research. When the data are assembled and analyzed, it becomes clear that the pendulum has not swung too far. Only a handful of criminals go free or escape punishment because of exclusionary rules, search-and-seizure laws, appeals, and other "technicalities" designed to protect defendants' rights.[38]

It is only in cases of so-called "victimless crimes" that any significant number of seemingly guilty offenders go free because tainted evidence—evidence acquired as a result of an illegal search, seizure, or arrest—is excluded from court; and even here, the number is considerably smaller than critics assume.[39]

Search-and-seizure problems play a larger role in drug cases, especially those where the defendant is charged with possession of a drug. Large numbers of drug arrests are made; in a Rand Corporation study of the prosecution of adult felons in Los Angeles, more than a third of the felony arrests were on drug charges, most of them for possession of marijuana, heroin, and other narcotics and dangerous drugs ("uppers" and "downers"). The prosecutor rejected over 40 percent of the arrests, either through outright dismissal or reduction to a misdemeanor. In the case of arrests for possession of dangerous drugs, most of the rejections were due to insufficient evidence (32 percent) or because they were "trivial offenses." Search-and-seizure problems, illegal arrests, and other violations of defendants' rights accounted for only 17.5 percent of the overall rejections and 25 percent of the outright dismissals.[40]

Punishment: When charges against an arrested felon are dropped or reduced to misdemeanors, it usually is not because prosecutors and judges are unduly lenient nor because their heavy caseloads force them to give away the courthouse. Nor, as we have seen, is it because the exclusionary rule "punishes the constable by letting the criminal go free." For the most part, prosecutors drop felony charges or reduce them to misdemeanors because they doubt the defendant's guilt, because they lack the evidence needed to prove guilt, or because they feel the crime was not serious enough, or the defendant not sufficiently culpable, to warrant the stigma and punishment that a felony conviction would bring.[41]

Studies by both the Vera Institute of Justice and the Institute for Law and Social Research (INSLAW) found that at the root of much of the crime brought to court is anger—simple or complicated anger between two or more people who know each other.[42] Until the Vera and INSLAW researchers analyzed the reasons why some arrests stand up in court and others do not, no one realized how much of a criminal court's workload involves cases in which victims and offenders know one another; nor had anyone understood the degree to which this affects what happens to those cases. Prosecutors and judges view crimes involving strangers as more serious offenses than crimes involving a prior relationship between victim and offender, but they also concentrate their resources on the former because it is so much harder to get a conviction in prior-relationship cases.

The reason, quite simply, is that when they know the offender, victims often refuse to press charges, testify, or cooperate with the prosecutor in other ways. No single factor has so large an impact on what happens to felons after they have been arrested: "complainant noncooperation" accounted for more than two-thirds of the dismissals of "victim felonies" in New York and well over half in Washington, D.C.[43]

Whether a crime involves strangers, relations, or friends, the weight that prosecutors and judges give to it reflects their evaluation of what the case is "worth." In effect, decisions about the worth of a case are decisions about the nature and amount of punishment offenders deserve—in particular, whether they need to be incarcerated or not. "Good guys should get breaks, and bad guys shouldn't," a California prosecutor explains, meaning that charging and sentencing decisions are based in good measure on an evaluation of culpability and of commitment to a criminal (or law-abiding) way of life.[44]

Differences in sentencing from one court to another are also a concern. In part, the disparity is due to the existence in each state (and in many states, each community) of an autonomous system of courts with jurisdiction over state and local crimes. That autonomy, in turn, means that sentences will reflect different state and local attitudes. Unless various states are willing to cede jurisdiction over intrastate crime to the federal government, it is hard to imagine how this kind of sentencing disparity could be eliminated.

Finally, critics of sentencing policy fail to make the distinction between differences in the sentences judges give and the sentences defendants receive. The distinction is neither specious nor academic; it explains an apparent paradox—that those who look at judges' behavior find enormous disparity in sentencing, while those who examine the sentences defendants receive (and equally important, the sentences they actually serve) find that sentences tend to be proportionate to the seriousness of the offense and of the offender's prior record.

The general impression of capriciousness is understandable. Every court has its hanging judges and its soft touches; and every court has judges who are harder to categorize—judges who are harsh with some kinds of offenses or offenders and lenient with others. But the same kind of discretion that enables individual judges to act capriciously makes it possible for prosecutors and defense attorneys to limit those judges' impact. What happens, quite simply, is that in large court systems hanging judges impose far fewer sentences than do judges who follow court norms. If defendants know that a judge will impose the maximum sentence whether they plead guilty or not, they have no reason to plead guilty and every incentive to insist on going to trial. There always is at least some chance that a jury will acquit, not to mention the chance that the case may be transferred to another, more lenient judge. And prosecutors, and often chief judges or court administrators, usually cooperate with defense attorneys in manipulating dockets so that cases will come before a judge who will impose a sentence commensurate with the plea that has been negotiated.[45]

The Real Conflict

Criminal courts are multipurpose institutions, charged with protecting society against criminals and with protecting the innocent individual against the coercive power of the state. Practitioners and scholars have tended to emphasize the conflict between these goals.[46]

So long as there is a certain tension between the desire to convict the guilty and the need to protect the innocent, the greater is the chance that we may acquit some guilty persons. The greater certainty we seek in convicting the guilty, the greater the probability that innocent people will be subjected to the burden of prosecution, and the greater the risk that some of them may be convicted. This tension is not unique to American courts; it is inherent in any system of justice, be it the inquisitorial approach characteristic of continental Europe or the adversarial approach of Anglo-American nations. Both systems of justice seek to convict the guilty, and both are concerned with protecting the innocent; they differ in the procedures used to achieve those goals and in the relative weight they give to each.[47]

In the past twenty years, as we have seen, considerable weight has been given to due process in American criminal courts. There are a growing number of Americans, however, who see this emphasis as favoring the guilty and punishing the innocent by encouraging criminal behavior. Yet, the evidence does not necessarily support this claim. "Real criminals" are not "getting away with it" in criminal court. As the authors of the Vera Institute study wrote, "Where crimes are serious, evidence is strong, and victims are willing to prosecute, felons with previous criminal histories ended up with relatively heavy sentences."[48] Although there is increasing pressure to swing the pendulum away from due process, it is doubtful that such a move will reduce criminal activity. Past experience and current data suggest that sending more criminals to jail or keeping them there longer will not bring about a significant reduction in criminal violence. Even so, the pendulum almost certainly will continue to swing from an emphasis on due process to one of law and order and back again.

JUVENILE JUSTICE

A special criminal justice system for the handling of juvenile offenders was established in the 1920s. Humanitarians, reformers, and social scientists saw it as a giant step forward in the search for justice.

This enthusiasm, however, has become muted, to say the least. "The great hopes originally held for the juvenile court have not been fulfilled," the President's Crime Commission declared in its 1967 report. "It has not succeeded significantly in rehabilitating delinquent youth, in reducing or even stemming the tide of delinquency, or in bringing justice and compassion to the child offender."[49]

"People have always accused kids of getting away with murder," a 1977 *Time* cover story declared. "Now that is all too literally true. . . . Especially in ghettoes of big cities, the violent youth is king of the streets. When he is caught, the courts usually spew him out again."[50]

Those fighting for the rights of juveniles in the 1920s were of course thinking in terms of their times and circumstances. The reality of the 1980s, as evidenced by the *Time* story, is very different. The juvenile today is likely to be on trial for murder, gang rape, arson, or mugging, perhaps for the third, fifth, even tenth time (see Box 6-1). This was not true in the 1920s, or nearly so true in the 1950s or 1960s.[51] The juvenile today usually has a defense counsel, and plea bargaining is common as the huge volume of cases demands accelerated handling. Even when declared delinquent for the third or fourth time, the juvenile is not likely to be institutionalized. Judges have learned that the institutions do not rehabilitate but are in fact prep schools for prisons. The advocates of community correction press for probation, an assignment to a group residence, an outpatient treatment program, or foster care.

If crime is be brought under control, juveniles above all must learn that there are limits to permissible behavior—that acts such as robbery, rape, burglary, and assault cannot and should not be tolerated.

Box 6-1
GETTING TOUGH WITH YOUNG OFFENDERS

In a 1982 decision, the Supreme Court took a get-tough attitude toward young offenders who commit crimes while they are in custody. In a case involving John Carroll Robinson, the Court ruled 6 to 3 that a judge can order young offenders jailed with adult criminals. The decision means that youthful criminals are not automatically entitled to stay in a rehabilitation program just because of their age. The justices held that the government is under no obligation to continue providing special treatment to John Carroll Robinson, who committed two violent acts while jailed under the youth program.

"Congress did not intend that a person who commits serious crimes while serving a sentence [under the youth program] should automatically receive treatment that has proven futile," wrote Justice Thurgood Marshall, who is noted for his usually liberal stand on prisoners'-rights issues.

Initially, at least, juveniles *expect* some kind of punishment when they are found guilty of behavior that threatens the safety and security of others. If "nothing happens" until the fourth or fifth offense (or later), young offenders are persuaded that they have an implicit contract with the juvenile court permitting them to break the law. Therefore, when something *does* happen—when a severe sanction is imposed at an earlier point—delinquents feel that their contract has been violated unilaterally, and their sense of justice is outraged.

It is hard to imagine a system better designed than our present one to reinforce delinquent behavior. This does not mean that delinquents (or adult offenders) are utilitarian creatures, rationally planning their acts and weighing and calculating their relative benefits and costs. What it does mean, David Matza explains, is "that the will to crime is encouraged when the predictable counteracting efforts of official authority are not seen as so menacing and thwarting that the potential offender is immobilized."[52] Juveniles' expectations of punishment are reflected in the streetcorner adage, "If you want to play, you gotta pay."

Some argue, however, that the price juveniles pay should be lower than for adults. Juveniles, they say, are less mature—less able to form moral judgments, less capable of controlling their impulses, less aware of the consequences of their acts. In a word, they are less responsible, hence less blameworthy, than are adults.

The diminished responsibility of juveniles flows from another equally important consideration, so the argument goes. The socialization of the young is an obligation of the whole society, not just of the parents involved; school attendance is compulsory, for instance, and courts have the power to take children away from parents who neglect or abuse them. Thus, society bears a responsibility for youth crime that it does not have in the case of adults. To point out that most juvenile criminals are victims as well as offenders is not just an expression of liberal guilt. Their acts must be condemned; but society has an obligation to do more than merely punish them for their offenses.

In the last analysis, so the argument continues, it is juveniles' malleability—their capacity for change—even more than their diminished responsibility that creates the need for a different and more lenient sentencing policy. As their stake in society increases, so do the pressures to conform to societal norms. Since the majority of juvenile offenders do in fact "grow out" of crime, it makes sense to respond to juvenile crime with that possibility in mind.

Finally, juveniles' capacity for change means that punishment ought to be accompanied by help. It has become fashionable of late to belittle (in some circles, almost to sneer at) rehabilitation. We may not know enough to help every troubled juvenile; we do not know so little that we ought to stop trying. If rehabilitation has largely failed (and it has), the remedy is not to abandon the effort with an air of sophisticated disillusionment; it is to try to understand why, and to intensify the search for approaches that offer some hope of working. The important point is that juveniles should not be incarcerated, or their liberty restricted in other ways, for the *purpose* of rehabilitation. But once the decision to punish has been made, there must be a serious attempt to provide whatever help youngsters need to become productive members of society.

THE LIMITS OF CORRECTIONAL REFORM

"The American correctional system today appears to offer minimum protection to the public and maximum harm to the offender," the 1973 Standards and Goals Commission declared in its summary report. "The system is plainly in need of substantial and rapid change."[53]

It always has been. Except for a brief period of euphoria in the early nineteenth century, when penal reformers from around the world came to the United States to study that American invention, the penitentiary, there never has been a time when the correctional system did not appear to be in need of rapid and substantial change. Since the Republic was founded, historian David Rothman has written, each generation has produced "a dedicated coterie" of prison reformers. Yet each generation "discovers anew the scandals of incarceration, each sets out to correct them and each passes on a legacy of failure. The rallying cries of one period echo dismally into the next."[54]

The Medical Model

The generally accepted theory of corrections for much of this century was based on the medical model. In its simplest terms, the medical model assumed offenders to be "sick" (physically, mentally, and/or socially); offenses were considered a manifestation or symptom of illness, a cry for help. It was believed that early and accurate diagnosis, followed by prompt and effective therapeutic intervention, assured a positive prognosis—rehabilitation. Diagnosis was the function of the presentence investigation; therapeutic intervention was decreed in the sentence and made more specific in the treatment plan devised by the correction officers; and the parole board decided (within certain legal constraints) when the patient was to be discharged back into the community as "cured."

However, today there is a shift away from the medical model to a new approach which says that justice should be based on individual responsibility with uniform penalties consistently imposed for like crimes. Out would go the indeterminate sentence (in which the number of years to be served are not fixed), virtually unlimited judicial discretion, parole, and coerced participation in rehabilitation programs. Deterrence, retribution, and incapacitation would be restored as respectable rationalizations for imprisonment; but in general, long prison terms would be reserved only for the habitually violent.

Changed Public Attitudes

The shift away from rehabilitation is due in part to changed attitudes among professionals, but also, as we have seen, it is due to changing attitudes of the public and lawmakers. Frightened by rising crime rates, the American public is demanding, in effect, that "retribution" replace rehabilitation as the purpose of incarceration. Apparently, the public's sense of fairness, fitness, and justice has turned to a punitive mood and a suspicion, bordering on contempt, about the workings of the justice system. The Victims' Bill of Rights passed by California voters in June 1982 represents growing public frustration toward criminal offenders (see Box 6-2). It contains provisions likely to be enacted elsewhere in the future.

In a 1977 study, the National Opinion Research Center found that close to 90 percent of the American public felt that the courts were "too soft on criminals." This is a dramatic increase from the 74 percent who felt that way five years earlier. Mounting concern for the debris of victims has ushered in demands for some kind of retribution. A Gallup Poll in the spring of 1978 showed 62 percent of Americans in favor of the death penalty. In a nationwide poll of high school juniors and seniors which has been conducted for many years, researchers found that 66 percent favored reinstating the death penalty in 1977—a startling shift from the 30 percent who advocated capital punishment in 1971.

Certainly, by the mid-1970s, the idea of "just desserts" was enjoying a certain vogue. Punishment, the argument went, should fit the crime and be based on no other criteria. Only so would it increase respect for the law and thus deter crime. Many elected officials used these claims in promoting mandatory sentencing laws. In any event, more people began going to jail more often. Between 1974 and 1979, the number of men in jail as a percentage of the adult male population jumped 40 percent.

Cost-Effective Justice

By the end of the 1970s, the most observable effect of tougher imprisonment policies was overcrowded prisons. As Figure 6-5 indicates, the prison population rose 94 percent between 1972 and 1982. Courts in thirty-one states soon decided that wretched prison living conditions required judicial intervention. In a typical action in 1976, Alabama judge Frank Johnson ordered state prison authorities to provide at least sixty square feet of space per inmate. State legislators soon counted up the costs of toughness—$50,000 to $70,000 for one new prison cell and $10,000 to $15,000 a year to keep a prisoner in it. During 1980–1981, voters in Michigan and New York turned down prison-building referendums. In New Mexico, the legislature approved a $107-million prison construction bill only after the worst prison riot in U.S. history left forty-three dead in the state penitentiary south of Santa Fe in February 1980.

The lesson of the 1970s seems to be that retribution as a crime-fighting philosophy has its limitations, too. While the crime

Box 6-2
THE VICTIMS' BILL OF RIGHTS

The Victims' Bill of Rights contains 10 major provisions for revising the state's criminal codes. They include:

■ Restitution: This section institutes a constitutional right to restitution for crime victims from the person convicted of the crime. Restitution would be mandated in every criminal case where a victim suffers a loss, unless extraordinary reasons exist to the contrary. Presently, restitution is provided for at the discretion of the court.

■ *Public Safety Bail:* Orders that public safety rather than surety be the key factor in granting bail or release, and provides that the seriousness of the offense charged, and criminal history, shall be considered in addition to the existing criteria regarding likelihood of appearance.

■ *Prior Convictions and Habitual Criminals:* Provides for longer terms for repeat, serious offenders. Individuals convicted of serious felonies will receive an additional five-year sentence for each previous felony conviction.

■ *Limitations of Plea Bargaining:* Prohibits plea bargaining with respect to serious felonies, or offenses of driving while under the influence of alcohol or drugs, except where there is insufficient evidence to prove the people's case, or testimony of a material witness cannot be obtained.

■ *Right to Truth in Evidence:* Would revise the so-called Exclusionary Rule, which invalidates evidence illegally taken by police, so that relevant evidence in criminal proceedings shall not be excluded, whether in an adult trial or juvenile hearing. This provision greatly expands admissible evidence.

■ *Diminished Capacity/Insanity Defense:* Abolishes the diminished capacity defense that allows evidence of mental trauma, illness, or defect on the question of whether the defendant is capable of malice or intent. The provision allows an insanity plea to stand only where it is proved that the defendant could not discern right from wrong, or understand the nature of the act at the time it was committed.

■ *Mentally Disordered Sex Offenders:* This section abolishes the Mentally Disordered Sex Offender designation that allows civil, rather than criminal, commitment of sex offenders.

■ *Victim's Statements/Public Safety Determination:* Orders that the victim or next of kin be notified of sentencing and parole hearings, and be permitted to attend and express his or her views regarding the nature of the crime.

■ *Right to Safe Schools:* Creates constitutional rights of students and staff of public K–12 schools to attend campuses that are safe and secure.

Source: San Francisco Chronicle, December 13, 1981.

Figure 6-5 THE PRISON POPULATION, 1972–1982

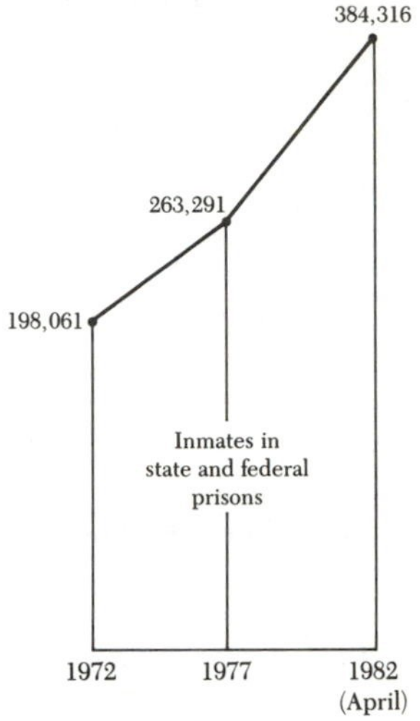

Source: U.S. Justice Department, *Bureau of Justice Statistics* (Washington, D.C.: U.S. Government Printing Office, 1982), p. 84.

rate seems of late to have steadied, population trends (i.e., we are an aging society) rather than tougher sentences are probably the reason. Meanwhile, because mandatory sentencing laws suffer from rigidity, the trend toward their adoption has slowed. New York has modified its drug laws to allow lesser offenders to plea bargain because juries often refused to convict them if conviction required harsh punishment. Among public officials, there is a new consensus that the *certainty,* not the *severity,* of punishment best deters crime.

Increasingly, criminal punishment today emphasizes cost-effectiveness above all other goals. *Incapacitation* is the byword of this new approach. The least expensive and most lenient treatment goes to criminals least likely to commit serious crimes again, regardless of the seriousness of their offense. The most expensive, that is to say, the harshest punishment goes to those who, in the words of Carnegie-Mellon University's Alfred Blumstein, "represent the greatest crime threat if they were outside, either because the crimes they will be committing are the most serious, because they will be committing them at the highest rate, or they can be expected to continue committing them for the longest time into the future." Legal attention in the 1980s focuses on the removal of the most dangerous at the least cost.

This philosophy may seem to be nothing more than common

sense, but considering how many long-accepted criminal justice goals it contradicts, it represents a significant development. The advocates of cost-effective justice take little interest in reforming the wrongdoer. They downplay the importance of "just deserts," an eye for an eye. They ignore the goal of putting away larger numbers of criminals. And they rely heavily on the unpopular sanctions of probation and parole.

Assessing "Client Risk"

Thus, the average convicted criminal is now likely to spend more time out on the streets: 1.5 million of the 2.3 million U.S. convicts in 1980 were under court-ordered "supervised release." Another 270,000 were on parole, the supervised release that follows incarceration. The number of convicts on probation or parole increased 24 percent between 1976 and 1981.

The probationer or parolee also submits to more sophisticated supervision than in the past. In Wisconsin, all convicts on release formerly met with staff supervisors once a month. Frequency of contact now ranges from once every fourteen to once every ninety days, with the figure determined by an "assessment of client risk scale" similar to ones used in release on recognizance (ROR) programs. (Taken into account are such things as the number of times the "client" has moved in the last twelve months of freedom, the percentage of this time spent employed, alcohol problems, and so on.) The test, variations of which are used elsewhere, has reduced violations by the most closely watched while not affecting violation rates among the least supervised.

Authorities are also making heavier use of halfway houses to help former prisoners become accustomed to community life. Such residences impose a certain amount of control on parolees, who must sleep at the halfway house and account for their whereabouts at work or with friends. They must take tests for alcohol and drug use—a once-cumbersome procedure now made easy by the development of portable electronic urinalysis equipment. ("Open an attaché case, perform a few simple steps . . ." begins a full-page Syva Company advertisement in an American Correctional Association directory.) Halfway houses cost half as much as prisons and are growing more common. To ease prison overcrowding during 1981–1982, California tripled the number of inmates assigned to halfway houses in major metropolitan areas. By using actuarial risk tables to select the people released, the state brought the halfway house escape rate to a twenty-year low.

Worth a Try?

Some judges have begun sentencing criminals to halfway houses with no initial stay in prison. Rather than halfway *out* of prison, these inmates are halfway *in*. With prison congestion unlikely to ease until the 1990s when, demographers say, the U.S. population of crime-prone young males will have greatly shrunk, the trend toward a "community-based" correctional system is likely to continue. In Massachusetts, halfway houses have entirely replaced reformatories for juveniles. However, the placement of halfway houses has ignited scores of "not-in-my-neighborhood" protests in places ranging from Prince George's County, Maryland, to Long Beach, California. Local opposition could retard the spread of such facilities in coming years, no matter how cost-effective they are.

While many low-risk lawbreakers may be safely placed back in the community, believers in incapacitation demand that high-risk offenders be incarcerated. Recent figures show this is happening. Between 1974 and 1979, the proportion of inmates serving time for violent crimes rose from 52 to 57 percent of all inmates. And this trend continues into the 1980s.

Whether an incapacitation policy can help lower the crime rate by locking up the most active criminals will not be known for years. Rand Corporation researcher Peter Greenwood asserts that because murder, rape, and assault are so rare for any one offender, the incidence of these crimes will not be affected by incapacitation. Nor, he believes, will "jail time" inhibit those convicted of larceny, fraud, and auto theft. And, because these offenders now go to jail infrequently, imprisoning more of them would put an intolerable burden on the prison system.[55]

"The crimes for which selective incapacitation principles appear most appropriate are burglary and robbery," Greenwood concludes. "They are the high volume predatory offenses of which the public is most fearful. They are also the offenses in which career criminals predominate, and they are the crimes for which a substantial number of convicted defendants are currently incarcerated."[56]

The logic of incapacitation appears sound, and its goal seems attainable. It offers, as other methods controlling crime once seemed to, a strategy for reducing crime without exceeding the country's capabilities. If not the most draconian solution to the problem, it is at least the best practical solution in a turbulent society where the financial cost of justice may soon rival the financial cost of crime.

SUMMING UP

There is no doubt that the United States is a violent country. A comparison of U.S. crime statistics with those of other economically developed countries rather dramatically shows the level of violence and crime in this country. In 1973, the U.S. homicide rate for males was 15.5 for each 100,000 people. In Canada, the figure was 3.2; in England, 1.0; in France, 1.1; in West Germany, 1.5; and in Japan, 1.6.[57]

Street crime is not the only crime we should be concerned with. Ironically, white-collar crime is far more pervasive and costly than street crime yet receives far less attention from the justice system, the press, and the public.

Although crime is on the rise in this country, there is every indication that the justice system is working more ineffectively than ever before. In 1974, for example, a total of $14.95 billion was spent on law enforcement by various governments in the United States. This compares with $3.35 billion in 1960. During this same period, over a quarter of a million police were added at the state and local levels.[58] Yet, crime rose sharply during this period.

There still is no consensus on whether the system can be made effective. Solutions have been proposed, and some have been tried on an experimental basis, but few people are optimistic. In fact, critics say that high levels of crime are virtually built into the nature of our society. Racism, unequal economic opportunity, and poor living conditions breed crime, and unless the fundamental problems of our socioeconomic system are eliminated, rampant crime will continue. Other observers do not believe that the poverty-leads-to-crime theory is factually correct. They argue that crime skyrocketed during the 1960s, when Americans, including blacks and other minorities, experienced considerable economic progress and opportunity. If anything, crime seems to be associated with more money and more social progress. Moreover, socialistic countries such as the Soviet Union also seem to be experiencing increased crime, so crime is not entirely a capitalist disease.

Another view of crime, also emphasizing its inevitability, sees the character of the population as the principal cause. According to this theory, young people (aged eleven to twenty-five) have traditionally been likely to commit crime. Following World War II, the U.S. experienced a baby boom, and as these postwar children began reaching adolescence in the early 1960s, crime increased dramatically. During the 1960s and 1970s, the eleven-to-twenty-five-year-old group comprised about a quarter of the population yet accounted for about 75 percent of those arrested for serious crimes.[59] People who argue this theory say the only solution is time. Eventually, as rambunctious youths mature and the birthrate declines, crime will likewise recede.

Even if this theory is true, there remain two problems. First, many of these same adolescents will have developed habitual criminal patterns and will therefore be likely to continue them into adulthood. The other problem is that many of us do not want to wait fifteen to twenty years for these children to grow up.

Frequent proposals to reduce crime now focus on rehabilitating criminals through such techniques as psychological counseling, behavior modification, job training, work-release programs, halfway houses, and education. Though some programs seem to work fairly well with certain types of people, the overall evaluation of rehabilitation efforts is fairly pessimistic.[60] Especially where "hard-core" criminals and repeated offenders are involved, rehabilitational efforts have produced meager results. It has proved very difficult to take people who have spent years being criminals and to transform them with a few months of therapy or vocational education.

The question on many minds today is: can we stop or at least greatly reduce crime? The answer is a qualified yes, if we are willing to make some difficult choices. Experience has shown that almost every type of crime *can* be drastically reduced *if* one is willing to bear the costs. For example, China once suffered from widespread opium addiction, but the problem was solved by making addiction a capital offense and executing thousands of addicts. Opium addiction is no longer a problem. Years ago, city police controlled thefts by keeping poor juveniles out of wealthy neighborhoods because "they had no business being there." Such practices are now politically unacceptable to most people.

The real issue of effectiveness, then, is how we move between our concerns for freedom and our desire to eliminate crime. A totally effective criminal justice system may be incompatible with a free society. And a totally free society would probably not last long unless people were reasonably well protected from crime. Obviously this is not an easy conflict to resolve. The indication is, however, that as violent crime increases (particularly outside of the ghettos) people will sacrifice much of their freedom in return for protection against crime.

NOTES

1. Federal Bureau of Investigation, *Uniform Crime Reports* (Washington, D.C.: U.S. Government Printing Office, 1976).
2. On homicide trends generally, see Lynn A. Curtis, *Criminal Violence* (Lexington, Mass.: Heath, 1974), esp. ch. 3; A. Joan Klebbon, "Mortality Trends for Homicide, by Age, Color, Sex: United States, 1960–1972," mimeo. (Rockville, Md.: National Center for Health Statistics, n.d.). I have updated Curtis's analysis of trends in stronger homicide through use of the FBI's *Uniform Crime Reports.*
3. A long-standing friend, who requests her name not be used. She practices law in Los Angeles, California.
4. For a discussion of the relationship of crime to race, ethnicity, and social class, see James Q. Wilson, *Thinking About Crime* (New York: Basic Books, 1975).
5. Joseph Newman, *Crime in America* (Washington, D.C.: U.S. News and World Report, 1972), p. 13.
6. Ibid., p. 23.
7. Philip H. Ennis, "Crime, Victims, and the Police," *Transaction* 4 (June 1967), 36–44; Law Enforcement Assistance Administration, National Criminal Justice Information and Statistics Service, "Criminal Victimization in 13 American Cities" (Washington, D.C.: U.S. Department of Justice, 1975); "Survey of Five Biggest Cities Shows Crime Double the Rate Reported," *Los Angeles Times,* April 15, 1976, p. A5.
8. "Tracking Crime," *Houston Post,* September 8, 1977, p. 2c.
9. John E. Conklin, *Illegal but Not Criminal: Business Crime in America* (Englewood Cliffs, N.J.: Prentice-Hall, 1977), p. 4.
10. Ibid., p. 4.
11. Gary F. Glenn, "Crime Doesn't Pay," *Readings in Criminal Justice* (Annual Edition Series, Duskin Publications, 1982), p. 107.
12. "Shoplifting Costly 'Gifts' on Holidays," *Houston Post,* December 7, 1978, p. 5a.
13. Ibid.
14. Conklin, *Illegal but Not Criminal,* p. 7.
15. John Pollock, *Figgie Report on Crime in America,* vol. 1 (sponsored by Figgie International of Willoughby, Ohio, 1980).
16. *The President's Commission Report on Law Enforcement and Administration of Justice, Task Force Report: Crime and Its Impact—An Assessment* (Washington, D.C.: U.S. Government Printing Office, 1967).
17. The relationship of race coupled with age to overall crime rates is so overpowering that Northeastern University criminologist James Alan Fox was able to project crime rates into the future with a model that employed only three "exogenous" variables. These were (1) the percent of population that is nonwhite and aged fourteen to seventeen; (2) the percent of population that is nonwhite and aged eighteen to twenty-one; and (3) the consumer price index. Fox's model is not really all that simple. In constructing it, he employed other pertinent data, such as previous local crime rates and the size of area police forces. But the three variables highlighted are important because they are the only factors that have to be estimated for the future in order to make forecasts. Furthermore, the accuracy of the Fox model has been high.
18. See Ferri's lecture given at the University of Naples, April 24, 1901, repr. in Stanley E. Grupp, ed., *Theories of Punishment* (Bloomington, Ind.: University of Indiana Press, 1971), pp. 231–233.
19. Henry W. Anclersau, "Separate Report of Henry W. Anclersau," in National Commission on Law Observance and Enforcement [Wickersham Commission], Report No. 13, *Report on the Causes of Crime* I (1931; repr. Montclair, N.J.: Patterson Smith Reprint Series, 1968), pp. LXVI, LXVIII.

20. See Wilson, *Thinking About Crime,* and Ernest van den Haag, *Punishing Criminals: Concerning a Very Old and Painful Question* (New York: Basic Books,1975). See also Macklin Fleming, *The Price of Perfect Justice* (New York: Basic Books, 1974).
21. Quoted in Raymond B. Fosdick, *American Police System* (1920; repr. Montclair, N.J.: Patterson Smith Reprint Series, 1972), p. 28.
22. Mark H. Haller, "Historical Roots of Police Behavior: Chicago, 1890–1925," *Law and Society Review* 10 (Winter 1976), 317–321. See also Yale Kamisar, "When the Cops Were Not 'Handcuffed,' " 1965, repr. in Arthur Neiderhoffer and Abraham S. Blumberg, eds., *The Ambivalent Force: Perspectives on the Police* (San Francisco: Rhinehart Press, 1973), pp. 312–317. On the nature and extent of police brutality in the 1920s and early 1930s, see Zechariah Chaffee, Jr., Walter N. Pollok, and Carl S. Stern, "The Third Degree," in National Commission on Law Observance and Enforcement [Wickersham Commission], Report No. 11, *Report on Lawlessness in Law Enforcement* I (1931; repr. Montclair, N.J.: Patterson Smith Reprint Series, 1968), pp. 13–261.
23. Robert J. diGrazia, "Police Leadership: Challenging Old Assumptions," *Washington Post,* November 10, 1976, p. 15.
24. See George L. Kelling et al., *The Kansas City Preventive Patrol Experiment: A Summary Report* (Washington, D.C.: Police Foundation, 1974), pp. 40–43, and Kelling Pate and Tony Pate, "Response to the Davis Knowles Critique of the Kansas City Preventive Patrol Experiment," *The Police Chief* (June 1975), pp. 33–34.
25. See Deborah K. Berman and Alexander Vargo, "Response-Time Analysis Study: Preliminary Findings on Robbery in Kansas City," *The Police Chief* (May 1976), pp. 74–77, and James F. Elliott, *Interception Patrol* (Springfield, Ill.: Thomas, 1973).
26. Under the exclusionary rule, evidence that was obtained illegally cannot be used in court. In a series of controversial decisions during the 1960s, the Supreme Court broadened the scope of the exclusionary rule. In *Miranda* v. *Arizona,* for example, the Court ruled that police officers must inform defendants of their right to counsel. (After the Court's ruling, Miranda was tried and convicted a second time.) The Burger Court has recently reversed many of the Warren Court decisions in this area. (See ch. 6.)
27. See Roger Lane, *Policing the City* (Cambridge, Mass.: Harvard University Press, 1967), and Clarence Schrog, *Crime and Justice: American Style* (Rockville, Ind.: National Institute of Mental Health Center for the Studies in Crime and Delinquency, 1971).
28. Herman Goldstein, *Policing a Free Society* (Cambridge, Mass.: Ballinger, 1977), p. 24.
29. David J. Bordua, "Comments on Police-Community Relations," *Law Enforcement Science and Technology* II (New York: Port City Press, 1969), 118.
30. According to the National Crime Survey for 1975, only 26 percent of the property crimes committed against individuals and 47 percent of the violent crimes were reported to the police. (The great majority of victims of commercial burglary and robbery reported these crimes.)
31. Personal interview with Joseph McNamara, Chief of Police of the City of San Jose, October 18, 1982.
32. Kelling et al., *The Kansas City Preventive Patrol Experiment,* p. 533.
33. Raymond Moley, *Politics and Criminal Prosecution* (New York: Minton, Balch, 1929), ch. 7. See also Arthur Rosett and Donald Cressey, *Justice by Consent* (Philadelphia: Lippincott, 1976), esp. pp. 53–54.
34. See James Eisenstein and Herbert Jacob, *Felony Justice* (Boston: Little, Brown, 1977).
35. See Arnold Enker, "Perspectives on Plea Bargaining," in President's Commission on Law Enforcement and Administration of Justice, *Task Force Report: The Courts* (Washington, D.C.: U.S. Government Printing Office, 1967).

36. Ibid., Appendix A.

37. See, for example, National Advisory Committee on Criminal Justice Standards and Goals, *Courts* (Washington, D.C.: U.S. Government Printing Office, 1973), pp. 42–45, and Albert W. Alschuler, "The Defense Attorney's Role in Plea Bargaining," *Yale Law Journal* 84 (May 1975), 1179–1314.

38. See, for example, Alan Carlson and Floyd Feeney, "Handling Robbery Arrestees: Some Issues of Fact and Policy," in Floyd Feeney and Adrianne Weir, eds., *The Prevention and Control of Robbery* II (Davis, Calif.: The Center on Administration of Criminal Justice, University of California–Davis, 1973), ch. 8, esp. p. 133; *PROMIS Research Project: Highlights of Interim Findings and Implications,* mimeo. (Washington, D.C.: Institute for Law and Social Research, 1977), pp. 59–60; Peter W. Greenwood et al., *Prosecution of Adult Felony Defendants in Los Angeles County: A Police Perspective* (Washington, D.C.: Law Enforcement Assistance Administration, 1973), table 46; and David W. Neubauer, *Criminal Justice in Middle America* (Morristown, N.J.: General Learning Press, 1976), pp. 166–167.

39. Vera Institute of Justice, *Felony Arrests: Their Prosecution and Disposition in New York City's Courts* (New York: The Vera Institute of Justice, 1977), pp. 166–167.

40. My own calculations from data presented in Greenwood et al., *Prosecution of Adult Felony Defendants in Los Angeles County,* tables 41, 42, 44.

41. See Vera Institute, *Felony Arrests,* and Brian E. Forst et al., *What Happens After Arrest?* (Washington, D.C.: Institute for Law and Social Research, 1977).

42. Ibid.

43. Vera Institute, *Felony Arrests,* p. 20, table E.

44. Lief H. Carter, *The Limits of Order* (Lexington, Mass.: Heath, 1974), p. 174.

45. Raymond T. Nimmer, "Criminal Justice Reform Impact: Models of Behavior and a Case Study," mimeo, Washington, D.C., May 4, 1982, pp. 72–79.

46. Roscoe Pound, "Criminal Justice in the American City—A Summary," in *Criminal Justice in Cleveland,* Report of the Cleveland Foundation Survey of the Administration of Criminal Justice in Cleveland, Ohio (1922; repr. Montclair, N.J.: Patterson Smith Reprint Series, 1968), p. 576, and Robert H. Jackson, "Criminal Justice: The Vital Problem of the Future," *American Bar Association Journal* 39 (April 1953), 743.

47. See, for example, Mirjan Damauska, "Evidentiary Barriers to Conviction and Two Models of Criminal Procedure," *University of Pennsylvania Law Review* 121, (January 1973), esp. pp. 575–576.

48. Vera Institute, *Felony Arrests,* p. 137.

49. *The President's Commission Report on Law Enforcement and Administration of Justice, Task Force Report: Crime and Its Impact—An Assessment* (Washington, D.C.: U.S. Government Printing Office, 1967).

50. "The Youth Crime Plague," *Time,* July 11, 1977, pp. 18–19. For other examples of this type, see Nicholas Pileggi, "Inside the Juvenile Justice System: How Fifteen Year Olds Get Away with Murder," *New York,* June 13, 1977; Ted Morgan, "They Think, 'I Can Kill Because I'm 14,'" *New York Times* Magazine, January 19, 1975; and Winston Groom, "Juvenile Justice System," *Washington Star,* June 7, 1975.

51. "Crime: Who, When, How, Why," *San Francisco Chronicle,* November 16, 1982, p. B-22.

52. David Matza, *Delinquency and Drift* (New York: Wiley, 1964), p. 186.

53. National Advisory Commission on Criminal Justice Standards and Goals, *Community Crime Prevention,* Washington, D.C.: U.S. Government Printing Office, 1973, p. 9.

54. David J. Rothman, "Decarcerating Prisoners and Patients," *Civil Liberties Review* 1 (Fall 1973), 8–9.

55. Peter Greenwood, "Career Criminal Prosecution: Potential Objectives," *The*

Journal of Criminal Law and Criminology, Vol. 71, No. 2 (Summer 1980), p. 74.

56. Ibid., p. 16.
57. These figures are cited in van den Haag, *Punishing Criminals,* p. 163.
58. U.S. Department of Commerce, Bureau of the Census, *Statistical Abstract of the United States, 1977* (Washington, D.C.: U.S. Government Printing Office, 1978), pp. 164–165.
59. See Titos Reid, *Crime and Criminology* (New York: Holt, Rinehart and Winston, 1976), pp. 58–59. According to the FBI, in 1975 those under twenty-five accounted for 95.5 percent of all criminal homicides, 77.0 percent of all robberies, 85.2 percent of all burglaries, and 84.6 percent of all motor vehicle thefts.
60. James Q. Wilson, *Varieties of Police Behavior: The Management of Law and Order in Eight Communities* (Cambridge, Mass.: Harvard University Press, 1968), pp. 168–170.

GLOSSARY

Adjudication: The formal giving, pronouncing, or recording of a judgment for one side or the other in a lawsuit.

Adjudicative facts: Facts about the person who have a dispute before an administrative agency. These are the "who, what, where, etc." facts that are similar to the facts that would go to a jury in a court trial. They are different from legislative facts.

Adversary system: The system of law in the United States. The judge acts as the decision maker between opposite sides (two individuals, the state and an individual, and so forth) rather than acting as the person who also makes the state's case or independently seeks out evidence. This latter method is called the *inquisitorial system.*

Bail: 1. A person who puts up money or property to allow the release of a person in jail until time of trial. 2. The money or property put up by the person in no. 1. This money, often in the form of a bail bond, may be lost if the person released does not appear in court. 3. The process of releasing the person for whom a bail bond was supplied.

Determinate sentence: An exact prison term that is set by law rather than one that may be shortened by good behavior or the actions of a parole board.

Diminished responsibility: A state of mind, less than complete insanity, that may lessen a person's punishment for a crime. For example, mental retardation is often accepted as a reason to lower the degree of a crime or lessen the punishment.

Exclusionary rule: 1. A reason why even relevant evidence will be kept out of a trial. 2. "The exclusionary rule" often means the rule that illegally gathered evidence may not be used in a criminal trial.

Felony: Generally, an offense punishable by death or imprisonment in a penitentiary.

Indeterminate sentence: A sentence for which there is not a determined or fixed number of years to be served.

Misdemeanor: Any crime not a felony. Usually, a crime punishable by a fine or imprisonment in the county or other local jail.

Parole: A release from prison, before a sentence is finished, that depends on the parolees "keeping clean" and doing what they are supposed to do while out. If parolees fail to meet these conditions, the rest of the sentence must be served. Parole decisions are made by a state or federal parole board or corrections board, and persons out on parole are supervised by parole officers.

Plea bargaining: Discussions between a prosecutor and a criminal defendant's lawyer in which the defense lawyer generally offers to have the defendant plead guilty in exchange for the prosecutor's agreeing to accept a plea to a less serious charge, to drop some charges, or to promise not to request a heavy sentence from the judge.

Probation: A penalty placing a convicted person under the supervision of a probation officer for a stated time, instead of being confined.

Procedural law: The rules of carrying on a lawsuit (how to enforce rights in court) as opposed to "substantive law" (the law of the rights and duties themselves).

Recidivism: The rearrest of an individual previously convicted of a crime.

Victimless crime: An act in which the parties involved knowingly and voluntarily engaged in the behavior, e.g., homosexuality, viewing of pornography.

SUGGESTED READINGS

Berns, Walter. *For Capital Punishment: Crime and the Morality of the Death Penalty.* New York: Basic Books, 1981.

Black, Charles L. *Capital Punishment: The Inevitability of Caprice and Mistake.* New York: Norton, 1981.

Clark, Ramsey. *Crime in America.* New York: Simon and Schuster, 1970.

Cloward, Richard A., and Ohlin, Lloyd. *Delinquency and Opportunity.* New York: Free Press, 1966.

Cohen, Albert K. *Delinquent Boys.* New York: Free Press, 1971.

Hirschi, Travis. *Causes of Delinquency.* Berkeley: University of California Press, 1969.

Ker Muir, William. *Police: Streetcorner Politicians.* Chicago: University of Chicago Press, 1977.

Prescott, Peter. *A Prison and a Prisoner.* Boston: Houghton Mifflin, 1978.

————. *The Child Savers.* New York: Knopf, 1981.

Silberman, Charles. *Criminal Violence, Criminal Justice.* New York: Random House, 1980.

Sutherland, Edwin H., and Cressey, Donald R. *Principles of Criminology,* 10th ed. New York: Harper & Row, 1978.

Walker, Samuel. *Popular Justice.* New York: Oxford University Press, 1980.

Wilson, James Q. *Thinking About Crime.* New York: Random House, 1977.

7

Fundamentalism and Politics: The New Religious Right

What is the traditional role of religion in American politics?

What people constitute the New Religious Right? What do they mean by *secular humanism*, and where did the term come from?

How does the New Religious Right conduct its campaign against selected targets?

Are the moral and social issues of the New Religious Right new to American politics? If not, why do they seem new to us?

What are the dangers of mixing politics and religion?

Social change is continuous and endlessly complex. To contrast the manners and morals of one historical "period" with those of another is surely to oversimplify and almost surely to exaggerate. Yet, the social climate does alter, just as the seasons do change.

Whether, as some say, the past two decades have been more socially and politically corrupt and disquieting than other periods in our history is open to debate. People in every generation undoubtedly wish for a *return* to a seemingly more tranquil and innocent past. Even so, it can be said that the social climate during the 1960s and 1970s has helped to make *morality* an important political issue. We have been rocked by scandal in high places, including government corruption and the sight of American youths living in cults or living together outside of marriage. Attitudes are changing, and so are life-styles. Such turbulent changes bring moral issues even closer to the experience of ordinary Americans.

220

RELIGIOUS FUNDAMENTALISM AND THE NEW RIGHT

The issue of morality has helped to bring together religious fundamentalism and the political New Right to form perhaps the most significant political feature on the American landscape today. According to Wesley McCune, head of Group Research, Inc., which for two decades has been monitoring radical political thought in the United States, "It is the most important development on the right since 1964" when Barry Goldwater was nominated as the Republican Party's presidential candidate. Aided particularly by fundamentalist Christian evangelists with vast television audiences and orchestrated primarily by quasi-religious organizations with an avowed political purpose, the movement has sought to unite right-wing conservative faith with right-wing conservative politics, largely around a dozen or so key issues. While the impact of this movement may not be measurable for some time to come, the alliance of religious fundamentalism with the political New Right during the past few years is not to be taken lightly. The movement's political power, for example, was very much felt during the 1980 elections. And although it fared less well in the 1982 elections, it nevertheless remains a potent political power. Clearly, fundamentalist Christians are forming a growing new force in American politics and are shifting away from their traditional view that "religion and politics don't mix."

In this chapter, we will look at the traditional place religion has held in the American political system. Although organized religion has been an important force in this country, we will find that today's fundamentalist movement, in both scope and character, is significantly different. These differences will be examined and their implications for the political system will be described. Finally, we will look at some of the moral issues expounded by the fundamentalist–New Right coalition.

THE ORIGINS OF SEPARATION OF CHURCH AND STATE

The political and social foundation of the American Revolution was the moral and intellectual revolution, known as the Age of Enlightenment, from which Jefferson, Madison, and the other major architects of American freedom drew their inspiration. But what was the force that these philosophers of the seventeenth and eighteenth centuries unleashed that so mightily transformed history? Essentially, they did an about-face from the doctrine of human nature that had prevailed for most of Christian history. They denied that human nature is essentially evil; they affirmed the human capacity for self-government; and they provided the moral foundation for a reasonable belief in human freedom and progress.

How, they asked, do we distinguish good from evil? What is the basis of morality and ethics? The orthodox religious answer had always been divine revelation. We can know the good only as God has revealed it to us through his prophets. Moses had received his tablets of the Law on Sinai. In Christian ethical thought, God had delivered his moral law through a succession of seers culminating in the advent of Christ. Scripture, interpreted by an authoritative church, was the final depository of moral truth. Theocracy follows as the logical government derived from such a moral philosophy.

Although most of the liberal thinkers of the late seventeenth century believed in a Supreme Being as the first cause and were either deists—believers in human reason rather than revelation—or liberal Christians, they turned their backs on the ancient authorities of Scripture and priesthood as the necessary depositories of moral knowledge. They reasoned that ancient holy books were fallible and could be further corrupted in transmission, while priesthoods were often self-serving and oppressive.

In effect, they concluded, we have no need for such uncertain and arbitrary authorities, which would keep the mind enslaved. The only revelation of the moral law we require, they argued, comes from an understanding of nature and human reason. By studying nature, including the social nature of humankind, we can discover the principles of morality and thus equip ourselves to live as morally free beings.

This was a bold declaration of spiritual independence, and on this foundation liberal philosophy and the *secular* constitutional democracy were constructed in their modern form. Jefferson welcomed this moral philosophy because it set the mind free. He believed that as our knowledge of psychology and of social behavior increased, we would be better able to understand nature, including moral nature.

While Jefferson stands out boldly as the most philosophically literate of the architects of American freedom (with at least Madison receiving far less public recognition than he deserves), he was not alone in his attachment to religious liberalism and tolerance. Frank-

lin, Madison, Monroe, the Adamses, and Washington were all het-
erodox or "liberal" in their religious beliefs and firmly committed
to the creation of a secular government that might be independent
of ecclesiastical ties or theological sanctions.

RELIGION AS A POLITICAL FORCE

Although church-state separation has been both a constitutional
and political reality in the United States, it would be difficult to conceive of a nation in which there has been closer interpenetration
of religion and society. Religion has played an important political
role in America and has not been relegated to the purely personal
and private concerns of citizens.

It is interesting, for example, that nineteenth-century European visitors to this country were impressed that here they found
on the one hand church-state separation and on the other the un-
mistakable influence of religion on the total life of the Republic. Indeed, it was this apparent paradox that prompted Alexis de Tocqueville, a French Catholic, "to inquire how it happened that the real
authority of religion was increased by a state of things which diminished its apparent force." Tocqueville came to see that church-state
separation had a direct relationship to the influence of religion on
American national life. The paradox of church-state separation and
interaction was perhaps never more succinctly stated than when
Tocqueville wrote, "Religion in America takes no direct part in the
government of society, but it must be regarded as the first of their
political institutions."[1]

While the U.S. Supreme Court has repeatedly interpreted the
First Amendment to ensure the separation of church and state, it
is significant that in church-state relations, the Constitution explicitly places prohibitions on the state and not on religion or the
churches. This does not mean that institutional independence of
both church and state is not clearly the intention of the Constitution, but it does indicate that organized religion is indeed legally
free to operate in the political sphere and, so far as the Constitution
is concerned, is guaranteed through "the free exercise of religion"
the right to engage in political action and witness in public affairs.
This the churches and synagogues have done through U.S. history,
from the colonial period down to the present.[2]

After all, it was religion, at least in part, which gave birth to
America. "Religious considerations," as Charles A. Beard wrote,
"entered in the founding of every colony from New England to

Georgia."[3] From the nation's beginning, religion played an important part in the election of public officials—local, state, and national. Religion figured prominently in presidential nominations and campaigns almost from the beginning of our history, as evidenced in the first campaign of Thomas Jefferson during the period of the Second Great Awakening.[4] In at least one-third of the presidential campaigns, religion has played a conspicuous role.[5]

At no time was organized religion in the United States more active politically than in the twenty years prior to the Civil War. The morality of slavery, for example, became a major issue in the nineteenth century.

THERE IS A DIFFERENCE

In both extent and character, however, today's Christian fundamentalism plays a radically different role than that previously played by organized religion in American politics. There are three basic differences worth remembering. First, there is the politicization of fundamentalism, which is itself a new and significant phenomenon (more will be said about this in a moment). There have been earlier political expressions of fundamentalism, such as its vigorous opposition to the teaching of evolution in the public schools during the twenties (and now recently revived), but such isolated excursions were narrowly confined to single-issue politics and were not a part of a comprehensive political agenda for action.

Second, the fundamentalist political crusade is neither a call to mere single-issue politics nor to Christians to become involved in politics for its own sake. Rather, it is a call to a political ideology, a political agenda, and partisan political action. The partisan politics being advanced is the inevitable result of an alliance between religious fundamentalism and the New Right—the religious far right joined with the political far right. This development is in marked contrast to the tradition of main-line religious denominations—Catholic, Protestant, and Jewish—which have generally seen their role in the political process to be one of advocacy of ideas in the formulation of public policy and not the advancement of partisan politics or the election of particular candidates.

The third difference is the massive attempt at political mobilization of one segment of organized religion, aimed at the implementation of a broad range of political objectives and, eventually, a political takeover. This activity is on a scale unprecedented in the nation's history. Through a mass communications network of thirty-six religious television stations and thirteen-hundred religious radio stations, fundamentalist preachers of the far right now reach an estimated weekly audience of 115 million. Jerry Falwell, leader of the Moral Majority, alone is programmed weekly through almost four hundred television stations in the United States. His organization pays $300,000 per week to buy radio and television air time, far more than is available to political candidates or even to American political parties on a week-by-week basis.

WHAT THE NEW RIGHT OPPOSES

The evil force that the New Right opposes is identified as "the religion of secular humanism." What is meant is any belief the new fundamentalists regard as unbiblical or "liberal"—especially beliefs and habits of thinking derived from modern science or the Age of Enlightenment.

The term *secular humanism* comes from a 1961 landmark opinion *(Torcaso* v. *Watkins)* of the United States Supreme Court which declared that those who hold ethical or nontheistic humanist beliefs are entitled to the same constitutional rights of religious freedom as those holding traditional beliefs. This straightforward application of the First Amendment to protect religious freedom for all deeply rankles those who think the religious protection clause of the Constitution should be restricted to traditional theological beliefs. The New Religious Right supports the freedom to be religious the "fundamentalist" Christian way, but not the freedom to be protected in holding differing beliefs.

In their confusion of issues, the proponents of the New Religious Right charge that the public schools are promoting secular humanism as a state religion. According to their logic, if the state refrains from promoting prayer in the schools, or does not teach the biblical account of creation, this restraint is tantamount to establishing humanism as the state religion. Since the Supreme Court noted that humanistic religions exist in the United States and are equally entitled to recognition as religions, the religious right makes a gigantic leap to the conclusion that all humanistic beliefs and values are religious. (It would be equally sensible to argue that since some dietary laws are religiously derived, all considerations of diet must be regarded as religious.)

Furthermore, the New Religious Right holds the humanists and "liberals" responsible for the wreckage of the American family and the "decadence" of the nation. One remembers that in the last days of the Weimar Republic, before Hitler's rise to power, liberals and "cosmopolitans" were similarly assailed by extremists of both left and right as the authors of social decay and corruption.

Thus, while most Americans have gone complacently about their business, the forces of intolerance have been gathering in a movement toward religious distrust and intolerance. This organized threat to religious liberty goes by many names: the Moral Majority, the New Religious Right, the Christian New Right, the New Fundamentalism. Whatever the name, it preaches distrust of religious pluralism and secular democracy.

The foremost champion of this cult of intolerance has described Americans who hold a liberal or humanistic philosophy in terms that invite scorn and rejection. The Reverend Jerry Falwell declares, "The godless minority of treacherous individuals . . . must now realize they do not represent the majority. They must be made to see that moral Americans . . . will no longer permit them to destroy our country with their godless, liberal philosophies."[6]

Another leader of the authoritarian right, Gary Potter, leader of Catholics for Christian Political Action, states baldly that liberalism is a sin, a rebellion against God, to which Falwell adds, "Secular humanism is nothing but communism waiting in the wings to be crowned with its political rights."[7]

Jean Belsante, a spokeswoman of a group calling itself Citizens United for Responsible Education, is even more direct in pointing an accusing finger at specific liberal religious, educational, and civic groups. Such people are part of an organized network, she alleges, which has been "working for decades to eradicate every trace of the Judeo-Christian heritage from our national life." She goes on gravely:

> This network is directed by an anti-God leadership that manipulates such organizations as the American Humanist Association, the American Ethical Union, the Unitarian Universalist Association, and the American Civil Liberties Union—the latter acting as the cartel's legal arm. The cartel works in concert with scores of atheistic "front-groups" including a number of "social health" agencies such as Planned Parenthood.[8]

But why is humanism so often singled out as the great devil of the new fundamentalists? Sixty years ago, the grandfathers of today's religious right deplored modernism and Darwinism. They still deny the overwhelming evidence for human evolution. Humanism is simply the current expression of their old bête noire, the spirit of free inquiry and scientific thinking applied to the problems of personal and social living.

Probably not one fundamentalist in a thousand could have defined a humanist before the Jerry Falwells, James Robinsons, and others like them made *humanism* a code word for infidelity, moral indifference, and selfishness. While it is flattering to a handful of humanistic philosophers and religious liberals to have such inordinate influence attributed to them, this inflated attack cannot simply be shrugged off as a bad joke played upon the ignorant. For the moment, "secular humanists" make an adequate devil, despite their limited numbers and power.

But as the authoritarian rightists flex their muscles and acquire a measure of political power, they will need other devils. Moderate political and business leaders and even responsible conservatives will not be immune from their venom. Former President Jimmy Carter, for example, a twice-born evangelical Christian of undoubted sincerity, was detested for his loyalty to the constitutional principle of church-state separation and opposition to an antiabortion amendment.

BUILDING THE AUDIENCE

There are a great many Americans who are tempted to blame the nation's troubles on one group or another labeled "immoral." The New Religious Right's leadership knows this and sees it as its opportunity to lead. While the inner circle of planners who have charted and organized the right is primarily motivated by secular, economic ideologies and interests, it was quick to recognize the religiously conservative and evangelical masses as an invaluable, perhaps essential, component in their design to build a majority.

The New Religious Right's problem was that evangelical religion, especially its ultraconservative fundamentalist form, had tended to be *apolitical.* Fundamentalist evangelists preached salvation in the world to come with little attention to the present life, except for the familiar denunciation of sin and worldliness. The faithful were urged to forsake godless civilization, soon to be destroyed in God's coming day of wrath, and to save themselves for life hereafter.

But astute right-wing organizers quickly recognized the growing importance of single-issue politics in bringing down liberal and centrist politicians; opposition to gun control and prayer in the schools and support of homosexual rights, the ERA, and, above all, the right to have abortions proved to be fatal controversies for politicians who collided with the locomotive of single-issue politics.

The New Right's intellectual leaders saw the possibility of altering the existing alignments of American politics. A vast population, numbering some 25 percent of the nation, was highly responsive to the "moral" issues of sex, family, and patriotism. By and large, they were the less-educated, less-privileged fourth of the nation. The majority of this target population were white, Protestant or ethnic Catholic, and working class—the "mid-Americans" who during the 1960s and early 1970s had displayed increasing resentment at what they perceived as special treatment or "coddling" of racial minorities, women, antiwar youth, homosexuals, and "Communists."

Their religious leaders, especially among southern and midwestern evangelicals, became increasingly vocal about pornography, drugs, relaxing sexual standards, and the weakening of stable family structures. Godlessness and immorality, fostered by permissive educators and the recently discovered bogeyman—"secular humanism"—provided convenient scapegoats for the stresses and traumas of social dislocation.

But the fact that liberals and "humanists" shared the same perplexities of rapid change and social disruption was lost on much of this population. If drugs were out of control, then permissive parents and teachers were to blame. Were marriages breaking down and children dropping out? Experts might be baffled by the human casualties of a technological civilization's exploding complexity—but the electronic preachers had no doubt: sin and rebellion against God were the root causes of our social distress. The willful agents of these evils were "secular humanists" and a decadent, degenerate "liberalism" that provided no moral absolutes.

We may not admire the New Right's political calculations or goals, but we can hardly convict its proponents of being stupid. While the two major parties and most political activists played familiar tunes to the usual audiences, New Right ideologues fetched a major constituency. At the time, very few even took notice.

If the nation's pundits had been paying closer attention instead of simply reprocessing each other's received wisdom, we would have recognized the emergence of the evangelicals as a political force in the precipitous rise of Jimmy Carter in the presidential primaries of 1976. The unexpected success and equally swift fall of President Carter must in large be explained by this phenomenon. The usual explanations of Carter's downfall are somewhat unsatisfactory in retrospect. Carter's real failure, beyond superficial explanations of "incompetence" and "vacillation," sprang from his inability to hold his original conservative Christian base. He was never favored or accepted by the Democratic establishment. From the outset he was the outsiders' candidate, and when in office Carter showed that his social philosophy was basically mainstream—his personal religious fervor notwithstanding—he was soon abandoned by his early evangelical boosters.

NEW RIGHT LEADERS—SHREWD AND LUCKY

The New Right's political architects have been skillful and shrewd. They have also been lucky. There are many diverse strands and conflicting interests in the fabric of their new conservative coalition, and despite their careful weaving, their alliance may soon begin to fray at the edges.

Contrary to the current identification of "moral" issues with the religious and ideological right, during much of American history, questions of morality have been addressed by humanitarian and progressive causes. The forcible removal of the southeastern Indian tribes in the 1830s was resisted by both liberal and evangelical religious groups as unjust and contrary to the spiritual vision of all people as children of God. The rejection of slavery on moral and religious grounds, beginning with the Quakers and spreading to the evangelical churches—as well as to the unorthodox and theologically liberal Unitarians and Universalists—is a story familiar to most of us. Perhaps less appreciated is the record of the early and determined hostility to slavery of the small farmers of the Piedmont and mountain South. These Calvinist and evangelical rural and highland folk hated the aristocratic planters of the tidewater and organized the southern reaches of the underground railroad that smuggled thousands of fugitive slaves to freedom.

The leaders of the New Right have effectively used fundamentalist religion's rejection of systematic theology and philosophy. They argue that the Bible is the only church law and admonish all believers to read and interpret for themselves, provided the interpretation is literal. The result is a predictable penchant to prove whatever one wishes to prove with an appropriate scriptural text, however far removed the text may be from the question at hand. Fundamentalist theology derives from the method of elevating a few favored biblical passages concerning creation and salvation to total and final authority, while the considerable bulk of biblical literature and history that might cast a different light on religion and ethics is steadfastly ignored or conveniently "harmonized" with whatever the beholder seeks to maintain.

The inclination to see all moral and religious truth as immediately available to all right-thinking, right-believing people makes it easy for politicians to tap religious prejudice by playing upon instinctive attitudes of moral superiority over novel and unfamiliar life-styles and beliefs. The real foundation of fundamentalism is unyielding rural American custom, before which even the meaning of the Bible must conform.

Yet the self-image of the conservative or fundamentalist evangelical remains that of the outsider, the saving remnant rejected by the world and suffering persecution for Christ's sake. To remain unstained by the world is a recurring admonition. One accepts "worldly" honors and power at risk to the soul. The resulting standoffishness of fundamentalist religion and culture, combined with its recurring proclivity to splinter into sects and factions, has made it a difficult base on which to build a stable political movement. Even so, single issues of a moralistic character—such as Prohibition early in the twentieth century and the antievolution laws of the 1920s—have provided platforms for political careers and national crusades.

CONTRADICTIONS WITHIN

Brilliant as their electoral strategy may have been in 1980, New Right leaders will find their religious partnership a highly volatile and difficult marriage of convenience. We saw evidence of this in the 1982 elections. A high unemployment rate, or a continued low in housing construction, may loom larger in the minds of bricklayers and roofers than questions of whether a political candidate attends church or favors prayer in school or abortion.

A basic contradiction eats at the heart of the "new conservatism." Paul Weyrich, the model "new conservative," illustrates the schism in the conservative philosophy. Weyrich states bluntly, "We are different from previous generations of conservatives. . . . We are radicals, working to overturn the present power structure of the country." We should note, however, that most evangelicals are not ideological zealots, however uncomfortable they may be in a fast-moving world that deals roughly with their most cherished institutions and values. They want stability and reassurance, an affirmation of familiar life patterns and inherited values, not new ideological ventures that threaten economic and social benefits they are just beginning to enjoy.

The contradiction imbedded in the effort of the New Right to be both conservative, in the accepted American sense, and "radical" in methods and objectives, is already producing stresses and confrontations. Senator Barry Goldwater's publicly expressed wish to kick the backside of the Reverend Jerry Falwell, which the senator later expanded into a speech condemning the moral arrogance and authoritarianism of the Moral Majority and other New Right preachers, struck many as surprising. Yet, except for the force of Senator Goldwater's expression and candor, there should be nothing unexpected in a statement highlighting the contradiction within the New Right movement. An irrepressible conflict brews within this incompatible marriage of traditional, liberty-loving American individualism—the essence of the "old" conservatism—and the authoritarianism and coerciveness of twentieth-century right-wing radicalism.

The New Right seeks to exploit the popular desire to "get the government off our backs and out of our lives." It proposes to achieve this objective by abridging the First Amendment to mandate state-sponsored "voluntary" prayer in public education, by amending the Constitution to overturn the right to privacy upheld by the Supreme Court with respect to abortion, by writing legislation to restrict the power of the courts to review violations of civil liberties, and so on. In short, the New Right's intrusion of state power into every facet of personal life is the antithesis of traditional American conservatism, which shared with Jeffersonian liberalism a profound respect for constitutional liberties and privacy of conscience. It is, therefore, hardly any wonder that a veteran conservative such as Senator Goldwater objects to this crusade against personal moral freedom masquerading as conservatism.

In the judgment of many evangelical theologians, the politicized fundamentalism of the New Right is a heresy. It perverts the gospel to a worldly purpose and violates the Pauline injunction to "be all things to all men" in order to serve the cause of bringing souls to Christ. Paul was not advising duplicity, as a modern reading of his words might imply. He was urging the true follower of the gospel not to violate the personality of others, to reach out on the basis of empathy and understanding of the nonbeliever's experience and moral awareness.

Many observers believe that evangelical Christians who are well grounded in their religion are not likely to be co-opted by the radical right, or by any other authoritarian political or economic movement. To do so would be to subordinate and deflect the purpose of their faith. When Billy Graham said of Jerry Falwell, "I told him to preach the gospel. That is our calling," Graham was perhaps pronouncing a prophecy of the ultimate failure of the New Right's effort to suborn religion for political ends.

But as prophetic as that may be for the future, the religious right has today assembled a formidable, often militant minority with a demonstrated ability to swing elections, shake legislators, and harass school boards. It is therefore worth examining some of the "moral" issues expounded by the New Right. We may be surprised by what we learn.

THE AMERICAN FAMILY

The New Religious Right and others tell us the American family is in a terrible state of collapse. True, the statistics seem alarming. The U.S. divorce rate remains the highest in American history, and the number of births out of wedlock among all American races and ethnic groups continues to climb. Yet, there are certain ironies about the much-publicized crisis that make one wonder.

What puzzles some is an ambiguity—not in the facts, but in what we are asked to make of them. A series of opinion polls conducted in 1978 by Yankelovich, Skelley, and White, for example, found that 38 percent of those surveyed had recently witnessed one or more "destructive activities" (for example, a divorce, a separation, a custody battle) within their own families or those of their parents or siblings. At the same time, 92 percent of the respondents said the family was highly important to them as a "personal value."

Can the family be at once a cherished "value" and a troubled institution? Perhaps we can say that the two go hand in hand. Like politics or athletics, the family has become a media event. Television offers nightly portrayals of lump-in-throat family "normality" *(The Waltons, Little House on the Prairie)* and even humorous "deviance" *(One Day at a Time, The Odd Couple, Three's Company)*. Family advisers sally forth in syndicated newspaper columns to uphold standards, mend relationships, suggest counseling, and otherwise lead their readers back to the True Path. Advertisers spend millions of dollars to create stirring vignettes of glamorous-but-ordinary families, the kind of families most eleven-year-olds wish they had.

All Americans do not, of course, live in such families, but most of us share an intuitive sense of what the "ideal" family should be—reflected in the precepts of religion, the conventions of etiquette, and the assumptions of law. And characteristically, Americans tend to project the ideal back into the past, the time when virtues of all sorts are thought to have flourished.

We Imagine the Past to Be Better Than It Was

We do not come off well by comparison with that golden age, nor could we, for it is as elusive and mythical as Brigadoon. More important, when judging today's family, we do not bother to ask how it was in yesteryear. For example, the White House Conference on Families in 1980 was "policy-oriented," which means present-minded. The familiar, depressing charts of "leading family indicators"—marriage, divorce, illegitimacy—in newspapers and news magazines rarely survey the trends before World War II. The discussion, in short, lacks balance.

Let us therefore go back to before the American Revolution. We find that perhaps what most differentiates the modern family from its colonial counterpart is its new-found privacy. Throughout the seventeenth and eighteenth centuries, well over 90 percent of the American population lived in small rural communities. Unusual behavior rarely went unnoticed, and neighbors often intervened directly in a family's affairs, to help or to chastise.

The most dramatic example was the rural charivari, prevalent in both Europe and the United States until the early nineteenth century. The purpose of these noisy gatherings was to censure community members for familial transgressions—unusual sexual behavior, marriages between persons of grossly different ages, or "household disorders," to name but a few. As historian Edward Shorter describes it:

> Sometimes the demonstration would consist of masked individuals circling somebody's house at night, screaming, beating on pans, and blowing cow horns . . . on other occasions, the offender would be seized and marched through the streets, seated perhaps backwards on a donkey or forced to wear a placard describing his sins.[9]

The boundaries between home and society were blurred during the colonial era. People were neither very emotional nor very self-conscious about family life and, as historian John Demos points out, family and community were "joined in a relation of profound reciprocity."[10] William George, a seventeenth-century Puritan preacher, called the family "a little community." The home, like the larger community, was as much an economic as a social unit; all members of the family worked, be it on the farm, in a shop, or in the home.

There was not much to idealize. Love was not considered the basis for marriage but one possible result of it. According to historian Carl Degler, it was easier to obtain a divorce in colonial New England than anywhere else in the Western world, and the divorce rate climbed steadily throughout the eighteenth century though it remained low by contemporary standards.[11] Romantic images to the contrary, it was rare for more than two generations (parents and children) to share a household, for the simple reason that very few people lived beyond the age of sixty. It is ironic that our nostalgia for the extended family—including grandparents and grandchildren—comes at a time when thanks to improvements in health care, its existence is less threatened than ever before.

Differences More Psychological

In simple demographic terms then, the differences between the American family in colonial times and today are not all that stark; the similarities are sometimes striking.[12]

The chief contrast is psychological. While Western societies have always idealized the family to some degree, the most vivid literary portrayals of family life before the nineteenth century were negative or at best ambivalent. In what might be called the "high tragic" tradition—including Sophocles, Shakespeare, and the Bible as well as fairy tales and novels—the family was portrayed as a high-voltage emotional setting, laden with dark passion, sibling rivalries, and violence. There was also the "low comic" tradition—the world of henpecked husbands and tyrannical mothers-in-law. It is unlikely that our eighteenth-century ancestors ever left the Book of Genesis or *Tom Jones* with the feeling that their own family lives were seriously flawed.

By the time of the Civil War, however, American attitudes toward the family had changed profoundly. The early decades of the nineteenth century marked the beginnings of America's gradual transformation into an urban, industrial society. In 1820, less than 8 percent of the U.S. population lived in cities; by 1860, the urban concentration approached 20 percent, and by 1900 that proportion had doubled.

Structurally, the American family did not immediately undergo a comparable transformation. Despite the large families of many immigrants and farmers, the size of the *average* family de-clined—slowly but steadily—as it had been doing since the seven-teenth century. Infant mortality remained about the same and may even have increased somewhat, owing to poor sanitation in crowded cities. Legal divorces were easier to obtain than they had been in colonial times. Indeed, the rise in the divorce rate was a matter of some concern during the nineteenth century, though death, not divorce, was then the prime cause of one-parent families, as it was up to 1965.[13]

Functionally, however, America's industrial revolution had a lasting effect on the family. No longer was the household typically a group of interdependent workers. Now men went to offices and factories and became breadwinners; wives stayed home to mind the hearth; and children went off to the new public schools. The home was set apart from the dog-eat-dog arena of economic life; it came to be viewed as a utopian retreat or, in historian Christopher Lasch's phrase, a "haven in a heartless world." Marriage was now valued primarily for its emotional attractions. Above all, the family became something for us to focus on and worry about.

In the late 1800s, science came into the picture. The "profes-sionalization" of the housewife took two different forms. One in-volved motherhood and child-rearing according to the latest scien-tific understanding of children's special physical and emotional needs. (It is no accident that the publishing of children's books be-came a major industry during this period.) The other was the do-mestic science movement—"home economics," basically—which focused on woman as full-time homemaker, applying "scientific" and "industrial" rationality to shopping, making meals, and house-work.

If anything, family standards became even more demanding as the twentieth century progressed. The new fields of psychology and sociology opened up whole new definitions of familial perfec-tion. "Feelings"—fun, love, warmth, good orgasm—acquired heightened popular significance as the invisible glue of successful families.

In an analysis of several decades of government-sponsored in-fant care manuals, psychologist Martha Wolfenstein has docu-mented the emergence of a "fun morality." In former days, being a good parent meant carrying out certain tasks with punctilio; if your children were clean and reasonably obedient, you had no cause to probe their psyches. Now, we are told, parents must commune with their own feelings and those of their children—an edict which has seeped into the ethos of education as well. The distinction is rather like that between religions of deed and religions of faith. It is one thing to make your children brush their teeth; it is quite another to transform the whole process into a joyous "learning experience."[14]

The task of twentieth-century parents has been further complicated by the advice offered them. The experts disagree with each other and often say different things at different times. The kindly Dr. Benjamin Spock, for example, is full of contradictions. In a detailed analysis of *Baby and Child Care,* historian Michael Zuckerman observes that Spock tells mothers to relax ("trust yourself") yet warns them that they have an "ominous power" to destroy their children's innocence and make them discontented "for years" or even "forever."

The Family In Transition

As we enter the 1980s, both family images and family realities are in a state of transition. After a century and a half, the web of attitudes and nostrums comprising the "sentimental model" is beginning to unravel. Since the mid-1960s, there has been a youth rebellion of sorts, a new "sexual revolution," a revival of feminism, and the emergence of the two-worker family. The huge postwar baby boom generation is pairing off, accounting in part for the upsurge in the divorce rate (half of all divorces occur within seven years of a first marriage). Media images of the family have become more "realistic," reflecting new patterns of family life that are emerging and old patterns that are reemerging. (We should note, however, that for all the talk of new life-styles, the traditional family is still the norm in this country. As Figure 7-1 shows, the 1982 population census found 73 percent of Americans—as opposed to 82 percent in 1970—to be living in households headed by married persons.)

Among social scientists, "realism" is becoming something of an idea in itself. For some of them, realism translates as pluralism: all forms of the family, by virtue of the fact that they happen to exist, are equally acceptable—from communes and cohabitation to one-parent households, homosexual marriages, and, come to think of it, the nuclear family. What was once labeled "deviant" is now merely "variant." In some college texts, "the family" has been replaced by "family systems." Yet, this new approach does not seem to have squelched perfectionist standards. Nor, therefore, has it

Figure 7-1 WHO'S AT HOME?

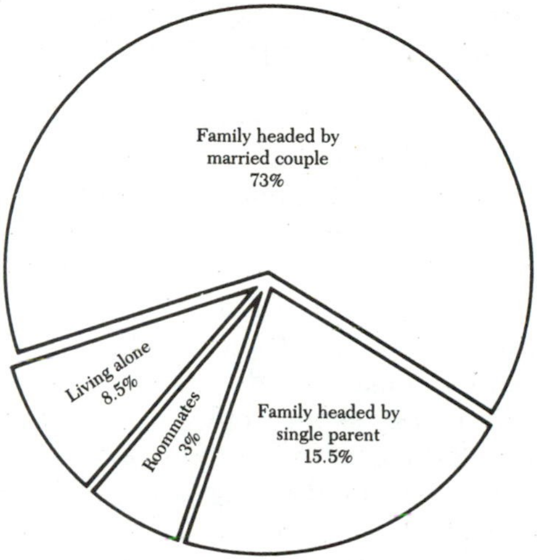

Family headed by
married couple
73%

Living alone
8.5%

Roommates
3%

Family headed by
single parent
15.5%

Source: San Francisco Chronicle, November 19, 1982, section I, p. 5.

caused less concern on the part of some media, religious, and political spokespersons.

Conflict and change are inherent in social life. If the family is now in a state of flux, such is the nature of resilient institutions; if it is beset by problems, so is life. The family will continue to survive.

Profamily as a Political Weapon

The New Religious Right recognizes the potential of the prolife, profamily issues in achieving a conservative majority and so has made them a cornerstone of its platform. "Paul Weyrich is very optimistic about the future impact of the pro-family movement," writes Richard Viguerie in *The New Right: We're Ready to Lead.* He attributes to the well-known conservative the opinion that "family issues in the 1980's could be what Vietnam was in the 1960's and environmental and consumer issues were in the 1970's for the left."

At the center of the "profamily" movement is a group of organizations that can hardly compete with the Moral Majority as a household word, yet that in Viguerie's estimate "has enormous political strength." Taking its name from the short street on Capitol Hill where it was first organized, the "Library Court" coalition by 1980 had grown to include some twenty organizations representing millions of members.

"In sheer numbers," Viguerie quotes Weyrich as saying, "the potential outreach of the Library Court group is greater than the whole range of conservative groups." It brings into alliance for political action such bodies as the Christian Coalition for Legislative Action, the Moral Majority, the American Association for Christian Schools, Citizens for Educational Freedom, the American Life Lobby, Conservatives Against Liberal Legislation, Family America, and the Conservative Caucus Research, Analysis and Education Foundation.

The alliance got off to a flying start in 1979, according to Viguerie, by organizing "a flood of mail" to thwart plans of the Department of Health, Education and Welfare to sponsor research on "test-tube" babies. It may seem ironic that a "prolife, profamily" coalition would undertake as its opening effort a campaign to halt fertility research to make childbearing possible for otherwise sterile couples.

But it is no more ironic than other Library Court manifestations of "support" for mothers and children. Many of the coalition's stands have taken legislative form in Senator Laxalt's family protection bill. This omnibus measure covers the spectrum of conservative "prolife" and "profamily" proposals, even including a ban on governmental "intrusion" into such private matters as a husband's freedom to beat his wife! (The same mentality in the recent past has blocked government funding of day-care centers for the children of working mothers on the argument that mothers should be "encouraged" to stay at home with their children.)

Other features of the proposed Family Protection Act would eliminate federal aid-to-education funds to states that forbid prayer in public buildings, deny funds for textbooks that fail to support the traditional image of the role of women, and forbid the use of funds by the Legal Services Corporation to support abortion cases, litigation on behalf of school desegregation, or legal aid for divorce or to challenge discrimination against homosexuals. Many other antireform and antiliberal provisions are included in this fifty-page bill in the guise of upholding the traditional roles of men and women and strengthening the family.

Viguerie describes a luncheon hosted by Senator Laxalt for "the nation's top evangelical leaders" who "promised an all-out effort" in support of his legislative proposal. Laxalt declared that "for years we have been debating on the terms of those who want to remake society. Now those groups *will have to explain* [emphasis added] why they oppose the traditional idea of the family."

Probably no other "moral" issue is more volatile, and therefore potentially more powerful a political weapon for the New Right, than *abortion*. It is obviously closely related to the "profamily" issue, and we will examine it next.

ABORTION: RIGHT TO LIFE OR RIGHT TO CHOOSE?

Of all the heated moral issues of our day, abortion is the one which cries the loudest for political solutions (see Box 7-1). Ever since World War II, however, we've seen a lot of political finger-pointing and very little compromise. Twenty years ago, for example, the key players in the abortion battle were the pope versus officials of the World Health Organization. The pope staunchly defended the traditional Catholic view that abortion is a sin while WHO leaders pointed to charts and graphs showing rapidly rising birthrates throughout the world's underdeveloped countries.

Though Third World overcrowding continues with alarming

Box 7-1
ABORTION

Since legalized in 1973, abortion has become the most frequently performed surgical procedure in the United States. Here are some of the more frequently heard arguments concerning abortion:

Pro: Every woman has the right to control her own body.
Con: Each unborn child has the right to be born.
Pro: A fetus is a person; therefore, abortion is legalized murder.
Pro: An expectant mother, or couple, has the right to abort a fetus which is either damaged or deformed.
Con: No one has the right to determine who shall survive and who shall die on the basis of physical perfection.
Pro: Scientifically, the issue of when life begins is unresolved. Politicians are the last group qualified to decide the question of when life begins.
Con: Major religious institutions and leading philosophers hold that life begins with conception. Therefore, abortion is the taking of a human life.
Pro: In the event of rape or incest, it is inhumane to require a woman to bear a child born of a forced pregnancy.
Con: Woman's lot is to bear children, regardless of the circumstances of the pregnancy. Abortion should not be used to end pregnancies that result from rape and incest.

---

speed, U.S. population growth has leveled off. Therefore, the abortion struggle in America now focuses on *individual* rights: the rights of a helpless fetus weighed against the rights of the woman who carries the child.

Abortion Is Not a New Issue

Although many Americans view abortion and birth control as predominantly modern controversies, the national debate over whether to prevent or terminate pregnancies goes back to colonial days. In fact, before the year 1821, *any* woman could have a legal abortion provided it was performed before the child in her womb "quickened"—that is, before she felt the baby move. Usually, this was no earlier than the fourth month of pregnancy. According to both the prevailing morals of the day *and* the American interpretation of British common law, an abortion before quickening was not equated with the taking of a life.

When the first antiabortion laws were written in America in the 1820s, they only outlawed the operations that took place *after* quickening. Nor was any of the first wave of antiabortion legislation directed at the mother; only the abortionist was deemed at fault. These early abortion laws were aimed at stopping malpractice, not abortion.

United States hospital records from the years 1840 to 1880 show that approximately one-third of pregnant mothers opted for abortions. Some people grew wealthy providing this service to American women. The financial records of one Madame Restell, a New York City abortionist, reveal that during the 1860s her advertising budget alone was approximately $60,000 a year. Restell's newspaper advertisements promised successful treatment of "private diseases" and "female complaints."

But popular sentiment began to shift after the Civil War: the birthrate had plummeted because so many potential fathers had been killed. Attorney David Wark was the leader of this era's antiabortion movement, and by the late 1870s, his followers had ensured that abortion was outlawed in every state. Punishments were severe, and in 1878, Madame Restell committed suicide rather than stand trial for performing illegal abortions.

As scientific tests for pregnancy became more reliable, abortion laws grew harsher. The Comstock Act of 1873 had made it illegal even to write about birth control and venereal disease! Meanwhile, birth control breakthroughs were generally suppressed. Although spermicidal douches and diaphragms were available by the 1880s, physicians did not conduct contraceptive research nor did they attempt to inform their female patients about the new contraceptives.

Although the "pill" has now been on the market for a full generation, the question remains: When does life begin? Many of the landmark cases concerning this controversy date back to the days of colonial America. The question is still being debated in our country's courts and legislatures—and in the hearts and minds of many Americans.

Roe v. *Wade* (1973), the Supreme Court's decision overruling all state laws that restricted a woman's right to obtain an abortion during the first three months of pregnancy, is still being condemned and lauded by "prolife" and "prochoice" groups respectively. Speaking for the prolife groups on the tenth anniversary of the court decision, President Regan vowed he would continue to support legislation to "end the practice of abortion on demand."

Pressure Builds for a Decision

As abortion activists, pro and con, step up their lobbying activities in the 1980s, legislators will have to make some tough decisions. Does the government have the right to tell a woman what she can or cannot do with her body? When poor women and teenagers need abortions, should taxpayers foot the bill? Does a fetus have legal rights? And can a husband step in to prevent his wife's abortions?

Polls show that our attitudes toward abortion depend heavily on the circumstances. A 1982 ABC/Harris Poll found that 60 percent of Americans approved of abortion in general. That same year, the National Opinion Research poll, on the other hand, revealed that 80 percent of the people surveyed supported abortion in cases of rape and incest, but only 40 percent favored it when the reasons were less dramatic.

Today's "situational ethics" are a sharp contrast to the prevailing attitudes in the 1940s, when abortion was seen without exception as wrong. Two events in the early sixties helped change that rigid outlook. In 1962, hundreds of women who had been given the drug Thalidomide gave birth to deformed children. And in 1964, many pregnant women caught German measles during a nationwide epidemic, risking damage to their unborn children.

Suddenly, many women who would never have considered abortion found themselves forced into a prochoice position. Even in these circumstances, abortion proved controversial: polls showed a surprisingly high number of Americans felt the Thalidomide babies should be brought to term. But these tragedies somehow served to legitimize the abortion procedure.

The stigma against abortion was further erased by *Roe* v. *Wade,* a ruling that women have a constitutional right to privacy, that bars government intervention. According to the antiabortion advocates, this landmark decision opened the floodgates. In the ten years since *Roe* v. *Wade,* the number of abortions in America has doubled.

Whatever one's position on abortion may be, it is obvious that some health benefits have resulted from the 1973 Supreme Court decision. Since 1973, for instance, women have been obtaining abortions earlier in their pregnancies, when the health risks to them are lowest. In 1973, fewer than 40 percent of women who had abortions did so before nine weeks (see Table 7-1). In 1978, more than half the procedures were performed before nine weeks, and more than 90 percent were performed during the first twelve weeks.

As we have said, the Supreme Court decision did not "invent" abortion. It did mean that the large majority of the crude and dangerous operations previously performed illegally have been replaced by legal procedures under proper medical supervision. In 1965, 235 deaths, or 20 percent of all deaths related to pregnancy and childbirth, were attributed to abortion. In 1978, there were 11 deaths from legal abortions and 7 from illegal ones.

Even so, in 1978 the pendulum began to swing back to the conservative side. The Hyde Amendment decreed that no Medicaid money could be used to fund abortions except in the case of rape or incest (reported within seventy-two hours) or when the mother's life was endangered. Today, most states have cut off funding even in cases of rape and incest.

President Reagan has gone on record as favoring a constitutional measure called the Human Life Amendment, based on the Helms-Hyde statute. The Helms-Hyde bill, which was defeated by the Senate on September 15, 1982, stated, "For the purpose of enforcing the obligation of the States under the 14th Amendment not to deprive persons of life without due process of law, human life shall be deemed to exist *from conception.*" The prolife forces have vowed to propose a new bill to the Congress in 1983 to undo *Roe* v. *Wade.* As President Reagan said on the tenth anniversary of the Court decision: "I have always believed that God's greatest gift is human life and that we have a duty to protect the life of the

Table 7-1
LEGAL ABORTIONS IN THE U.S., 1973–1979

LEGAL ABORTIONS ACCORDING TO SELECTED CHARACTERISTICS OF THE PATIENT

	1973	1974	1975	1976	1977	1978	1979
	615,831	763,476	854,853	988,267	1,079,430	1,157,776	1,251,921
AGE CHARACTERISTICS							
Under 20 years	32.7	32.7	33.1	32.1	30.8	30.0	30.0
20–24 years	32.0	31.8	31.9	33.3	34.5	35.0	35.4
25 years and over	35.3	35.6	35.0	34.6	34.7	34.9	34.6
MARITAL STATUS							
Married	27.4	27.4	26.1	24.6	24.3	26.4	24.7
Unmarried	72.6	72.6	73.9	75.4	75.7	73.6	75.3
PERIOD OF GESTATION							
Under 9 weeks	36.1	42.6	44.6	47.0	51.2	53.2	52.1
9–10 weeks	29.4	28.7	28.4	28.0	27.2	26.9	27.0
11–12 weeks	17.9	15.4	14.9	14.4	13.1	12.3	12.5
13–15 weeks	6.9	5.5	5.0	4.5	3.4	4.0	4.2
16–20 weeks	8.0	6.5	6.1	5.1	4.3	3.7	3.4
21 weeks and over	1.7	1.2	1.0	0.9	0.9	0.9	0.9

Source: The World Almanac (New York: Newspaper Enterprise Association, 1983), p. 961.

unborn child. Until someone can prove the unborn child is not a life, shouldn't we give it the benefit of the doubt and assume it is? That's why I favored legislation to end the practice of abortion on demand and why I will continue to support it in the new Congress."[15]

A third issue that is used by the New Religious Right to condemn the teachings and practices of the liberal establishment is the problem of drugs—the subject of the next section.

DRUG USE

The much publicized "drug problem" isn't news—it's ancient history. Since the founding of our country, psychoactive substances have been used, abused, and regulated.

America's most popular drug is alcohol, and its consumption is ages old. According to figures gathered by William J. Rorabaugh, a history professor at the University of Washington, between 1790 and 1840, Americans—for the most part males—routinely drank about half a pint of hard liquor every day. This was the hardest-drinking era in the nation's history. An early surgeon general warned that if the U.S. Army was to bar recruitment or reenlistment of "habitual drunkards," the army would have to be disbanded due to the resulting lack of recruits.[16]

Nor have Americans been prudent in their use of other drugs. For example, cocaine was fully legal until 1914. The "speedy" alkaloid of the coca leaf was so popular in the United States during the late nineteenth century that some social historians have called the period "the Great Cocaine Explosion." Cocaine parlors catering to the middle class functioned in many American cities at the time and, according to Robert Sabbas, author of *Snowblind,* a history of cocaine use, "The drug was available in saloons, served in whiskey shots, and the hoi-polloi could buy cocaine preparations from any number of door-to-door salesmen." Most users, however, got their hit of cocaine in patent medicines sold over the counter "in syrups, tonics, liqueurs, capsules, tablets, hypodermic syringes, cigars, cigarettes, and nasal sprays—everything from Agnew's Powder to Ryno's Hay Fever 'n-Catarrh Remedy. Until it was made illegal, cocaine was endorsed by the Hay Fever Foundation and touted by American doctors as a cure for everything from alcoholism to the common cold."[17]

Cocaine was not the only drug which reached vast portions of the public via patent medicines. Before 1906, when the Federal Pure Food and Drug Act made strict regulation of over-the-counter preparations possible, some $80 million a year was spent in the United States for commercial medicines, which often contained opium and morphine.

The 1906 Sears and Roebuck catalogue carried twenty pages of mail-order patent medicine and nostrums and included "cures" for opium and morphine addiction as well as a substance called "the Sears White Star Secret Liquor Cure." Analysis showed the liquor cure to contain sufficient narcotic to put a drinker to sleep within twenty minutes. Alcohol, sometimes as much as 23 percent, was an important ingredient in numerous popular nostrums of the era.

Among these potent patent medicines was Coca-Cola, introduced in 1886 as a headache remedy and general "nerve tonic." Its original formula contained a tidy dose of cocaine. The ingredients were changed in 1903, but many other "soft" drinks continued their reliance on drugs until the 1906 federal law.

It was not only the entrepreneurs of the patent medicine industry who supplied drugs to the unwary. Science, too, occasionally lent moral respectability to drugs later discovered to be dangerous or addictive. Heroin, now the most feared of drugs, was developed and initially marketed—over the counter—as a nonaddictive substitute for morphine.

As passage of the 1906 Pure Food and Drug Act indicates, Americans of the past were wary of drug misuse. From about 1810, America was home to a growing and powerful antiliquor movement—the temperance crusade which, a century after it began, culminated in Prohibition, the Eighteenth Amendment to the Constitution.

"The Noble Experiment," as Prohibition was dubbed, proved a disaster. According to a study published by the University of North Carolina, the only people who stopped drinking during Prohibition's first years were moderate drinkers. Alcoholics and heavy drinkers merely ignored the law, with the help of an illicit liquor industry which appeared seemingly overnight.

By the beginnings of the 1930s, consumption had reached pre-Prohibition levels. It was not until the 1940s, with the establishment of the Center for Alcohol Studies at Yale University, that the concept of alcoholism as a disease began to take hold. The American Medical Association didn't accept this theory until 1958.

Today's Use of Soft Drugs

In every region of the country, parents, teachers, religious leaders, and drug counselors express great concern over the increased use of "soft" drugs among their children and teenagers. Law enforcement officials now glumly admit that marijuana and cocaine are readily available to anyone. They also concede that the soft drug explosion is not just a ghetto problem. If anything, the drugs tend to follow the money out to the suburbs.

Even though our nation's drug woes deepened during the 1970s, most parents and civic leaders wanted to believe that the crisis was over. Despite their denials, marijuana and other soft drugs became even more widely used. By 1979, a total of 90 percent of the students questioned in a *New York Times* survey said that "pot" was "easy to obtain."[18] The survey further revealed that in some communities, marijuana use is common among eleven- and twelve-year-olds.

The professionals who deal daily with drug abuse cases are quick to point out that children in the 1980s are smoking marijuana for totally different reasons than the ones which prompted their older brothers and sisters to try it in the 1960s. The Woodstock-era kids smoked pot to have a good time and to experience a new thrill. Now that the novelty has worn off, many high school students are using marijuana the way a problem drinker uses alcohol—as a crutch.

"For some of our young people, drugs are not used to enhance life; they're used to *get through* life," says Dr. Mitchell Rosenthal, president of Phoenix House, the largest private residential drug treatment program in the United States. "We are moving from parental self-medication and seeing it fed back among our children."[19]

Dr. Rosenthal's concern is echoed by Arthur Jaffe, director of the New York City school system's antidrug program. "Drugs aren't frightening to the students," notes Jaffe. "Society's message is always, 'Don't ever feel anything. If you feel tense, take a tranquilizer. You feel like eating, take an appetite suppressant. You feel pain, take an aspirin."[20]

It's extremely difficult for youths to say no to soft drugs when their parents are taking more mood-altering prescription pills and drinking more alcoholic beverages than ever before. Because our lives are getting more stressful, marijuana—just like the legal drugs that help people cope with everyday life—is still much in demand and therefore easy to obtain.

The final issue to be looked at in this chapter has to do with the New Religious Right's desire to censor what is taught in the classroom.

UNFIT FOR CHILDREN: CONTROLLING THE CLASSROOM

The Moral Majority and other New Religious Right organizations believe American schoolchildren are being taught that it is all right to lie, cheat, steal, and kill. They say that through values clarification, sex education, and drug abuse education, liberal, humanistic public schools are teaching there are no objective moral principles, that anything one wants to do is acceptable. American parents must fight back, or else remove their children to private schools under conservative religious direction.

What are the objectives of the educational right wing? Among them are censorship of library books (both to remove obscene material and to monitor social and intellectual philosophies), the abolition of sex education, the teaching of the fundamentalist doctrine of creation (disguised as "creation science"), and eliminating the teaching of ethics or values by the method of stimulating the child's powers of moral reasoning.

If the previous statement seems overdrawn, consider this widely quoted portrayal of public education circulated by an organization called the Network of Patriotic Letter Writers of Pasadena, California:

> IT'S OK TO LIE—IT'S OK TO STEAL—IT'S OK TO HAVE PRE-MARITAL SEX—IT'S OK TO CHEAT—IT'S OK TO KILL—if these things are a part of *your own* value system and you have clarified these

BLOOM COUNTY   **by Berke Breathed**

values to yourself. The important thing is not *what* values to choose, but that you have *chosen* them yourself. . . . That in essence is what values clarifiers teach children in schools today.

Right-wing opponents of values clarification publicly burned forty copies of a book setting forth its principles and methods. While book-burning may be an isolated phenomenon in America, the crusade against what has come to be known as humanistic education is a major concern to educators and defenders of academic freedom. Teachers' unions and professional educational organizations are being forced to defend both their methods of teaching and the personal integrity and patriotism of their members.

Always just below the surface—and often rising above it—is the accusation that humanistic educators are inspired by totalitarian philosophies and harbor subversive intentions. In an article entitled "Why Johnny Can't Tell Right from Wrong," Margaret Baldwin writes:

> Although it has many names and disguises such as values education, moral education, citizenship education, moral development, and character education, values clarification is the hedonistic grandchild of Communist brainwashing and the offspring of sensitivity training. Using this powerful psychological technique, humanists are seeking to replace the traditional values of the school children of the United States with situation ethics.[21]

Baldwin further tells us: "A basic assumption which teachers and students are to accept is that no idea is wrong, no matter how immoral or ludicrous."[22]

Why is so much attention paid to values and values clarification? What is it, and why is it so widely feared by those of the political and religious right?

Values clarification is the name of a technique or method of moral education based on John Dewey's principle that effective learning involves thinking about one's experience. It seeks to use the young person's powers of observation and reasoning to examine attitudes about behavioral questions. For example, is it ever right, under any circumstances, to steal a loaf of bread? Is it usually right to tell falsehoods or to take what does not belong to you? If not, why not? How do we decide that one act is right and another wrong?

These questions were not invented by the small group of teachers who only a few years ago developed the technique of teaching now known as values clarification. The method of teaching by asking questions and examining the answers is as old as Socrates, and the emphasis on the consequences for human beings as a standard of judgment is at least as ancient as the New Testament teaching that the Sabbath was made for man, not man for the Sabbath.

When values clarification was first attacked, its proponents believed they were simply the victims of mistaken identity: they were being confused with the atheistic or agnostic advocates of the religion or life philosophy known as secular humanism. They quickly pointed out that they were not humanists in that sense of the word. Indeed, thousands of their teachers and thinkers were priests, ministers, and rabbis or lay members of traditional religions.

There is no question that the radical right endeavored to confuse the issue by throwing humanistic religious groups, such as many Unitarian Universalists, Ethical Culturists, and other "nontheistic" humanists, into the same bag with groups having no religious connotation or connection. The extreme right attacks values clarification by attributing to its developers a religious position that most of them do not hold while also claiming that the values clarification movement, from which many religious and secular humanists emphatically dissent, represents the official ethical philosophy of humanism—which the religious right further narrows down to "situation ethics."

The truth of the matter is not so simple. Most religious and secular humanists, those accepting humanism as their religion or life philosophy, would recognize the usefulness of values clarification as an educational tool in awakening the powers of critical thinking essential for moral growth and for participation in democratic dialogue. These are the stalwart Jeffersonian traits of reasonable discussion and the untrammeled testing of ideas, without which a free classroom, or a free society, cannot exist. At the same time, those who embrace humanism as a personal religion or life philosophy would go well beyond values clarification in asserting a distinctive moral philosophy they are prepared to defend on rational grounds. The principles of such an ethical faith include upholding the worth of each person as a unique moral agent in a community of unique selves and the values of freedom, reason, and tolerance within a free society. From such an ethical system, it follows that needlessly, willfully inflicting avoidable pain, harm, or death on any creature is always evil; that denying the moral freedom or dignity of human beings is universally wrong; and that serving to advance the development of free, self-directed, socially responsible human beings within a mutually supportive democratic community is the greatest good. Is this situation ethics? Perhaps, with sufficient qualification, it is, but not as the radical right misinterprets and abuses a moral philosophy that it appears to be incapable of or unwilling to describe fairly.

Most decent human beings accept "situation ethics" if that means believing we would be right in not disclosing to the Gestapo the direction in which the fugitive Jew ran into the forest. We could, under those circumstances, deceive the would-be killer of the innocent and sleep with clear consciences. If, on the contrary, we became the killer's collaborators by a misapplied rectitude, we could not sleep. If this is what situation ethics means—and in fact this is what its proponents have in mind when they use the term—then most human beings as a matter of course practice situation ethics and are completely justified in doing so. But this does not mean that we lie, steal, or kill in any but the most morally tortured and extreme circumstances, and only then to avoid committing a great wrong.

To point this out, and to enable students to grasp the dilemmas that arise when two or more moral principles are in conflict, is not to concede that humanistic moral philosophers have no principles, or that their highest value is more sensual pleasure or self-expression. Morally autonomous people—the goal of humanistic ethics—are people capable of self-determination and responsible self-governance; moral autonomy does not mean just "doing your own thing," as uninformed or deliberately misleading critics claim. But such misrepresentations proliferate because of their usefulness to extremist propagandists.

Noting the range and power of the fundamentalist assault on the public school, Betty Brout commented in the Moral Democracy Bulletin, "The attack on public education by the New Right seems to be taking on the characteristics of an octopus." Counting off some of the principal points in the New Right campaign, she noted:

> The issues now include the massive drive to legislate prayer in the public classroom; the push to enact laws allowing tax tuition credits for the support of non-public schools; the bitter controversy over the teaching of "creationism" as science on a par with evolution; the steam gathering to ban busing—with no accompanying safeguards to insure unsegregated public education; and the censorship of textbooks and school libraries to keep books that children read pure from the viewpoint of the Religious Right.

She also found that the book censors sometimes reveal their complete ignorance of the contents of the books they propose to ban.

A *New York Times* story, for instance, reported a right winger's index of forbidden books that includes two suggestive titles: *Mr. and Mrs. Pig's Evening Out,* an innocent children's story of porcine domesticity, and *Making It with Mademoiselle,* which proved to be a home-sewing instruction book for teenagers published by *Mademoiselle* magazine.

The simple fact is that intellectual freedom in the teaching of science, the humanities, and social sciences is imperative for a nation that is not to decline into a second- or third-rate power. America's influence as a force for freedom requires the moral and technological vitality that only a spirit of free inquiry can sustain. Protecting the integrity of science and improving the quality of science teaching in the United States, free from ideological or religious control, must be a common concern of all friends of public education.

In the long run, a tolerant society is one in which diversity is prized as a necessary condition for freedom and social progress. Teachers must not be forced into a common mold, and while it is improper for teachers to indoctrinate students into a particular religious or ideological viewpoint, it is equally wrong to force educators into conformity to a politically imposed social or moral orthodoxy. Democracy in education requires students to develop critical skills—the ability to question, reason, and explore various options. Teachers cannot elicit or encourage these capacities if they themselves lack or fear to express them.

SUMMING UP

Problems of family life, drugs, abortion, pornography, and censorship are very much with us today, but they are *not* unique to this generation. Controversial public issues are frequently determined by changing social norms, economics, and the ever swinging pendulum. Certainly today's moral and political questions are serious—but reasonable people can argue whether they are more or less serious than those of other eras. The real problem, however, is not only deciding what the desired ends should be, but also finding the means to those ends. History is replete with examples of the use of religion in the struggle for political power, the maintenance of the status quo, or the advancement of nationalism. We see examples today in Iran and the Middle East. As Martin Marty observed in regard to the New Religious Right, "The echoes of the Iranian militants are loud and clear." When moral absolutes are confused with public policy, anyone who dissents is identified with immorality and is in conflict with the will of God. The New Religious Right ignores the pluralism of America's faiths, the almost eighty million persons who remain without any religious affiliation, and the essential safeguards of a free society.

To identify any nation with God is to distort the prophetic role of religion and to deny the fundamental basis of a free and democratic society by making an idol of the state. Fortunately, for both historical and theological reasons, many Americans have a strong bias against the blending of religion and politics. The temptation of religious leaders to use political means for the accomplishment of religious ends is no less dangerous than the temptation of public officials to use religion for political ends.

There is no question of the right of fundamentalists to be involved in politics; it is the *nature* of that involvement which is at issue. Not only does the New Religious Right presume to make political issues into moral absolutes and moral absolutes into political issues, but also it holds forth a political agenda which must be ruled as both morally and politically deficient. With all of its espousal of morality in public policy, one looks in vain for the movement's concern with the sins of injustice, poverty, bigotry, racism, and war.

The present resurgence of America's theocrats (i.e., those who believe they are divinely guided), with their enculturation of a particular and strident form of religious faith, does not bode well for the prophetic role of religion, the separation of church and state, or a pluralistic and free society. Reinhold Niebuhr perceptively warned some years ago, "The temper and integrity with which the political fight is waged is more important for the health of a society than any particular [public] policy." This truth is one worth remembering for the future course of religion and politics in America.

NOTES

1. Alexis de Tocqueville, *Democracy in America* (New York: Vintage Books, 1945, Phillips Bradley Edition).
2. For an excellent history of the United States, see Mary Beth Norton, David Katzman, Paul Escott, Howard Chudacoff, Thomas Paterson, and William Tuttle, *A People and a Nation* (Boston: Houghton Mifflin, 1982).
3. Charles A. Beard, *An Economic Interpretation of the Constitution of the United States* (New York: Macmillan, 1933), p. 22.
4. For a discussion of the Second Great Awakening and the role of religion in Jefferson's presidential campaign, see Norton, et al., *A People and a Nation,* pp. 185–191.
5. Ibid., pp. 308, 309, 312, 325, 326, 357, and 517.
6. Jerry Falwell, *Listen America* (Garden City, N.Y.: Doubleday, 1980), p. 12.
7. A discussion of Gary Potter's views can be found in Jerry Falwell, ed., *The Fun-*

damentalist Phenomenon: The Resurgence of Conservative Christianity (Garden City, N.Y.: Doubleday, 1981).

8. *Los Angeles Times,* June 10, 1981, Section IV, p. 38.
9. Edward Shorter, *The Making of the Modern Family* (New York: Basic Books, 1975).
10. John Demos, *A Little Commonwealth: Family Life in Plymouth Colony* (New York: Oxford University Press, 1970), p. 43.
11. Carl Degler, *At Odds: Women and the Family in America from the Revolution to the Present* (New York: Oxford University Press, 1980).
12. For a detailed discussion of the differences and similarities in American family life throughout our history, see Norton et al., *A People and a Nation.*
13. See Mary Ellen Reilly, *The Family Population People* (Washington, D.C.: Center for Information in America, 1977), for a complete review of statistics through 1976 on marriage, divorce, childbirth, and education.
14. There are indications that the pendulum is swinging once again in the other direction. Parents and educators are beginning to recognize that "progressive education" and "permissive" childrearing haven't worked all that well. There is a movement back to traditional educational methods and subjects and more discipline in the home. There are even organizations forming to give support and reinforcement to the parents of "problem" children. Such parents know now they are not alone and not necessarily to blame.
15. *San Francisco Chronicle,* January 23, 1983, p. 2.
16. William Rorabaugh, *The Alcoholic Republic: An American Tradition* (New York: Oxford University Press, 1979), p. 82.
17. Robert Sabbas, *Snowblind: A Brief Career in the Cocaine Trade* (New York: Bobbs-Merrill, 1977), p. 104.
18. *New York Times,* March 14, 1979, p. 3.
19. *Los Angeles Times,* December 8, 1981, Part IV, p. 46.
20. *San Francisco Chronicle,* October 26, 1982, p. 10.
21. *Margaret Baldwin,* "Why Johnny Can't Tell Right from Wrong." *Conquest* (Kansas City: Kansas City Youth For Christ), 1981, p. 10.
22. Ibid., p. 11.

GLOSSARY

Bill of Rights: The first ten amendments to the United States Constitution. Bills of rights, sometimes called declarations of rights, are also found in all state constitutions. They contain a listing of the rights a person enjoys that cannot be infringed upon by the government. Many important rights, such as trial by jury and the guarantee of habeas corpus, are stated in other parts of the United States Constitution. All bills of rights contain provisions designed to protect freedom of expression, rights of property, and rights of persons accused of crime. No rights are absolute, however, and all are subject to reasonable regulation through law.

Censorship: The curbing of ideas either in speech or in writing *before* they are expressed. Accountability *after* expression is provided by laws regulating libel and slander, obscenity, incitement to crime, contempt of court, or seditious utterance. Except in time of war or other national emergency, any prior restraint upon freedom of speech or of the press is forbidden.

Civil liberties: Those liberties usually spelled out in a bill of rights or a constitution that guarantee the protection of person, opinions, and property from the arbitrary interference of governmental officials. Restraints may be placed upon the exercise of these liberties only when they are abused by individuals or groups and when the public welfare requires them.

Civil rights: Positive acts of government designed to protect persons against arbitrary or discriminatory treatment by government or individuals. Civil rights guarantees are sometimes written into constitutions but frequently take the form of statutes. Though the term is often used interchangeably with *civil liberties,* the latter generally refers to restraints upon government as found in bills of rights. The term *civil rights* is also to be distinguished from *political rights,* which generally refer to the rights to participate in the management of government through such practices as voting, and *equal rights,* which has been used mainly in connection with the movement to achieve equality between men and women.

Freedom of religion: Freedom of worship and religious practice. The national government under the First Amendment, and the states under their constitutions and the Fourteenth Amendment, may not abridge this right of worship. Any religious practice that is contrary to public peace or morality may be outlawed, such as snake-handling or polygamy.

Freedom of speech: The right to speak without prior restraint, subject to penalties for abuse of the right. Abuses include slander, obscenity, incitement to crime, contempt of court, or sedition. By virtue of the First and Fourteenth Amendments and state bills of rights, neither the national government nor the states may abridge the right of freedom of speech.

Privacy: The right to determine one's personal affairs free of governmental interference and to control dissemination of information about oneself. The Constitution makes no mention of a right of privacy but the Supreme Court has recognized it as falling within the "penumbra" (borderline) of the First, Fourth, Fifth, Ninth, and Fourteenth Amendments. In the Privacy Act of 1974, Congress provided, for the first time, that individuals may inspect information about themselves in public agency files and challenge, correct, or amend materials. Agencies may not make their files on an individual available to other agencies without that person's consent. Exempted from the law, however, are law enforcement agencies, the Central Intelligence Agency, the Secret Service, and certain files pertaining to federal employment.

Radical: Although no precise use of the term exists, a radical is generally regarded as a leftist or rightist who is extreme in demands for change.

While the term usually refers to extremist individuals and parties of the political left, it can be used to describe anyone who favors drastic political, social, or economic change.

Separation of church and state: A basic principle of American government that prohibits the mingling of church and state. The principle rests on the First Amendment clause forbidding the passage of any law "respecting an establishment of religion." In a series of controversial cases, the Supreme Court has held that the state must be committed to a position of neutrality and may neither advance nor retard religion. No public funds may be expended on behalf of any church nor may the government favor one church over another. Public schools may not be used for sectarian religious observances, and official requirements for Bible reading or prayer recitals are forbidden. Laws that have a predominantly secular effect, such as public bus transportation for parochial schools or Sunday closing laws, have been upheld.

The permissible extent of public aid to church-related schools, however, remains unresolved. Under the Elementary and Secondary Education Act of 1965, the national government provides for aid to parochial schools, as do many state governments. The Supreme Court has struck down state programs that pay the salaries of teachers in church-related schools, for instruction in nonreligious subjects, as "excessive entanglement between government and religion" and, on similar grounds, voided programs of tuition aid through reimbursement or tax relief to families of children attending nonpublic schools. At the same time, however, the Court upheld federal and state construction grants to church-related colleges. The distinction was made by the Court on the grounds that precollege parochial schools are more involved in religious indoctrination, and that the state programs would involve continuing controversy over public support.

SUGGESTED READINGS

Abraham, Henry J. *Freedom and the Court: Civil Rights and Liberties in the United States.* 2nd ed. New York: Oxford University Press, 1972.

Cranston, Maurice. *What Are Human Rights?* New York: Taplinger, 1973.

Dierenfield, Richard B. *Religion in American Public Schools.* Washington, D.C.: Public Affairs Press, 1962.

Dolbeare, Kenneth M., ed. *American Political Thought.* Monterey, Calif: Duxbury, 1981.

————, and Hammond, Philip E. *The School Prayer Decisions.* Chicago: University of Chicago Press, 1971.

Dorsen, Norman, ed. *The Rights of Americans: What They Are—What They Should Be.* New York: Pantheon, 1970.

Hartz, Louis. *The Anguish of Change.* New York: Norton, 1973.

Hofstadter, Richard. *The American Political Tradition and the Men Who Made It.* New York: Knopf, 1948.

Reitman, Alan, ed. *The Pulse of Freedom: American Liberties, 1920–1970s.* New York: New American Library, 1975.

Roelofs, H. Mark. *Ideology and Myth in American Politics: A Critique of a National Political Mind.* Boston: Little, Brown, 1976.

Sigler, Jay A. *American Rights Policies.* Homewood, Ill.: Dorsey Press, 1975.

Spicer, George W. *The Supreme Court and Fundamental Freedoms.* 2nd ed. New York: Appleton-Century-Crofts, 1967.

8

The Arms Race:
Salvation or Ruin?

What is meant by *deterrence?* Can we afford to let it fail?

What is meant by *arms control?* How does it differ from disarmament?

Where is the high-tech race taking the world?

Whatever happened to détente?

How is President Reagan's "war-fighting posture" different from past U.S. positions regarding nuclear arms? Are movements in the United States and Europe opposing the arms race influencing his nuclear policies?

Out among the mesquite, yucca, and Joshua trees on the vast arid landscape, drilling rigs are penetrating thousands of feet into the desert basin. They are opening more holes into which more nuclear weapons will be deposited and then exploded in the continuing effort to understand and advance this awesome technology.

In a tunnel far into the side of a mesa, another test is being prepared to determine what effects an enemy nuclear blast in space might have on American missiles in the vicinity. This new test, code-named Huron Landing, was conducted in late 1982.

The research and testing continues in the seemingly never-ending search for bigger and more accurate nuclear weaponry. Yet, most of us cannot conceive of conditions which would warrant fighting a nuclear war. The modern consensus has been that the conditions giving a war relative moral sanction must include defense of biological survival or of overriding societal values such as freedom; a reasonable chance of success without an unacceptable cost in blood, treasure, and those values being defended; protection of civilian populations; and a ban on causing unnecessary suffering.

Nuclear weapons have made a mockery of these conditions. The atom bomb and its even deadlier cousin, the hydrogen bomb, were no mere leaps from bow to crossbow, from arrow to bullet, from peasant infantry to Napoleonic conscript, from horse to tank, from artillery to airplane. From 1945 on, it was no longer a tribe, city, or nation whose existence might be threatened by war. Now entire civilian populations—and civilization itself—were at stake.

A PARADOX

The nuclear genie loosed by a team of scientists at Los Alamos, New Mexico, has rendered obsolete Clausewitz's maxim that war is the continuation of politics by other means. But the two superpowers—the United States and the Soviet Union—continue to threaten the use of nuclear weapons in an effort to win their political battles. Do they really mean to fight a nuclear war if other means of winning their political cause fail? Do they expect to win a nuclear war if they do choose to fight one? And if they don't expect to fight or win a nuclear war, why continue to spend vast sums of money on the research and development of nuclear weaponry? These are some of the questions we will attempt to answer in this chapter.

Whatever the answers, we must remember that they are asked in a world in which the nuclear genie can never again be imprisoned in the bottle of ignorance. Thus, the modern world is faced with a terrible paradox. It has been best described by the British general Sir Hugh Beach, who said, "It is necessary both to possess nuclear weapons *and to form the intention* that in certain circumstances we would use them—and yet their actual use in any circumstances must be morally outrageous—which is absurd." This absurdity, Sir Hugh continues, "is a paradox which no logic nor any alternative line of policy which I know of, can mitigate. It remains to live with it!"[1]

NUCLEAR STRATEGY

The strategy for survival in the nuclear age can be summed up in the novel concept of *deterrence.*[2] Of course, deterrence as such is not new. The idea was first practiced (one assumes) when the first cave dwellers averted a raid by holding aloft bigger stones than their rivals wielded. What is new is the central importance of deterrence. In the past it didn't matter too much to the human race if deterrence broke down and disputes over home and societal values and national honor were resolved by battle rather than by one side's timely retreat. One person, one family, even one generation of young men might be slain—but others would survive, return to normal lives, and procreate.

The bomb changed this. Scenarios for an all-out nuclear war project tens of millions of deaths in a few moments through fire, radiation, and the explosion itself. As Figure 8-1 shows, the blast effects of *one* MX missile can destroy an area sixty times as large as that destroyed at Hiroshima. Mankind can no longer afford to have deterrence fail.

Why Deterrence?

To understand why deterrence has been the cornerstone of American and Soviet strategy in the nuclear age, we must go back to the first American debate over whether any defense was possible against the atom bomb. President Truman thought in 1945 that "every new weapon will eventually bring some counter defense to it." So did the United States Navy. The U.S. Air Force, however, was skeptical.

The air force proved right. Defense was difficult enough against planes carrying nuclear bombs. (Unless a defender destroyed 100 percent of incoming aircraft, it would still suffer devastation.) And defense became impossible against missiles that could fly from one continent to another in minutes.[3] Once both the United States and the Soviet Union had nuclear weapons, the first premise of security planning was that both superpowers, and especially their major civilian cities, were inescapably vulnerable to any attack. The corol-

Figure 8-1 AREA DESTROYED BY NUCLEAR BLASTS (LETHAL RADIUS FROM EPICENTER)

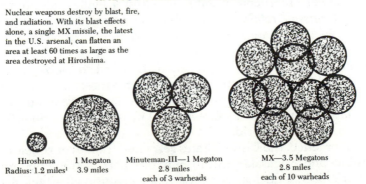

Nuclear weapons destroy by blast, fire, and radiation. With its blast effects alone, a single MX missile, the latest in the U.S. arsenal, can flatten an area at least 60 times as large as the area destroyed at Hiroshima.

| Hiroshima Radius: 1.2 miles[1] | 1 Megaton 3.9 miles | Minuteman-III—1 Megaton 2.8 miles each of 3 warheads | MX—3.5 Megatons 2.8 miles each of 10 warheads |

Source: Ruth Leger Sivard, *World Military and Social Expenditures* (Leesburg, Va.: World Priorities, 1982), p. 43.

lary quickly came to be that the only possible "defense" was *retaliation*.

In other words, the aggressor cave dwellers had to be deterred from ever throwing the first nuclear rock by the certainty that if they did so, a second nuclear rock would flatten them, too.

Anticonventional Military Thinking

The irony is that since 1945, we have provided the military with increasingly sophisticated weapons that can *never* be used. As early as 1946, Bernard Brodie, a pioneer nuclear strategist, concluded, "Thus far the chief purpose of a military establishment has been to win wars. From now on its chief purpose must be to avert them. It can have almost no other useful purpose."[4]

This hard nuclear truth established itself—not without resistance—after the Soviet Union broke the American monopoly on the atom bomb in 1949, and especially after both sides developed the even more terrible hydrogen bomb in 1952–1953. It was after the testings of the hydrogen bomb that Winston Churchill realized there would be a stalemate between superpowers and, therefore, a paradoxical enforced peace. "Then it may well be that we shall by a process of sublime irony have reached a state in this story where safety will be the sturdy child of terror, and survival the twin brother of annihilation." President Eisenhower's secretary of the air force, Donald A. Quarles, agreed. War was now an "unthinkable catastrophe" from which "neither side can hope by a mere margin of superiority in airplanes or other means of delivery to escape."

Massive Retaliation

Eisenhower's secretary of state, John Foster Dulles, adopted a doctrine of *massive retaliation* which acknowledged in part this stalemate. Nuclear weapons were to be used only in response to an attack, and deterring wars, not winning them, was the main objective. But Dulles also preached the need to "seize the initiative," and he rejected any restrictions on targets or weapons. His policy envisioned the firing of American nuclear weapons in reaction either to nuclear or conventional incursions in various trouble spots around the world.

In practice, the United States refrained from ever repeating Hiroshima and Nagasaki. And in only one part of the globe did the threat of a U.S. nuclear response to a conventional attack become fixed policy. This was in Western Europe, America's top defense priority abroad and an area in which the United States felt a need to compensate for Western inferiority in conventional weapons.

The second stage of evolution in American thinking about deterrence came in the early 1960s, in the heady years of John F. Kennedy's presidency. Defense Secretary Robert McNamara completed the wresting away of nuclear strategy from military commanders to give to civilian academics; Dulles had begun this process. McNamara became fascinated by the idea of limited wars (including limited nuclear wars) and pushed development of battlefield nuclear weapons. He eventually wrote a definition of how many nuclear weapons were enough in the approaching world of nuclear plenty. His thesis was called *mutual assured destruction* and was dubbed MAD by its detractors.

MAD

McNamara's concept was based on the distinction that Albert Wohlstetter, a think-tank analyst, made in 1959 between first and second strikes. A first strike was the opening shot of a nuclear war and was specifically directed against the nuclear weapons of the enemy with the aim of wiping out the means of retaliation. A second strike force was one that could survive an incoming first strike and still cause unacceptable damage (even if only to cities) in its return blow.

All that was necessary or desirable for purposes of deterrence, in McNamara's estimation, was an assured second strike. An important change in thinking was that a first strike force would be superfluous—and, American strategic thinking increasingly believed,

FEIFFER

dangerous. It would add nothing to American security and would simply feed the Soviet feeling of insecurity, inducing a jittery trigger finger in Moscow, thus increasing "instability"—all of which works against deterrence.

On the other hand, an assured second strike would promote the ideal of stability. By enabling the nation to ride out a first strike, it would allow time for calm assessment of a real or suspected attack before any decisions were made as to response. It would reduce "use 'em or lose 'em" pressure for a policy of overhasty "launch on warning." It would leave time to distinguish between a deliberate attack and, say, an accidental launch or a deceptive firing by some third nuclear state. This emphasis on a defensive, second-strike capability strategy helped to give rise to the concept of arms control.

The Birth of Arms Control

It is a mistake to confuse the concept of arms control with a desire for disarmament. The pursuit of arms control, begun in the mid-1960s, never sought to end the arms race, nor even necessarily to cut numbers of weapons. Instead, it accepts the arms race as a given and attempts to render it less explosive by maintaining a stable balance that neither side would be tempted to break out of. If stability is greater at higher rather than lower levels of weapons (by making any cheating or even surprise attack so marginal that it would not destroy the effective balance), then so be it.

Arms control also differs from traditional disarmament efforts in its fundamental analysis of the arms race. Arms controllers reject the disarmers' vision of any arms race (whether of nuclear missiles or of battleships) as the source of tensions between rival nations. To arms controllers, the arms race is an aspect of some more basic clash of perceived national interests. They might cite, for example, the fact that Canada doesn't get alarmed by any U.S. buildup of missiles or tanks. The problem today, of course, is that the arms race—especially in a thermonuclear age—could dangerously fuel fears and lead to overreaction, miscalculation, and possibly a disastrous war that no one really intended. There is growing evidence that these fears are alive and active among most peoples around the world—including the very young (see Box 8-1).

The new arms control theory, therefore, tried, in the mathematical and "systems analysis" jargon that came into vogue, to write rules for a "non-zero-sum" rather than a "zero-sum" game. The latter term describes a contest in which one player's gain is necessarily

Box 8-1
THE KIDS WHO DON'T EXPECT TO LIVE TO BE THIRTY

At the Urban High School graduation at Fort Miley a weekend ago, a young girl in a white dress stood on an abandoned gun emplacement on a bluff overlooking the Pacific and talked about life and death and nuclear war, and I thought Good God, I've heard this song before.

It was a lullaby of a Sunday afternoon, warm with an easy west wind that fluffed the ocean like a pillow. The children of the nuke generation did not enjoy the scenery. They had things like survival on their minds.

"Most of my friends do not believe we will live to be 30 years old, or have children," the 17-year-old graduate said.

The day before, many of her classmates had marched in the big national Nuclear Freeze demonstration; perhaps there were as many as 30,000 here in Union Square, perhaps as many as 700,000 in New York in Central Park. In a season of nuclear despair, this is the poor arithmetic of hope.

Today, the anti-nukers will be on the asphalt again, this time in the East Bay. They'll be blockading the highway into the Lawrence Livermore National Laboratory, the cradle of atomic warheads, where nukes are nursed to perfection. Today, a lot of them intend to get arrested, and a lot of them will be children.

"Darn right I'm going to get arrested," said Amy Bomse, who is 14. She wrinkled up her forehead into something resembling a frown. "We kids are told to go to school and prepare for the future—but the adults won't create a world that guarantees a future for us. The way the world's going, we might as well be majoring in oblivion."

Amy talked about being vaporized in a nuclear attack the way kids talk about what's on TV. It's become so common.

Amy was a freshman at Urban this year. Urban, a private high school in the Haight, is so antinuke that it rescheduled its graduation last weekend from Saturday to Sunday so the students and faculty could go on the nuclear freeze march. Next fall Amy is going to high school in Berkeley, where a recent survey of junior high kids found that 66 percent of them believe they won't live out their normal lifetime, but will go up in some nuclear holocaust. No wonder kids cut school.

She said that other kids—aged 8 to 16—had been training with her in nonviolent protest tactics in antinuke "affinity groups." She said that "at least 20" kids had decided to get arrested with her. "After a nuclear war, you won't have to worry about your arrest records," she said.

If one wonders where the current national antinuke craze is coming from, one explanation is that the movement is, in part, a children's crusade. This is at least cost-effective; they have the most to lose.

History is the hard-knock door these kids are going to have to walk through.

There were The Hague conferences on disarmament in 1889 and 1907, and then there was World War I. There was the 1925 Kellogg-Briand pact to "renounce war," which all the good guys signed, and the Geneva Disarmament Conference of 1932, and then there was

World War II. There was the 1963 Test Ban Treaty, and the nuke testers burrowed like rats underground, and the warheads kept stockpiling.

Now most everyone says there are too many nukes, and even Ronald Reagan talks like a peace monger. When the leaders speak of peace, the common folk know that war is coming, said Bertolt Brecht.

"I'm getting arrested and my kids are getting arrested and my husband is going to get arrested at Livermore today," said Daral Rucker, who is 26 and in a wheelchair.

"Our entire family is going to be arrested," she said. That included two kids aged 8 and 10. The family who protests together, stays together.

"The only place for people who care about peace in America today is to be in jail," said her husband, Terry.

Tom Bowman is 55 and an East Bay insurance executive. He's been on the Oakland Symphony board and the Oakland Museum board and heads the local Boy Scout Council. He smokes a pipe and has button-down Oxford white shirts and is straighter than the ruler that Ronald Reagan measures his old film reviews with.

He had an arm around one of the kids who planned to be arrested in Livermore today—the man from the establishment had been arrested during a demonstration in the same place just a couple months ago for the same thing.

How could he and these kids—nuclear holocaust predictions notwithstanding—believe anything they could do today would change the sad routine of history?

The insurance executive puffed his pipe. "Look, I've written letters and voted and done all the normal things, but at a certain point in time, you have to put your body where your mouth is," he said.

Bowman said that being against nuclear weapons was not a political issue. "Hell, I'm a Republican," he said.

The kids nodded and they all went out to get arrested.

Warren Hinckle, *San Francisco Chronicle,* June 21, 1982.

the other player's loss—the traditional view of any arms race. The innovation was to be a contest in which some moves might be seen to benefit both players, with a premium placed on certain aspects of cooperation (such as, for example, survival).

To conventional military thinkers, all this was highly suspicious. It was bad enough to say in the abstract that no defense was possible against nuclear weapons, let alone to renounce both defense and victory. And it was the greatest heresy of all to think that the Soviet Union should be encouraged to develop an invulnerable second-strike capability. Such an elevation of the fact of mutual vulnerability into a principle of unilateral relinquishment of a first-strike option defied all common sense.

Even more difficult for conventional thinkers was the value-free neutrality inherent in treating both the Soviet Union and the United States as equivalent players in a game. Furthermore, the view that the arms race itself might be more of a danger to Americans than the Soviet threat itself seemed to downplay the differences between the two societies. Even so, McNamara prevailed. The "balance of terror" was acknowledged as the state of mankind in the second half of the twentieth century, and stabilizing this balance of terror through MAD became America's policy goal.

The Cuban Missile Crisis

The first major test of the balance of terror came with the 1962 Cuban missile crisis, when Khrushchev attempted to place nuclear weapons secretly in Cuba to compensate for the developing American superiority in intercontinental missiles. (The disparity resulted because the two countries had gone in different directions in the first few years of the missile age, with the United States concentrating on intercontinental-range missiles and the Soviet Union on intermediate-range missiles, with Europe as the target.)

It is possible, in retrospect, to view the Cuban missile crisis as both alarming and reassuring. It was alarming in the immediacy of the threat of ultimate resort to nuclear weapons, and reassuring in its resolution—Khrushchev withdrew his missiles. (Although he backed down partly because the United States then enjoyed a considerable superiority in nuclear weapons.)

Analysts were already exploring the policy of arms control, but the Cuban missile crisis helped to speed up the superpowers' willingness to pursue it in earnest. Shortly after the crisis, they agreed to ban nuclear testing in the atmosphere and to prevent the spread of nuclear proliferation to other countries (see Box 8-2). They set up a hot line so that each side could avoid miscalculation in crises and reassure the other about what it was doing or not doing. They devised rules for preventing accidental and unauthorized use of nuclear weapons and formalized these in the Measures to Reduce the Risk of the Outbreak of Nuclear War.

Probably the most significant outcome of the emphasis on arms control was the 1972 SALT I treaty (see Box 8-2), which put a mutual ceiling on offensive nuclear launchers and called for a minimal antiballistic missile defense.[5] SALT I seemed to corroborate the perverse new peace based on invulnerable nuclear weapons and vulnerable civilian populations. As Laurance Martin, vice-chan-

Box 8-2
TREATIES CONTROLLING NUCLEAR ARMS

Limited Test Ban Treaty: On August 5, 1963, the Soviet Union, Britain, and the United States agreed to ban the testing of nuclear weapons in the atmosphere, in outer space, and under water. More than one hundred other nations followed suit. France and the People's Republic of China did not sign.

Outer Space Treaty: Britain, the United States, and the Soviet Union agreed in January 1967 to ban the placement of weapons of mass destruction in orbit or on any celestial body. The treaty also restricts the use of celestial bodies to peaceful activities. The treaty was signed by fifty-four other nations.

Treaty on Nonproliferation of Nuclear Weapons: The United States, the Soviet Union, and Britain agreed in 1968 to establish safeguards to deter the spread of nuclear weapons and to keep new nations from using nuclear material to build weapons. One hundred thirteen other nations also signed the agreement.

Ocean and Seabed Arms Control Treaty: The United States, Britain, and the Soviet Union agreed on February 11, 1971, to ban the placement of weapons of mass destruction on the ocean or sea floor outside of a twelve-mile coastal zone. Fifty-six other nations also signed the agreement.

Antiballistic Missile Limitation Treaty: The United States and the Soviet Union agreed in 1972 to limit the placement of antiballistic missiles to two sites in each country, with no more than one hundred launchers or missiles at each site. The treaty, which is of unlimited duration, was amended in 1974 to restrict the ABM missiles to one site. The Soviet Union opted to place its ABM missiles around Moscow. The United States selected a site in Grand Forks, North Dakota, built it, and then abandoned it. The United States now has no ABM launching sites.

Salt I: An interim plan in 1972 resulted in a five-year agreement on offensive weapons. Both sides agreed to freeze the number of strategic ballistic missile launchers in operation or under construction, with complicated exceptions. The agreement was supposed to be a holding action to be replaced by SALT II.

Threshold Test Ban Treaty: In July 1974, the United States, Britain, and the Soviet Union agreed to prohibit underground nuclear tests with a yield of more than 150 kilotons. The treaty has never been ratified by the Senate, although the United States abides by it. The United States revealed on March 29, 1983, that it had asked the Soviet Union to reopen negotiations on this treaty to strengthen verification provisions but was turned down.

Salt II: Designed to limit strategic offensive weapons, SALT II was signed in December 1981 but never ratified by the U.S. Senate.

Strategic Arms Reduction Talks (START): Proposed by President Reagan during a speech at Eureka College in May 1982, the talks began in Geneva a month later. At issue are U.S. and Soviet long-range missiles and warheads. The latest U.S. proposal suggests a limit for both sides of 5,000 warheads on no more than 850 long-range missiles (land- or sea-launched). It would restrict the number of land-based warheads to

2,500. The Soviet counterproposal suggests a limit of 1,800 for long-range missiles and bombers, accompanied by a freeze on new production of strategic weapons.

Intermediate-Range Nuclear Forces: Started in November 1981, the negotiations deal with limits on nuclear missiles based in Europe. Under discussion are the 572 U.S. missiles (108 Pershing II and 464 Cruise missiles) scheduled to be placed in Western Europe starting in December 1983. These would replace the current, shorter-range Pershing-I now in place in West Germany. The U.S. missiles carry one warhead. The Russians reportedly have 351 mobile SS-20 missiles armed with 999 warheads (one-third targeted on Asia) and 300 older SS-4 and SS-5 missiles. The starting U.S. position in these talks was labeled the zero or double-zero option. The United States said it would not station its 572 missiles if the Soviet Union would dismantle all its SS-20, SS-4, and SS-5 missiles. The Russians replied by offering to cut their European missiles to 162 if the United States canceled the new missiles. On March 30, 1983, President Reagan offered to cut back the number of new American medium-range missiles to be placed in Europe if Russia would reduce its missiles in Europe and Asia. The cutbacks by the two sides would leave each with the same number of warheads on such missiles. This new proposal stresses equality of warheads rather than missiles.

---

cellor of the University of Newcastle, said, deterrence was enthroned and widely regarded "as the crowning achievement of postwar strategic thought." But by 1981, when Professor Martin spoke these words in the BBC Reith Lectures, he was already using the past tense as a prelude to discussing the "severe limitations" in this theory of nuclear deterrence.

WHERE IS THE HIGH-TECH RACE TAKING THE WORLD?

For nearly a decade and a half, the concepts of deterrence, stability, and arms control first promoted by Robert McNamara have been generally accepted and, more important, seem to have worked. The unprecedented thirty-seven years of peace in Europe in this century are due to the nuclear stalemate and faith in deterrence. The proponents of deterrence argue that despite the Berlin crises in 1948, 1958, and 1961—events that in any previous era might well have led to combat—the fear that any conflict might escalate to nuclear war has averted even subnuclear war in Europe. In an age that has achieved an appalling degree of destructiveness even in "conventional" weapons, this is a laudable accomplishment.

Yet, in the 1980s, the consensus that deterrence through the balance of terror is essential to our survival is showing signs of fraying under new technological and political strains. The technological strains are developing as nuclear weaponry becomes more and more sophisticated. Some experts believe that today's technology undermines predictability in any crisis, increasing anxiety and placing a premium on fast rather than considered action. In short, technological developments threaten the breakdown of deterrence.

Technological advances have been accompanied by a steady deterioration in world politics, including the relationship of the two superpowers. As our capacity to control arms through technology appears to be slipping away, so does the spirit of political control of arms. World politics has maximized rather than minimized the growing technological risks.

In this section, we will examine the technology of the arms race. We will discuss the type and number of weapons that presently exist and what is likely in the future. In the section that follows, we will look at the politics of the arms race.

The Nuclear Arsenal

No one knows the exact number of nuclear warheads in the world today, but according to a recent and authoritative United Nations report it is probably "in excess of 40,000," with their explosive power ranging "from about 100 tons up to more than 20 million tons equivalent of chemical high explosives."[6] The report states, "The largest weapons ever tested released an energy approximately four thousand times that of the atomic bomb that leveled Hiroshima, and there is in principle no upper limit to the explosive yields that may be attained."

The total strength of present nuclear arsenals may be equivalent to about one million Hiroshima bombs—some thirteen thousand million tons of TNT. It is often pointed out that this is equivalent to more than three tons for every man, woman, and child on the earth. The armory of nuclear weapons now includes free-falling bombs, warheads for ballistic missiles, artillery shells, depth charges, and nuclear-tipped torpedoes with yields ranging from a kiloton to several megatons. "Small" weapons have also been devised to use in field warfare.

According to Ruth Leger Sivard, "The trend is toward expansion, whether measured in government budgets, men under arms, research effort, number of weapons, or their kill-power."[7] In the 1970s, the United States increased its stock of deployable nuclear warheads from 3,950 to 10,000 while the Soviet stockpile grew from 1,659 to 7,400 (see Figures 8-2 and 8-3). As Henry Kissinger noted, it is bombs and warheads rather than missiles that destroy targets. The Soviets have, however, far surpassed the United States in deployment of new missiles. Since 1969, they have installed three new models of intercontinental ballistic missiles and three new submarine-launched ballistic missile systems. In the same period, the United States deployed the Minuteman-III, the Poseidon, and a few Trident-I submarine-launched missiles. The result is the much-publicized numbers gap. The Soviets now have 2,592 "delivery vehicles" (the standard euphemism for bombers and missiles), while the United States, having eliminated more than 200 obsolete missiles, has only 2,048.

There are two levels at which this gap can be considered—the technical and the strategic. As a technical matter, there is much less of a gap than the numbers suggest because the new inertial guidance installed on 550 Minuteman-IIIs has enormously increased their accuracy. According to calculations of D. C. Kephart of the Rand Corporation, each warhead is nearly three times more likely to destroy a concrete-hardened Soviet ICBM silo than the missile system it replaced. The Mk-12A warhead now being added to 300 Minuteman-IIIs doubles the explosive yield and further increases the probability of destroying hard targets. Whether these improvements increase or decrease U.S. security is itself a matter of debate and will be discussed later, but the impression that the United States has been standing still in the 1970s is erroneous. As Congressman Les Aspin summarizes the decade in the *Bulletin of Atomic Scientists,* "The power of U.S. warheads has thus kept pace with the Soviet Union's, even with additional missiles."[8] The cost is "several orders of magnitude cheaper than building a new missile." According to Aspin,

> The Soviets have spent tens of billions of dollars on new missiles, but we have continued to overwhelm them in deployment of new warheads; we have matched them in hard-target kill capability with just a billion dollars' worth of new guidance systems and warheads; and we have degraded Soviet missile power by upgrading our missile silos at low cost.[9]

The United States has also developed the air-launched Cruise missile, which can fly lower than one hundred feet from the ground and deliver within one hundred feet of a target warheads eleven times more powerful than the bomb that destroyed Hiroshima. Because of the obsolescence of the Polaris and Poseidon submarines,

Figure 8-2 NUCLEAR WEAPONS DEPLOYED, 1982

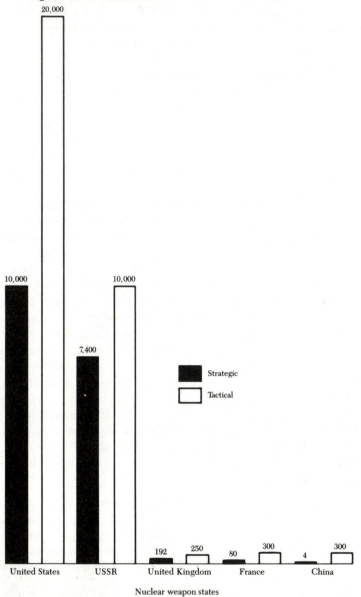

Source: Ruth Leger Sivard, *World Military and Social Expenditures* (Leesburg, Va.: World Priorities, 1982), p. 42.

Figure 8-3 STRATEGIC NUCLEAR WEAPONS OF THE TWO SUPERPOWERS

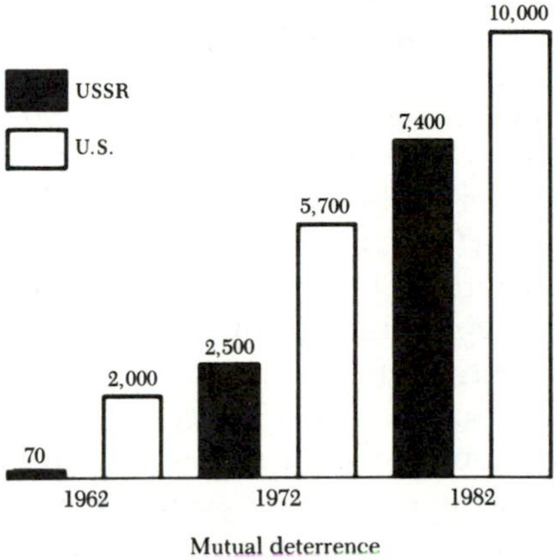

Mutual deterrence

¹Level of "mutual deterrence," on the assumption that 200 warheads on each side, assuring the destruction of 100 of the opponent's cities, should be sufficient to deter deliberate attack by a rational leader.

Source: Ruth Leger Sivard, *World Military and Social Expenditures* (Leesburg, Va.: World Priorities, 1982), p. 11.

which are normally retired after twenty-five years, the number of U.S. submarine-launched missiles will be reduced from 656 to 384 by 1992. But a substantial portion of these missiles are being fitted with vastly more powerful and more accurate warheads (Trident-I missiles carry eight one-hundred-kiloton warheads, replacing missiles bearing forty-kiloton warheads). The new Trident-II will carry fourteen warheads. This means that each submarine commander will be able to land the equivalent of eleven Hiroshima bombs on 336 separate and dispersed targets.

The superpowers have been proceeding inexorably with the nuclear arms race throughout the last decade, each in its own way. But increasingly strident critics of the defense establishment demand a quantum jump in military spending, claiming that Soviet weapons developments have given Moscow new political capabilities. Let us now look more closely at one of the major breakthroughs of the arms race: increased missile accuracy.

The "Window of Vulnerability"

In military thinking, there is a peculiar logic to the theory of deterrence. For example, in this logic, the recent dramatic increase in missile accuracy threatens international stability. The increase in accuracy was not the result of a single discovery or scientific breakthrough but of what has been called *technological creep*. Several small improvements suddenly added up to a leap in precision that caught everyone—and especially the theorists of deterrence—by surprise.

More important, this new technology was no monopoly of the United States. The United States pioneered the changes, but the Soviet Union has generally been only half a generation behind, testing weapons with performance characteristics equivalent to those of weapons the United States is already deploying. American ICBMs currently have accuracies of six hundred to one thousand feet; Soviet ICBMs have accuracies of one thousand to fifteen hundred feet, with the Soviet Union expected to match the present American achievement within a few years. One very important consequence of these new levels of accuracy is that not even "superhardened" concrete can protect missile silos.

Herein lies the peculiar logic mentioned a moment ago. "Normal" military thinking undoubtedly would welcome greater accuracy. After all, it would mean that military targets could be hit with fewer civilian casualties. But in the topsy-turvy world of nuclear deterrence "normal thinking" doesn't apply. The overall nuclear balance—and therefore deterrence—depends on keeping each superpower convinced that it cannot wipe out the other's missiles in a first strike—and that its own military establishment and civilian populations would pay a gruesome price if it were so foolish as to try.

However, the new accuracy holds out the tantalizing hope that just around the corner there may be a "disabling" first strike—a capacity to demolish the opponent's best weapons in a surprise attack. Under certain circumstances, that prospect might look tempting, thereby weakening the power of deterrence.

The by-now famous American "window of vulnerability" and Soviet "window of opportunity" which President Reagan speaks about are the result of the increased accuracy *and* an earlier innovation: multiple independently targetable reentry vehicles (MIRVs) on single missiles. With the original single-warhead missiles, an attacking nation would always have expended more of its own missiles than the enemy missiles it would have knocked out, given the low accuracies and therefore low kill ratios of the time. The attacker would have always have left a risky inferior residual balance for any further combat.

With MIRVs, however, an attacker could use, say, ten warheads from a single missile (at the standard two warheads per target) to wipe out five of the opponent's ICBMs in a first strike—a very favorable ratio of 1 to 5. The surviving balance after the initial strike would then strongly favor the attacker in any subsequent exchanges.

The result is the so-called window of vulnerability. According to Paul Nitze, chief U.S. negotiator at the Geneva Euromissile arms control talks, this window of vulnerability will arise by 1985. Nitze says that given the disparity between American nuclear forces (more warheads) and those of the Soviet Union (more missiles, much greater megatonnage of strategic nuclear explosives), the Kremlin could shortly launch a surprise attack that would wipe out 90 percent of America's land-based ICBMs. (The United States, with its far fewer ICBMs, could not wreak the same damage on the Soviet Union in any first strike until the late 1980s since the accuracy required currently resides only in land-based ICBMs and not in air- or sea-launched systems.)

Following a Soviet first strike under those conditions, Mr. Nitze argues, the United States would be crippled because its few remaining ICBMs and its inferior residual nuclear megatonnage would be outclassed by the remaining Soviet ICBMs. Washington would of course lack sufficient ICBMs to have the choice of retaliating against Soviet missiles. More significantly, it might not even dare to retaliate against Soviet cities—since it could do so only in the knowledge that American cities would then receive a much more devastating counterretaliation.

Add to this concern the political concern of people like Richard Pipes, a Harvard historian and current National Security Council advisor, and you have cause for alarm. Mr. Pipes suggests that precisely because Moscow now feels pressed by severe economic problems, potential crises with conflicting nationalities within Soviet borders, and the death of Brezhnev, the Kremlin might be tempted to exploit anti-Western chauvinism to divert Soviet citizens' attention from domestic troubles.[10]

Others, however, think this scenario is far-fetched. They argue that the Soviet Union has never displayed the kind of political adventurism the scenario presupposes—and especially not in a cautious succession period. They also maintain that from a military standpoint, there are also too many imponderables for the Soviets to risk a bolt-out-of-the-blue attack. These uncertainties include firing missiles over the North Pole, made tricky by the magnetic field, in trajectories that have obviously never been tested; coordinating a massive, simultaneous launching of ICBMs (in which the explosions of the first might very well alter the impact point of the following ones); and banking on the United States to accept millions of deaths and still decide rationally that retaliation is unprofitable.

The American Triad

Still others argue that the Soviet Union would be reluctant to take advantage of its "window of opportunity." The reason is that only a quarter of American warheads are on vulnerable, immobile ICBMs. The U.S. strategic weapons—on land, in the air, and at sea—form a "triad." Even if the Soviet Union did knock out 90 percent of our land-based ICBMs, there would still be more than six thousand U.S. warheads left on invulnerable mobile submarines and bombers.[11] The latter, as noted, do not yet have the accuracy of the ICBM. But they would flatten Moscow, Murmansk, and Vladivostok along with all but the most hardened silos and command posts. And the Kremlin displays no more eagerness than does the White House to gamble away its entire civilization for the sake of political one-upmanship. Therefore, argue critics of the window of vulnerability, deterrence holds.

Still, those who traditionally fight for arms control take the window of vulnerability seriously in its more general application. The adversary's theoretical first strike capability against one's own most accurate, flexible, and reliable missiles makes everyone much more jittery and events more unpredictable. Experts maintain that the Soviet Union poses a *theoretical* threat to U.S. ICBMs in the early 1980s, while the United States will pose a *theoretical* threat to Soviet ICBMs in the late 1980s, when its MX and Trident-II submarines will have attained accuracies close to the present-day precision of the ICBMs. Theoretically, again, these developments should present an even greater threat to the Soviet Union in the late 1980s than the Soviet threat to the United States today since the Soviet ratio of vulnerable land-based missiles and invulnerable bomber and submarine missiles is just the reverse of America's. Three-quarters of Soviet strategic warheads are on land and will be subject to first-strike destruction. In addition, Soviet bombers do not have the range of U.S. bombers and—most important—Soviet submarines are noisier and much more easily tracked and destroyed than their American counterparts.

On the other hand, the Soviet Union, with its intermediate-range missiles, can theoretically counterbalance this weakness by continuing to hold Western Europe hostage against any U.S. first strike (as it did during the most dramatic period of American missile superiority in the 1960s). While Soviet retaliation against any American first strike could conceivably be limited to "only" several tens of millions, Soviet retaliation against Western Europe could not be minimized, even if all Soviet ICBMs were demolished.

What this means, at least to a great many analysts, is that the mutual balance of terror still holds, asymmetrical in detail but symmetrical in horror. It also seems, however, that both superpowers have new fears that the balance may not be holding. Such fears can lead to rash judgments, hair-trigger alerts, and missile "launch on warning" rules that could leave decisions about war and peace up to computers—and computer error.

War by Accident?

There are two especially worrisome possibilities in this age of increased technological sophistication in nuclear weaponry and heightened political tensions around the world. Many experts fear war by *accident* or by *miscalculation.* Thus, the unusual interaction of technology and politics in the nuclear age produces what is called *crisis instability.*

In a tense confrontation (like the 1962 Cuban missile crisis or the 1973 Middle East war), there might be an impassioned escalation of encroachments and commitments to allies and tests of credibility. Clashes of wills and interests could reach a point at which one or both sides might fear that the other was about to launch a nuclear attack. (In the abstract this sounds outlandish, of course, but then so did a British-Argentine war before mid-1982.)

The future looks even more frightening. Antisatellite weapons, now on the way, could threaten the reliability of second strikes more than they would endanger first ones because of their threat to our communications system. The elements of nuclear-age "C_3I"—command, control, communications, and intelligence—are all so fragile that they compound anxiety in any period of tension and would surely deepen the "fog of war" in any outbreak of nuclear hostilities.

Antiballistic Missile Systems

In spite of the excessive strength of the nuclear armories on both sides, each superpower fears lest the other gain some advantage in the nuclear arms race. Nowhere is this more true than with the promised development of an *antiballistic missile system.* Like their

American counterparts, the Soviet leaders listened to the exaggerated claims of their research and development chiefs that an antiballistic missile (ABM) system could be devised which would destroy incoming enemy missiles either in outer space or after they had reentered the earth's atmosphere. Khrushchev boasted that the Russians had it in their power "to hit a fly in space." Technicians on both sides have worked feverishly to develop such a system, with complicated radars linked to computer communication networks and then to batteries of nuclear-armed missiles which would be launched instantaneously into automatically calculated ballistic paths to meet incoming enemy warheads. At the same time, other technical teams focused their efforts on means whereby enemy ABM systems could be defeated. They designed decoys to be carried in the terminal stage of a ballistic missile to confuse the antiballistic missile radars. The decoys would be released at the same time as the nuclear warheads, making it difficult or even impossible for the defending radar systems to differentiate the right objects to track and destroy in flight. But the ABM system was a mirage.

These matters are never kept completely secret in the United States. In the late 1960s, there was a spirited public debate between technicians who, in spite of one costly failure after another, still claimed that it was possible to devise an effective ABM system, and those who said it was not. In 1967, when ABM fever was at its most acute, and with strong pressure from many quarters for the continued development and then deployment of a system of defenses against missiles, President Johnson summoned his top military and science advisers. Dr. Herbert York, former director of defense research and engineering in the Pentagon, describes how the discussion led the president to ask two simple questions about a defense system against a possible Russian missile attack: "Will it work and should it be deployed?"[12] All present agreed that the answers were no. For the president wanted to know whether it was possible to devise a defense which could destroy *all* incoming warheads. It was not sufficient to destroy, say, one in every two, since if only one warhead got through, it would be enough to destroy Washington.

Once both sides were ready to admit the technical and functional futility of work on ABMs, work which could only "destabilize" the state of mutual deterrence, the first of the SALT talks was embarked upon. Negotiators reached agreement in 1972, by which time Nixon was president and Kissinger was both National Security Advisor and Secretary of State. Work on the main ABM deployment programs in the United States and the USSR was then halted, although research and development continued. It still goes on, despite the irrefutable logic of the technical argument that no ABM system can ever be devised that will provide either side with a guarantee that it can escape disaster in a nuclear exchange.

In fact, on March 23, 1983, President Reagan announced a plan to begin work on a futuristic defense system designed to destroy Soviet missiles in flight and render "these nuclear weapons impotent and obsolete."[13] The plan envisions laser and particle-beam technology, which exists more in theory than fact. Reagan admits that it could be the turn of the century before such new defense weapons could be produced, and on both sides of the Iron Curtain, experts doubt the effectiveness of this "star wars" technology. To cite one example, a team of physicists at the Massachusetts Institute of Technology studied the concept of charged-particle-beam weapons; they concluded that not only are there sound scientific reasons why such systems could not work, but also that even if orbiting space vehicles carrying the necessary machinery to generate laser or other beams could be devised, it would be even easier to develop relatively inexpensive countermeasures by which they could be neutralized or destroyed.[14]

IN QUEST OF A BOMB

When asking where the high-tech race is taking the world, we must consider the dangers of the proliferation of nuclear weapons. What has been called *technology seep* will cause the bomb to be spread to other nations outside the two superpowers and the four (possibly six) medium powers that now possess it.

The fear of technology seep was dramatized in the daring Israeli air strike of June 1981 against Iraq's Osirak nuclear research center. This attack did not end Iraq's drive for atomic weapons, however. Scarcely had the smoke cleared above the pile of the reactor's rubble than a determined Iraqi President Saddam Hussein went before his cabinet to declare, "Any country in the world which seeks peace and security . . . should assist the Arabs . . . to obtain the nuclear bomb in order to confront Israel's existing bombs."

It is true that the experts believe the Israelis have the bomb or the capacity to quickly assemble one. Someday, one of the oil-rich Arab nations will have the bomb too. This potential Middle East nuclear confrontation offers a dramatic specter of the nuclear-proliferated world of the 1980s—a world in which new atomic arsenals threaten to collapse a system of international controls crafted to prevent nuclear bombmaking.

Iraq had played by the rules of that system. It had signed the Treaty on the Nonproliferation of Nuclear Weapons (see Box 8-2) and had submitted to nuclear-plant safeguard inspections under the eye of the International Atomic Energy Agency. But that facade didn't reassure the Israelis, who dealt a deathly blow to confidence in the system.

The United States and the world depend on that system, the nonproliferation treaty signed by 115 nations in 1968. Each has foregone the development of nuclear weapons and submitted to inspections to ensure that nuclear fuel hasn't been diverted into bombmaking in exchange for assistance in the peaceful development of nuclear energy.

How well does this so-called system work? Most nuclear analysts say the problem isn't yet totally out of control, but that it is getting worse. Surprisingly, however, other experts contend that the nonproliferation efforts over the last twenty-five years have largely succeeded. In the early 1960s, President John F. Kennedy envisioned that by the 1980s, more than twenty nations would possess the deadly atom bomb. Yet, there are still only five major nuclear nations—the United States, Russia, France, England, and China—although India detonated a so-called peaceful nuclear device in 1974 (see Figure 8-4). Another nine countries—South Africa, Israel, Pakistan, Japan, Italy, Switzerland, West Germany, Sweden, and Canada—are said to be capable of joining the nuclear club now, and sixteen more members—Brazil, Argentina, Australia, Egypt, Libya, Taiwan, South Korea, Iraq, Yugoslavia, Spain, Austria, Belgium, the Netherlands, Denmark, Norway and Finland—are expected by 1990.

What triggers alarm bells, however, is the character of the nations now gaining nuclear capability. They are increasingly unstable nations in high-conflict regions of the globe. Experts fear some countries may emulate Israel and choose to bomb a rival's nuclear facilities rather than trust the international safeguard system.

Some see a kind of nuclear-terror poker game being played out; bargaining power is derived from the perception of being able to use a bomb while keeping it hidden to avoid world condemnation. "The best tactic is to have a bomb in the basement," explains Jack Hamilton, a former staff aide to retired New York Congressman Jonathan Bingham, who chaired the House subcommittee which oversaw nuclear export policies. "Everybody knows you have a

Figure 8-4 NUCLEAR TESTS, 1945–1981

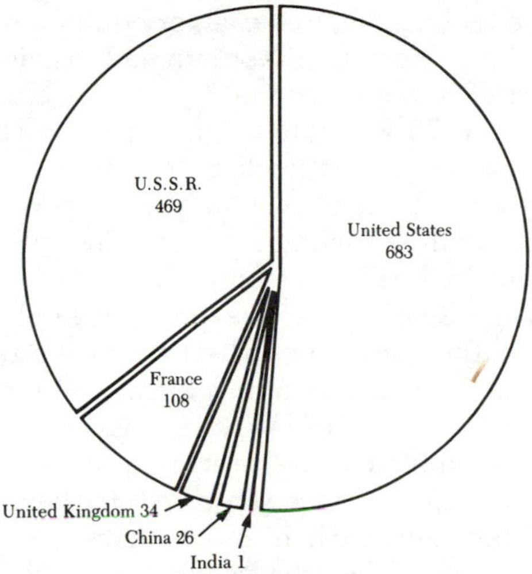

U.S.S.R.
469

United States
683

France
108

United Kingdom 34
China 26
India 1

State of the World's
Military Machine

The trend is toward expansion, whether measured in
government budgets, men under arms, research effort,
number of weapons or their kill-power.

Further growth will be on top of new records in all
indicators of military development. In financial terms,
this means current annual outlays of:

$600,000,000,000 in military expenditures
50,000,000,000 in weapons research
35,000,000,000 in arms trade

And a record weapons inventory, including
150,000 tanks
40,000 combat aircraft
50,000 nuclear weapons

Source: Ruth Leger Sivard, *World Military and Social Expenditures* (Leesburg, Va.:
World Priorities, 1982), p. 11.

bomb, but you don't use it, so you have the best of all possible
worlds."

Paradoxically, nonproliferation efforts have been sabotaged by
international cooperation, which has spread nuclear know-how,
material, and equipment. As we noted, by 1983, more than one
hundred nations had signed the nonproliferation agreement in
order to gain assistance in the peaceful development of nuclear energy.

Attempts at restrictive export controls, drawn up and agreed
to by the major supplier nations in 1976 and known as the London
Nuclear Suppliers Group Guidelines, were full of loopholes. They

failed to ban many types of "sensitive technology" (atomic-weapons–usable technology, material, or equipment) and pledged only "restraint" in exporting plutonium and uranium enrichment facilities—the stuff of bombmaking.

Although the 1976 guidelines tightened export controls, they are still lax and invite covert nuclear trading. For example, Pakistan has secretly used "dummy" companies to purchase components for a uranium enrichment plant. In 1980, Iraq openly bought an Italian "hot cell"—a facility for training in reprocessing techniques which also can make weapons-grade plutonium. These transactions raise the question of whether the Western powers are engaged in atoms for peace or atoms for war. Whether the developing nations use the cloak of legitimate nuclear trade for peaceful purposes or for military ones remains a murky and controversial area. India's nuclear device shattered illusions that there was no connection between civilian and military use. Many nuclear policy analysts believe that the technology and knowledge for atomic bombmaking is so disseminated that any determined country can build one.

Many nuclear experts are also frightened by what they call the growing *plutonium economy.* Plutonium is the fuel ingredient of nuclear weapons. It's either chemically separated from spent uranium reactor fuel or "bred" from uranium in a breeder reactor which produces more fuel than it actually consumes. Dependence on plutonium use has grown, as has the controversy over its economic justification (opponents say it's too expensive). But the International Atomic Energy Agency predicts that by the end of the 1980s, forty countries will be using plutonium fuel in their reactors without adequate safeguards and inspections to handle the increase.

Plutonium is very difficult to safeguard, and nuclear experts fear terrorists will inevitably obtain some. It takes a mere ten to twenty pounds of plutonium to make a bomb. What's more, assembling a crude bomb is easier than getting the fuel itself. "Even making fission weapons is relatively easy compared to acquiring the material (weapons-grade fuel)," says Dr. Theodore Taylor, a nuclear physicist who designed atomic bombs at the Los Alamos nuclear weapons laboratory and later became a staunch nonproliferation advocate. One estimate reports today's power plants produce enough plutonium to make 7,700 bombs a year. It is estimated that by 1990 there will be 760 tons available, or the equivalent of 167,200 bombs.

EAST-WEST RELATIONS: AN UP-AND-DOWN AFFAIR

The 1970s opened with the high point of Western optimism about the Soviet Union, East-West relations, and taming the nuclear Frankenstein. The decade closed with renewed American gloom about Soviet militarism, expansionism, and the "window of opportunity."

The cause for optimism in the early 1970s is summed up in a word: *détente.*[15] While not everyone agreed that détente would work, there was a general consensus that it was a good thing. Henry Kissinger, the architect of détente, saw it as an attempt to cope with an adversary superpower that was on the rise militarily while on the decline economically and ideologically. American planners hoped that the Soviet Union, having achieved relative prosperity and approximate nuclear parity with the United States, might finally mature from a revolutionary into a status quo power. That is, in setting foreign policy priorities, the Kremlin might come to the conscious calculation that it had more to gain from preserving its attained position than from trying to broaden its world influence by military means. For the United States, the prerequisite for accepting détente was recognition that the Pax Americana of the immediate postwar years was over.

A Renewed Cold War in the 1980s?

Détente was indeed short-lived. For various reasons, the Reagan administration and much of the American public are unwilling to accept the limits on American power necessary for détente. Furthermore, there are renewed charges by the administration that the Soviet Union is actively seeking military and political dominance in the world. The Reagan campaign platform of military superiority over the Soviet Union, for example, suggested a nostalgia for the 1950s era of Pax Americana. So does the Defense Department's continuing wish to build a position of strength before getting down to the real bargaining in strategic arms talks—and to outspend Moscow in military procurements into a real Soviet economic crisis.

At the same time, however, President Reagan (in a pattern that emulates the evolution of almost every American president in the nuclear age) shifted from the uncompromising line of his election campaign once he had the awesome responsibility of the finger on the button. After sixteen months in office, Reagan overruled his Defense Department and resumed strategic-arms-control talks on much the same premises as his predecessors. Significantly, on the eve of the opening of the SALT talks—rechristened START, or Strategic Arms Reduction talks—Reagan even pledged formally not to undercut the very SALT II treaty he had branded, while out of office, as "fatally flawed."

On the Soviet side, too, some ideologues and military commanders have resisted the undermining of Leninist verities that has occurred in the nuclear age. The status quo "stability" imposed on relations between potentially mortal enemies contradicts the Marxist-Leninist view in which there can be no stability until the final worldwide triumph of the Communist system. The change violates the fundamental precept of the inevitable historical victory of the Communist camp. After some squabbling, however, the ideologies squared this circle by proclaiming that détente itself would advance the world in a direction favorable to Moscow.

To Western hard-liners, this new Soviet ideological formulation seemed to be a very accurate description of the détente they opposed. Détente was shifting the economic, social, and, therefore, political forces in Moscow's favor; it was lulling the West into a misplaced conception of amity; it was, through a Western fear of escalation from local to nuclear war that was unreciprocated by the Russians, paralyzing Western resistance to local Soviet interventions.

Like their American counterparts, a few Soviet commanders at first held a dim view of their country's prospects under détente and nuclear parity. They resisted Brezhnev's goal, stated in 1971, of equal security for both superpowers as well as his 1974 warning about nuclear devastation for both sides and his explicit 1977 rejection of the goal of Soviet superiority. By 1977, however, the generals too fell into line, echoing Brezhnev's sentiments in their own public declarations.[16]

There is now considerable uncertainty about the overall political environment surrounding the new START talks. Initially, the United States and the Soviet Union thought they had worked out a mutual political understanding through their 1972 vow accompanying SALT I (and marking the real beginning of détente) that neither side would seek "unilateral advantage at the expense of the other, directly or indirectly." This turned out to mean very different things to Washington and Moscow, however, and became the subject of endless recriminations.

Two Interpretations of Détente

For the United States, détente (as first expressed in the promise that neither side would seek "unilateral advantage at the expense of the other"), meant roughly that the Soviet Union would not introduce its own or proxy troops into local conflicts in numbers that would sharply alter the local balance. (Moscow could still supply arms to "national liberation" movements in the Third World.) For Moscow, it meant equal status with America around the world—while Soviet promotion of national liberation movements around the world would proceed as usual.

The American hope was shattered in the mid-1970s when the Soviets ferried twelve to fifteen thousand Cuban combat troops into Angola to give victory in the postcolonial civil war to the minority Popular Movement for the Liberation of Angola (MPLA) faction.

Shortly afterward, the Soviets introduced three Soviet generals, twenty thousand Cuban troops, and $1 billion worth of tanks, armored personnel carriers, artillery, and other military equipment into Ethiopia. This was approximately double the amount of America's military input in that country in the previous quarter century.

In Moscow's interpretation, its actions—marking the first time the tide had been turned in Africa by Soviet rather than Western-sponsored military force—were the natural adjunct to full superpower status. In Kissinger's view, the Soviet entry into a region where Moscow had little discernible national interest suggested instead aggrandizement for its own sake. It showed precious little Kremlin willingness to set rational priorities in foreign policy and to subordinate marginal Soviet gains in the world to the shoring up of the wary cooperation forced on the superpowers by the nuclear age.

Afghanistan

The Soviet invasion of Afghanistan in 1979 provided an even sharper contrast in interpretations. For Moscow, the action was a natural ensuring of Soviet security in a border region where political instruments were failing. In any case, the Soviets felt they had little to lose. The advantages of détente had proved to be more meager than the Kremlin had hoped. Because the U.S. Senate had linked most-favored-nation tariff status to the domestic Soviet issue of Jewish emigration, the Soviets had failed to win the full trade benefits the Nixon administration had promised. Furthermore, the United States achieved full normalization of relations with China. The United States further turned out to be unreliable on SALT, inasmuch as it continued to do research and development (R&D) on ABM systems, and was stalling on ratifying the signed SALT II treaty even before the Soviet invasion of Afghanistan. And Washington kept using the Helsinki agreement (i.e., an agreement with European nations providing national and economic security and protection of human rights) to nag the Soviet Union about the domestic issue of human rights.

Perhaps most important, at the time of the Soviet invasion of Afghanistan, the United States was preoccupied with its hostages in Iran and suffering from memories of the Vietnam War. The Soviets therefore felt confident that America would not react vigorously to any Soviet military adventure in far-off Afghanistan.

Western policymakers, however, were shocked by the Kremlin's casual breaking of its own cautious postwar rules. The invasion marked the first time the Soviet Union ever sent its own army to occupy territory outside the area of Soviet hegemony wrested in the wake of World War II. It suggested a dangerously lowered threshold of risk-taking and an increase in assertiveness in Soviet actions abroad.

Afghanistan sounded the final death knell for Senate ratification of SALT II and may have been a factor in the election of Ronald Reagan to the White House. As President Carter said, the invasion certainly taught us "what the Russians are really like." The principle of "linkage" between general Soviet behavior and arms control talks was firmly established in Washington, with the talks regarded more as a reward to the Soviet Union for good conduct than as a joint attempt at survival.

THE PASSING OF THE BREZHNEV ERA

One of the big questions of the 1980s—whether an effective arms control package with Moscow can be negotiated—must be answered at a time when the Soviets are undergoing a change in leadership. The expeditious appointment of Yuri Andropov to succeed Brezhnev in the top post of general secretary of the Party is the most dramatic event in a process that will inevitably involve far-reaching replacement of leading elites in all governing hierarchies within a relatively brief time.

Who is this new leader of the Soviet Union? And what direction is he likely to pursue in foreign policy? The answer to the first question is a little easier to provide. The Politburo has chosen a leader whose experience supremely qualifies him to act in certain major areas of actual and projected difficulty while offering no evidence of serious competence in others. Andropov's professional biography may indicate how the Politburo assesses its priorities. Following his tenure as Central Committee official in charge of supervising Eastern Europe, Andropov served a good part of his career in the KGB (the Soviet secret police), with responsibilities for the domestic secret police and the foreign intelligence services. Indeed, he headed the KGB longer than any of his forerunners. He has extensive knowledge of the affairs of the Soviet Union abroad as well as those of his country's foreign adversaries. Of all members of the Politburo, he is best trained to conduct domestic policies stressing law and order, and social and labor discipline; to contain the potentially explosive non-Russian republics within the Soviet Union; and to handle the troubled and troublesome Eastern European empire. But he has very little visible experience in management of the economy and can probably be expected to rely on old and new subordinate specialists.

Both inside and outside Russia, Andropov is regarded as potentially a very strong leader, a man whose intelligence and experience prepare him well for his considerable burdens. It seems Andropov possesses the skill, the vision, and the will to become a powerful leader of the Soviet Union. At the same time, on the basis of past performance it is impossible to predict how he will conduct himself and which policies he will pursue. The combination of a highly centralized and bureaucratized system together with the premium placed on personal loyalty did not encourage subordinates like Andropov to dispute superiors like Brezhnev. It is too early to anticipate the direction of Soviet policy that will proceed from continuing debates and struggles behind the screen of a smooth passage of authority.

If the past can be taken as a guide, however, succession periods have an impact on Soviet foreign policies. During a succession period, the key goals of Soviet leaders are to insulate domestic politics and policies from foreign crises and challenges and to minimize the potential vulnerability of an unconsolidated leadership; to defend against foreign incursions and stabilize vital Soviet international positions; and—as happened after both Stalin and Khrushchev—to reverse as quickly as possible the corrosive damage of dubious foreign ventures inherited from the old leadership. It is likely that the new leaders will initially display considerable caution in their expansionist drive and in many respects continue the holding pattern of their predecessors. In an effort to avoid more international confrontation, they are likely to combine greater pliability in arms control negotiations and new proposals on arms reductions with concerted efforts to fan the growth of peace movements in the West and to launch a major peace offensive in Western Europe and the United States. At the same time, we must realize that in the initial period of a succession, the new leader cannot afford to appear weak and must therefore respond forcefully to any challenges from abroad. And, as we will learn in the next section, President Reagan is certainly challenging the Soviet Union.

REAGAN'S NUCLEAR-WAR–FIGHTING POSTURE

President Reagan and his advisers came to Washington intending to reestablish the United States as the leading nuclear power. In the process, Reagan's administration has assumed what many call a *nuclear-war–fighting* posture. Such a position is not new to the American government. In July 1980, for example, President Carter issued Presidential Directive 59 which, in the words of then New York Times writer Richard Burt, "requires American forces to be able to undertake precise limited nuclear strikes against military facilities in the Soviet Union, including missile bases and troop concentrations . . . [and] to develop the capacity to threaten Soviet political leaders in their underground shelters in time of war."[17]

However, Reagan's advisers have gone further than any of their predecessors in suggesting that countervailing nuclear threats are not enough. They argue that to be fully credible, the U.S. nuclear deterrent must be able to limit damage to the United States in a protracted nuclear war. Ideally, this capability would be composed of an imposing preemptive threat against Soviet missile silos, submarines, bombers, warning systems, command and control systems, and air defenses; an "active" ABM defense against any "residual" Soviet reentry vehicles that escaped destruction in a preemptive U.S. attack; and "passive" civil defense measures such as evacuation from "high risk" areas and "expedient shelters" against fallout from any nuclear warheads that penetrate the ABM system and explode on American territory (remember that previous presidents rejected the idea that an ABM system could ever be realized). Looking toward the future, Reagan's advisers advocate yet another layer of defenses to be deployed in space—the zone they call the "high frontier"—to further reduce the size of any residual Soviet retaliatory attack. With such an imposing array of offensive and defensive military capabilities, we are told, U.S. leaders would appear less afraid of war—and therefore more willing to pursue vital national interests eyeball-to-eyeball and fireball-to-fireball with the Russians.

As described in congressional testimony by Richard DeLauer, undersecretary of defense for research and engineering and a former TRW vice-president, a strategy of fully credible nuclear deterrence means that "we must improve the capability to control U.S. forces throughout crisis situations *up to and including protracted nuclear war*, improve the survivability and endurance of strategic offensive forces and intelligence resources, protect the U.S. population in order to reduce the risks of coercion and blackmail, and counter Soviet capabilities and initiatives by exploiting their weaknesses" (emphasis added).

Reagan's Spending Plans

The president's strategic program, DeLauer testified, "is designed to take control of the U.S./Soviet strategic balance and shape it to our benefit." To implement this program, Reagan would like the nation to buy 100 B-1 strategic bombers (at an estimated total program cost of $40 billion); more than 100 radar-evading, high-tech "stealth" bombers ($56 billion); 100 MX missiles ($20 billion); 20 Trident submarines ($30 billion); 480 Trident-II submarine-launched missiles ($30 billion); 3,400 air-launched Cruise missiles (ALCMs) and advanced-stealth ALCMs ($8 billion); 3,000 sea-launched Cruise missiles ($7 billion); bomber, missile, and civil defense systems ($29 billion); and "enduring" nuclear command, control, communications and intelligence (C_3I) systems ($22 billion)—for a grand total of at least $242 billion. And that is just the beginning; the administration has been toying with plans for the deployment of possibly thousands of lightweight and potentially mobile single-warhead intercontinental missiles that would cost another $30 to $40 billion as well. Then there is Reagan's provocative and risky proposal to deploy an ABM system in space—a project that could cost hundreds of billions of dollars for research alone.

Gen. John W. Vessey, chairman of the Joint Chiefs of Staff, testified before Congress in 1982 in defense of this extremely expensive and unabashedly aggressive program. Vessey said that the crux of America's security problem is that Soviet acquisition of a massive and survivable nuclear retaliatory force allows Moscow "to build an atmosphere in which they can pursue their own political objectives in the world without the United States threatening to interfere with their pursuit of those objectives." In a classic explication of the object of U.S. strategy, Vessey added, "We don't want a war and we certainly don't want a nuclear war. But at the same time we don't want to be paralyzed by the fear of a war as we pursue our economic, political, social and cultural objectives."

Prepared for Any Fight

Given the existence of massive conventional forces and tactical nuclear munitions on the Soviet side, and given the steady growth of an invulnerable long-range Soviet second-strike capability, the Pentagon's strategic logic now dictates that threats to begin the process of nuclear escalation—ostensibly to defend American interests in specific overseas theaters—can only be rendered credible by continuous modernization of U.S. nuclear and conventional warfighting capabilities "across the full spectrum of conflict," from brush-fire engagements to major regional conflicts and then to protracted intercontinental nuclear wars.

In order to convince the Russians that the United States is prepared to use its nuclear deterrent, we must show that our vital interests are at stake. This is the mission of U.S. "power projection" forces—the Rapid Deployment Force and other units formed for military intervention overseas. Once deployed, these forces must appear to be such a firm expression of Washington's commitment to protect its interests that the Russians could reasonably expect nuclear retaliation should they succeed in overrunning them.

To heighten such Soviet fears, the Reagan administration is modernizing the tactical nuclear weapons stockpile and accelerating the production of "dual-capable" delivery systems, which could deliver nuclear or conventional munitions. Old F-4 Phantom attack planes in the Marine Air-Ground Task Force that were not certified for delivering nuclear weapons are being replaced by F-18 Hornets that are certified. Nonnuclear AV-8A Harrier jump-jets are being replaced by the nuclear-capable AV-8B. Nonnuclear 105-millimeter howitzers are being replaced by the dual-capable 155-millimeter gun, almost doubling the marines' nuclear artillery arsenal. Army and marine eight-inch howitzers will also be equipped to fire the W-79 "neutron" warhead, about eight hundred of which are now being stockpiled in the United States for potential deployment overseas.

According to Pentagon planners, the United States must have the ability to deter Moscow from launching limited strategic nuclear attacks by threatening the prompt destruction of Soviet counterforce weapons, particularly the more accurate ICBMs deployed in hardened silos. From a nuclear-war–fighting perspective, if these missiles and their command and control systems are perceived as being vulnerable, an American president or a Soviet premier might be less inclined to threaten their deliberate limited use in a crisis, out of fear that such threats might spark a preemptive attack. It follows from such reasoning that the side with the most accurate and survivable weapons will be able to "dominate" the process of nuclear escalation, and achieve its national objectives, before the conflict becomes all-out nuclear war.

As interpreted by Gen. Bennie L. Davis, commander of the Strategic Air Command, this outlook means that "for combatant commanders to meet today's defense policy requirements, they must possess . . . strategic forces which are capable of destroying, neutralizing or disrupting the enemy in a measured and selective manner across the conflict spectrum, whether nuclear or conventional, spasmodic or protracted." Davis's strategy, in contrast with that of the 1960s and early 1970s, called for "flexible targeting options which destroy both hard and soft targets, yet keep civilian fatalities at the lowest possible level."[18]

This is the principal reason, Davis explained to the Senate Armed Services Committee, that the Pentagon seeks deployment of the highly accurate MX missile. "As we go from a strategy of assured destruction to one which stresses warfighting capability, that is, the priority targeting of military and leadership targets, you need weapons that are more accurate—that give you a capability against Soviet military and leadership elements."

Defensive War-Fighting

Once the MX and other counterforce weapons are in production, the next step on the Reagan agenda is to acquire a defensive war-fighting capability, combining an antiballistic missile system and civil defense. Although always described as defensive weapons, ABMs could play an *offensive* role in a U.S. first strike, reducing the effects of Soviet retaliation by intercepting enemy missiles that survive an initial U.S. assault. In such a scenario, civil defense measures would provide shelter for the population from any Soviet weapons that do not penetrate the ABM system.

In line with this long-term perspective, top military and civilian officials in the Reagan administration have become openly hostile to the existing ABM treaty. Secretary of Defense Weinberger, for example, incorrectly informed the Senate Armed Services Committee in December 1982 that "there is no change in the treaty needed" if the administration opts for an ABM system to defend the proposed "dense pack" MX deployment, in which MX missiles would be placed close together in superhardened silos. Displaying (or feigning) ignorance of the fact that the 1972 ABM treaty and its 1974 protocol permit the United States to move its ABM system from Grand Forks, North Dakota, *only* to Washington, D.C., he testified, "Instead of Grand Forks, we could put an ABM system on Fort Warren, in Wyoming." Weinberger further declared, "I am fully prepared to make that notification any time it is determined that an ABM system be constructed. . . . The sooner we get it, the better I like it."

According to Maj. Gen. Grayson Tate, the army's Ballistic Missile Defense (BMD) Program manager, "This Administration has made it very plain that they intend to restore some sort of balance between offense and defense. . . . We have been told to accelerate the work we are doing on low-altitude defense." For fiscal 1984, the administration is requesting $709.3 million for BMD development, and the proposed funding for 1985 more than doubles that amount, to nearly $1.6 billion. The only explanation Weinberger's fiscal 1984 annual report offers for this large expenditure in a field supposedly foreclosed by treaty is that the "program is structured . . . so that we could field an advanced and highly effective BMD system quickly should the need arise.

We have already seen that in his television address of March 23, 1983, President Reagan proposed an open-ended program to develop a whole array of antimissile systems. This effort, which according to Reagan "may not be accomplished before the end of this century," would make use of lasers, particle-beam weapons and other space wars technology.

If President Reagan or his successors manage to abrogate the ABM treaty and deploy a ballistic missile defense system, then the only stone missing from the administration's nuclear-war–fighting arch would be a serious civil defense program. And here too, the evidence suggests that the president and his civil defense director, Louis Giuffrida, actually believe that civil defense would be effective. According to Giuffrida, the president has directed that the U.S.

civil defense program be strengthened so as to "reduce the possibility that the United States could be coerced in time of crisis," and to "provide for survival of a substantial portion of the U.S. population in the event of a nuclear war . . . and for continuity of government."

The Drawbacks of Reagan's Approach

Reagan's nuclear-war–fighting doctrine can be opposed on many grounds. First, in a crisis it places the burden of making a rational moral choice about whether to escalate on Moscow; this may not be the way to ensure U.S. security. Second, none of the nuclear-war–fighting weapons are likely to perform with the degrees of accuracy and reliability that the scenarios require. Third, limiting a nuclear conflict requires assured communications with the enemy as well as one's own forces, something that is likely to be impossible in the radioactive frenzy of the nuclear battlefield. Finally, efforts to negotiate meaningful arms control agreements will surely be overtaken by the rush to deploy new war-fighting systems on both sides.

It seems very likely that the Reagan administration will not attain a reliable and usable nuclear-war–fighting capability. But the Soviet-American enmity, and the potential for miscalculation engendered by its quest, contain the seeds of an unprecedented genocidal catastrophe.

GRASS-ROOTS MOVEMENTS AGAINST THE ARMS RACE

In the 1960s and 1970s, there was considerable apathy toward nuclear weapons and the arms race. But the breakdown of détente, increased tension around the world, and Reagan's request for the largest-ever peacetime defense budget (including a considerable increase in nuclear weapons research and development appropriations) have aroused new public concern about nuclear issues in the 1980s.

In just a few months in 1982 and 1983, more than 624 local town meetings or councils passed nuclear freeze resolutions—an impressive showing considering this is a policy arena in which local governments have no authority. Grass-roots antinuclear organizations—not on radical campuses but in the suburbs and the promilitary South—are growing rapidly. In the 1982 election, several states, including California, passed nuclear freeze resolutions intended to send a clear message to Washington. Even more significant was the passage of the nuclear freeze resolution by the United States House of Representatives on May 4, 1983. Religious leaders are also concerned about the arms race. On May 2, 1983, three hundred American bishops met in Chicago and overwhelmingly voted to adopt a controversial "pastoral letter" on nuclear weapons. The bishops were trying to reconcile Christian morality with a defense policy based on a threat to kill millions of innocent people.

Two years of work by a committee of the National Conference of Catholic Bishops culminated in a battle between liberal and conservative factions over a document that places the nation's largest church in opposition to many elements of the Reagan administration's defense policy.

The letter is entitled "The Challenge of Peace: God's Premise and Our Response." Its various sections discuss whether Catholic theories of "just war" can be applied to nuclear weapons, review the Catholic traditions of nonviolence and conscientious objection to wartime service, call for a "no-first-use" policy in nuclear weapons, and advocate "clear public resistance" to military statements regarding "limited, winnable and survivable" nuclear war.

The increased public interest in nuclear issues in this country as well as in Europe raises some important questions. How will the yearning for a durable peace affect nuclear arms policy? Can the public, through the democratic process, restore a saner world? Will new popular opposition force politicians to formulate concrete policies that promote survival? Can we turn our balance of terror into something our consciences can live with? In other words, can we have an impact on what has clearly a crazy ordering of priorities in this world? (See Box 8-3.)

Or will the superpowers conspire to ignore the longing for peace and press on unrestrained with their deadly macho games? Will the Kremlin be content merely with exploiting—and Washington merely with pacifying—grass-roots sentiment in the West without ever really responding to it? And finally, will the peace movements, in turn, simply promote warm feelings of righteousness without ever translating this emotion into real policy?

More must come from the new nuclear consciousness-raising than the rejection of the one thing that has worked for the past thirty-five years—mutual deterrence. After all, the balance of terror has

Box 8-3
PRIORITIES, 1982

- The world's stockpile of nuclear weapons is equivalent to 16,000 million tons of TNT. In World War II, 3 million tons of munitions were expended, and 40–50 million people died.
- The U.S. government is spending a minimum of $4,500 million a year on a rapid deployment force to protect its vital interests in Middle East oil, vs. $400 million for research on renewable energy sources as alternatives to oil.
- In 24 countries, food consumption averages 30 to 50 percent above requirements; in 25 countries, the average is 10 to 30 percent below requirements.
- The richest fifth of the world's population has 71 percent of the world's product; the poorest fifth has 2 percent.
- The international policing effort to control the proliferation of nuclear weapons has an annual budget of $30 million, half the size of the average police budget of a medium-large U.S. city.
- In 32 countries, governments spend more for military purposes than for education and health care combined.
- Nuclear missiles can go from Western Europe to Moscow in 6 minutes, but the average rural housewife in Africa must still walk several hours a day for the family's water supply.
- The NATO and Warsaw Pact forces between them have 100,000 tanks. Tailgating each other, they would form a column stretching from Paris to Budapest.
- The efficiency of a U.S. car (fuel use to weight) has doubled since World War II; the efficiency of a nuclear weapon (destructive yield to weight) has increased 150 times.
- In the U.S., the world's first superpower, the infant mortality rate is over twice the average for other developed countries.
- The family breadwinner in industrial countries works one and one-half weeks per year to pay for national military forces; 4 minutes a year to pay for international peacekeeping.

Source: Ruth Leger Sivard, *World Military and Social Expenditures,* (Leesburg, Virginia: World Priorities, 1982), p. 5.

averted wars in Europe since 1945. But as Lawrence Freedman says,

Nonetheless, we ought to be disturbed by the permanence of nuclear arsenals, having an entrenched position in the international order. . . . An international order that rests upon a stability created by nuclear weapons will be the most terrible legacy with which each succeeding generation will endow the next. To believe that this can go on indefinitely without major disaster requires an optimism unjustified by any historical or political perspective.

We can only hope that the new antinuclear movement in this country and abroad will help us find a way to control the nuclear genie which escaped its bottle in 1945.

SUMMING UP

The "American century" that Henry Luce spoke of in 1941 lasted less than thirty years. Of course, we still have the largest economy, the most powerful military, and the greatest cultural influence in the world. But we are not the "number-one" nation in quite the way we once were. And we never will be again. But for the same reasons that it is no longer the American century, it cannot now become the Soviet century either. The world is too complex a place in the 1980s for any one nation to dominate as the United States did after World War II.

The big question to be answered in this decade is whether the nuclear arms strategy of deterrence can continue to work —particularly at a time when no single nation (not even a superpower) can dominate international politics. The Reagan administration seems to believe that deterrence will work so long as the United States shows its determination to stay abreast, if not ahead, of the Soviets in the arms race. Consequently, Reagan is asking for a massive military buildup in both conventional and nuclear forces.

On the other side, however, increasing numbers of experts and citizens are questioning the logic of a continued arms race. They are saying that the uncontrollability of the arms race is the greatest threat we face. War is not a national security option in the nuclear age. Even President Reagan has recanted his statement that a nuclear war could be won.

The opponents of the arms race say that the decline in our power to control our destiny should indeed worry us, but that it has nothing to do with a lack of nuclear hardware. Instead, it stems from an increasingly uncontrollable international environment in which the superpowers risk being sucked into other people's wars. It stems also from a failure to manage our society. Nothing could restore American prestige and influence faster than a dramatic reduction of our foreign-oil dependence and a workable approach to the control of inflation that did not tear the country apart. Our influence

Box 8-4
THE POWER OF AN ATOMIC EXPLOSION

It is all too easy, when discussing nuclear weapons strategy, to lose sight of the horror that would be wrought if such weapons ever were actually used to fight a war rather than to deter one. Let us therefore review the probable effects of a nuclear attack on an urban population center like San Francisco.

A single explosion, a one-megaton airburst at seven thousand feet over downtown San Francisco, is likely to produce the following: within a radius of about one and one-half miles is an area in which the overpressures are twenty pounds per square inch, which will destroy everything; winds are five hundred mph; reinforced concrete and steel buildings of the strongest construction will either collapse totally or will have all of their floors swept out from within the structure.

The heat is such that almost everybody will be either vaporized or killed by third degree burns, if indeed they're not killed by other traumas.

Within a radius of three miles are overpressures of over ten pounds per square inch and winds at 160 mph. Brick and wood are destroyed; exposed people are seriously burned. Even at a range of eight and one-half miles, you have overpressures of more than two pounds per square inch. And overpressures of anywhere from one-half pound per square inch to two pounds will take a glass window and turn it into a thousand particles of glass traveling in excess of one hundred mph.

If one wants to think about twenty megatons, everything that happens within a radius of three miles at one megaton is happening within a radius of eight and one-half miles at twenty megatons. If you are standing that far away, you will have a fifty-fifty chance of survival.

As a nuclear bomb explodes, a huge pressure wave traveling faster than the speed of sound spreads out from the center of the explosion, followed by winds at speeds transiently exceeding five hundred mph. The winds create a low-pressure area as they move outward, and the surrounding air rushes in, fanning the many fires started by the thermal radiation and initial blast damage. Once can expect such fires within a radius of anywhere from eight to sixteen miles, depending on the megatonnage.

At one megaton, of the 3,613,000 people in the San Francisco metropolitan area, 780,000 would be killed outright. Total casualties are 1,162,500, almost every third person. We have never, in the Western world at least, had an event in which every third person was killed or injured in such a short time.

But again, I'm talking about conservative assumptions. What of a multiple strike? What of a 10 A.M. and 4 P.M. strike? . . . I'm not going to numb you with specific details—two one-megaton explosions of that type would kill or seriously injure 2.2 million, or 61 percent of the Bay Area's population. And just two twenty-megaton weapons—a very small percentage of the superpowers' arsenal—really do the job; 3,407,000 killed. That's 94 percent of the population, and all of those who are not killed are seriously injured or incapacitated.

What type of injuries would result? Overwhelmingly, first of all, third-degree burns—certainly thousands, probably tens of thousands. In the case of the multiple twenty-megaton explosions, there would be hundreds of thousands. And this, of course, exceeds the total number of burncare beds in the United States. Second-degree burns and crushing injuries due to the collapse of buildings and related traumas would also result. Other common injuries would include ruptured internal organs, especially rupture of the lungs, [and] penetrating wounds of the skull, thorax, and the abdomen, because all kinds of objects have been turned into missiles traveling at high speeds. Also common: simple and compound fractures of all kinds, including skull fractures because people have been turned into missiles traveling at high speeds until they hit the nearest wall, or whatever.

And there are two things that aren't mentioned very often: significant numbers of wounded survivors will suffer ruptured eardrums, and even more people—anybody within thirty-five miles who takes a reflex glance at the fireball—will be blinded by retinal burning.

What about radiation effects? Whole-body doses of several thousand roentgens produce a central nervous system syndrome with inevitable death within hours or days, preceded by hyperexcitability, loss of coordination, respiratory distress, and intermittent stupor. Doses of fifteen hundred roentgens may produce only gastrointestinal syndrome before death.

To talk of response becomes a kind of absurdity and a kind of delusion when we look at the data. Who will respond? And what will they respond with?

Physicians and hospitals will be destroyed at rates greater than that of the general population because they tend to be concentrated in downtown urban areas, in the zones of highest lethality. It is a conservative calculation that there would be fewer than two thousand physicians in the San Francisco metropolitan area able to function. And that includes physicians who haven't seen blood in years. . . .

. . . The doctors and other health workers will be working without equipment, without diagnostic aids, without laboratories, without caches of blood supplies or any of the other things that are needed for contemporary medical management of trauma, burns, or even lesser injuries. . . .

You must remember that there will be no electric power. There will be no transportation system. Most of the buildings and streets and terrain will be unrecognizable. There will be no organized systems of civilian communication. And in the scenario we are describing, there is no probability of help from the outside. . . .

Then there is the problem that's not looked at very much. Even making the generous assumption that a twenty-megaton attack consumes everything in a sixteen-mile radius with a firestorm, there will still be three hundred thousand to five hundred thousand human corpses, not counting the animal corpses and the like. Again, an event unprecedented in human experience. One can assume that most of those bodies will decay, spreading disease. . . . There is no survival in any sense of the word that has social meaning. . . .

Speech delivered by Dr. H. Jack Greiger in the film, "The Last Epidemic," produced for the *Physicians for Social Responsibility,* 1982.

in the world, say opponents of the arms race, is directly related to our ability to confront successfully unprecedented problems of advanced industrial society and to create a legitimate social order within the limits of a slow-growth economy.

To step up the arms race as President Reagan wants at a time when the economy is in decline forces difficult choices. The opponents of increased military spending see an acute distortion of priorities in the administration's desire for a massive increase in military spending while essential services in every major American city are being cut.

Furthermore, the whole purpose of modern war is to demoralize the enemy population. But we now run the risk of demoralizing ourselves. Even if nuclear war never comes, the psychological toll on our people is enormous (see Box 8-4). Exactly how this awesome threat affects child development, family life, and the rise of an uncharacteristic mean-spiritedness in our political arena cannot be calculated. But two generations of life under the shadow of the bomb have taken their toll.

NOTES

1. For two excellent overviews of the basic dilemmas of the nuclear age, particularly in terms of the moral issues, see Barrie Paskins and Michael Dockrill, *The Ethics of War* (London: Duckworth, 1979), and Michael Walzer, *Just and Unjust Wars: A Moral Argument with Historical Illustrations* (New York: Basic Books, 1978).
2. Geoffrey Goodwin, ed., *Ethics and Nuclear Deterrence* (London: Croom Helm, 1982) does an excellent job of explaining the concept of deterrence. Also, see Michael E. Quinlan, "Preventing War: Why Deterrence Becomes an Inexorable Policy," *The Tablet,* July 18, 1981.
3. At first no technology existed to protect missiles; now some partial technology exists, but its cost-effectiveness means that it is cheaper for an assailant to add one more warhead than for a defender to add sufficient interceptors to stop the incoming warhead.
4. For an overview of U.S. nuclear strategy, see Lawrence Freedman, *The Evolution of Nuclear Strategy* (London: Macmillan, 1981).
5. See John Newhouse, *Cold Dawn: The Story of SALT* (New York: Holt, Rinehart & Winston, 1973).
6. *Comprehensive Study on Nuclear Weapons.* Report of the secretary general to the General Assembly of the United Nations, p. 62.

7. Ruth Leger Sivard, *World Military and Social Expenditures* (Leesburg, Virginia: World Priorities, 1982), p. 6.
8. Les Aspin, "Judge Not by the Numbers Alone," *Bulletin of Atomic Scientists* 36 (June 1980), 28–33.
9. Ibid., p. 30.
10. Richard Pipes, "Why the Soviet Union Thinks It Could Fight and Win a Nuclear War," *Commentary* (July 1977), pp. 21–35. See also Daniel Seligman, "Our ICBMs Are in Danger," *Fortune*, July 2, 1979, pp. 50–58; and Richard Pipes, "Soviet Global Strategy," *Commentary* (April 1980), pp. 31–40.
11. W. K. H. Panofsky, "Looking Through the Window of Vulnerability," *San Jose Mercury News*, October 7, 1981.
12. H. F. York, *Race to Oblivion* (New York: Simon & Schuster, 1970).
13. *San Francisco Chronicle*, March 31, 1983, p. 1.
14. K. Tsipis, "Directed Energy Weapons Feasibility and Effectiveness," Paper presented at IFRI Colloquium for Science and Disarmament, Paris, January 1981.
15. For a discussion on détente as Henry Kissinger envisioned it, see Henry Kissinger, *White House Years*, (Boston: Little, Brown, 1979). See also Paul Nitze, "Assuring Strategic Stability in an Era of Détente," *Foreign Affairs* 54 (January 1976), 207–233, and "The Death of Détente?" *International Security* 5 (Summer 1980), 22–31.
16. John Collins, *American and Soviet Military Trends Since the Cuban Missile Crisis* (Washington: Georgetown University, 1978), and "President Brezhnev and the Soviet Union's Changing Security Policy" (U.S. Foreign Broadcast Information Service Analysis Report, May 25, 1979).
17. Richard Burt, *New York Times*, July 16, 1980, p. 1.
18. *San Francisco Chronicle*, January 4, 1983, p. 10.

GLOSSARY

ABM: antiballistic missile (defense).

ALCM: air-launched cruise missile.

BMD: ballistic missile defense.

C_3I: command, control, communications, and intelligence.

Counterforce: U.S. strategy in which military installations, for example, missile silos, are the primary targets in retaliation against nuclear attack.

Countervalue: U.S. strategy in which cities and other civilian complexes are the primary targets in retaliation against nuclear attack.

Cruise: a low-flying pilotless Aircraft with either a conventional or a nuclear warhead (medium and long-range).

Détente: relaxation of tension or strained relations between the United States and the Soviet Union.

ICBM: inter-continental ballistic missile.

IRBM: intermediate-range ballistic missile.

MAD: mutually assured destruction.

Minuteman: a U.S. land-based intercontinental ballistic missile.

MIRV: multiple independently targetable reentry vehicles fitted to ballistic missiles.

MX: the code name for a projected US mobile intercontinental ballistic missile.

PD 59: Presidential Directive 59 (1980), defining U.S. counterforce strategy.
Pershing-II: a U.S. medium-range ("theater") ballistic missile.
Polaris: a submarine-launched intermediate-long-range ballistic missile.
SALT: Strategic Arms Limitation Talks/Treaty.
SS-20: a Soviet mobile intermediate-range ballistic missile.
START: Strategic Arms Reduction Talks.
Trident: a submarine-launched long-range ballistic missile.

SUGGESTED READINGS

Barnet, Richard J. *Real Security: Restoring American Power in a Dangerous Decade.* New York: Simon and Schuster, 1981.

Baylis, J., and Segal, G. *Soviet Strategy.* London: Croom Helm, 1981.

Collins, John. *American and Soviet Military Trends Since the Cuban Missile Crisis.* Washington: Georgetown University, 1978.

Douglass, Joseph J., and Hoeber, Amoretta. *Soviet Strategy for Nuclear War.* Stanford: Hoover Institution Press, 1979.

Fallows, James. *National Defense.* New York: Vintage, 1981.

Leebaert Derek, ed. *Soviet Military Thinking.* London: Allen & Unwin, 1981.

Millar, T. B. *The East-West Strategic Balance.* London: Allen & Unwin, 1981.

Paskins, Barrie, and Dockrill, Michael. *The Ethics of War.* London: Duckworth, 1979.

Walzer, Michael. *Just and Unjust Wars: A Moral Argument with Historical Illustrations.* New York: Basic Books, 1978.

Index